The ADMIRE

Framework *for* Inclusion

Positive Strategies That Pave the Way
for Students of All Abilities

Toby J. Karten

Solution Tree | Press

Copyright © 2024 by Solution Tree Press

Materials appearing here are copyrighted. With one exception, all rights are reserved. Readers may reproduce only those pages marked "Reproducible." Otherwise, no part of this book may be reproduced or transmitted in any form or by any means (electronic, photocopying, recording, or otherwise) without prior written permission of the publisher.

Figure 5.1 created with the assistance of rhyme.cool.

555 North Morton Street
Bloomington, IN 47404
800.733.6786 (toll free) / 812.336.7700
FAX: 812.336.7790

email: info@SolutionTree.com
SolutionTree.com

Visit **go.SolutionTree.com/specialneeds** to download the free reproducibles in this book.

Printed in the United States of America

Library of Congress Cataloging-in-Publication Data

Names: Karten, Toby J., author.
Title: The ADMIRE framework for inclusion : positive strategies that pave
  the way for students of all abilities / Toby J. Karten.
Description: Bloomington, IN : Solution Tree Press, 2024. | Includes
  bibliographical references and index.
Identifiers: LCCN 2024003797 (print) | LCCN 2024003798 (ebook) | ISBN
  9781960574244 (paperback) | ISBN 9781960574251 (ebook)
Subjects: LCSH: Inclusive education--United States. | Children with
  disabilities--Education--United States. | Motivation in
  education--United States.
Classification: LCC LC1201 .K365 2024 (print) | LCC LC1201 (ebook) | DDC
  371.9/0460973--dc23/eng/20240222
LC record available at https://lccn.loc.gov/2024003797
LC ebook record available at https://lccn.loc.gov/2024003798

Solution Tree
Jeffrey C. Jones, CEO
Edmund M. Ackerman, President

Solution Tree Press
President and Publisher: Douglas M. Rife
Associate Publishers: Todd Brakke and Kendra Slayton
Editorial Director: Laurel Hecker
Art Director: Rian Anderson
Copy Chief: Jessi Finn
Production Editor: Paige Duke
Proofreader: Anne Marie Watkins
Text and Cover Designer: Abigail Bowen
Acquisitions Editors: Carol Collins and Hilary Goff
Content Development Specialist: Amy Rubenstein
Associate Editors: Sarah Ludwig and Elijah Oates
Editorial Assistant: Anne Marie Watkins

Acknowledgments

This book is dedicated to the people who believe in high standards for individuals of all ability levels. That includes my publisher, Solution Tree Press. Thanks to the students, the families, and the professionals I have been blessed to collaborate with in my personal and professional endeavors to ensure that we ADMIRE inclusion, beyond the pages of this resource, with our actions and within our hearts. Infinite gratitude to my dear family and friends. Without you, I am not me. xoxox

The ADMIRE Framework for Inclusion is also dedicated to Randie, my cousin. Randie taught me at a very young age that no one has a monopoly on how or what to learn. Randie, who had an intellectual difference, led me to choose my career as a special education teacher. My cousin taught me that the word *exceptional* never capped a person's potential. Randie taught me about equity and inclusion before the legislation spelled it out. Randie taught me patience. Randie taught me that life is a process, never a race nor a competition with pecking orders on who owns the answers. Randie taught me about perspectives as I experienced the world through her eyes.

Solution Tree Press would like to thank the following reviewers:

Doug Crowley
Assistant Principal
DeForest Area High School
DeForest, Wisconsin

Jenna Fanshier
Principal
Marion Elementary School
Marion, Kansas

Erin Kruckenberg
Fifth-Grade Teacher
Jefferson Elementary School
Harvard, Illinois

Kim Timmerman
Principal
ADM Middle School
Adel, Iowa

Sheryl Walters
Senior School Assistant Principal
Calgary, Alberta, Canada

Visit **go.SolutionTree.com/specialneeds** to download the free reproducibles in this book.

Table of Contents

Reproducibles are in italics.

About the Author ix

Introduction 1
    Attitudes Toward Inclusion 2
    ADMIRE Inclusion Supports and Actions 3
    About This Book 3

CHAPTER 1
What Students and Staff Need to Know 9
    Common Myths About Inclusion 9
    Seven Questions to Guide a Definition 11
    Inclusion in the Research 15
    ADMIRE the Competencies 20
    Conclusion 26
    Creating Classroom Norms 27
    Admiring What Students and Staff Need to Know 28

CHAPTER 2
Think Individuals, Not Categories 29
    Focus on Functional Skills 29
    ADMIRE Exceptionality as a Difference, Not a Deficit,
    Definition, or Limitation 32
    Recognize Student Diversity as Strength 34
    ADMIRE Student Realities 43
    Conclusion 46
    Admiring Individuals, Not Categories 47

CHAPTER 3
Connect to the Realities That Teachers, Students, and Families Face 49

    Assess and Activate Awareness. 49

    Decide and Delineate Inclusion Structures. 54

    Plan With and for Learners 56

    Collaborate With Families 69

    Conclusion. 70

    Interest Survey *71*

    Learner Profile. *73*

    Admiring the Realities of the Teachers, Students, and Families . . . *74*

CHAPTER 4
Practice Supportive Classroom Management 75

    ADMIRE Classroom Management. 76

    Positive Classroom Environment 76

    Routines and Expectations 81

    Individualized Support. 82

    ADMIRE Inclusion Principles. 85

    Student Realities 86

    ADMIRE Inclusion Principles, Revisited. 92

    Conclusion. 93

    Admiring Supportive Classroom Management Practices *94*

CHAPTER 5
Inclusion Challenges Generate Solutions 95

    Innovations, Inventions, and Solutions 96

    Adjust Complexity and Delivery. 98

    Proactive Inclusion 101

    Climate for Inclusion Acceptance. 104

    Adaptations 107

    Collaborative, High-Tech, Individualized, Low-Tech, Data-Driven Approaches. 113

    Conclusion. 120

    Documenting Specially Designed Instruction *122*

    Admiring How Inclusion Challenges Generate Solutions *123*

CHAPTER 6
Manage Inclusion Anxiety 125
    Acknowledge and Reduce Inclusion Anxiety 125
    Include Small-Group Activities 128
    Offer Voice-Choice Assignments 129
    Empower Students to Be Successful 132
    Collaborative Framework 139
    Conclusion. 142
    Create a Choice Board *143*
    Use an MTSS Planning Template *144*
    Create a DSLO Chart *146*
    Admiring Ways to Manage Inclusion Anxiety *147*

CHAPTER 7
ADMIRE Wellness. 149
    Wellness Competencies 150
    Support the Person in the Mirror 151
    A Ten-Step Intervention Plan 155
    ADMIRE Relationships 157
    Conclusion. 161
    Admiring Wellness *163*

Epilogue. 165
    Inclusion Word Cloud. 165
    True or False Questions 166
    An Edutaining Pictograph 167
    A Digital Platform. 168

References and Resources. 169

Index. 183

About the Author

Toby J. Karten is an award-winning special educator, dynamic presenter, and author who is passionate about sharing her knowledge with others. Throughout her career, she has taught students with and without exceptionalities from preschool to the graduate level. Toby works with school districts across the United States and internationally as a staff developer, an inclusion coach, an educational consultant, an author, and an adjunct professor. Toby focuses on creative, practical solutions for helping all students gain not only access to but also ongoing successes in inclusion classrooms. She has collaborated with administrators, staff, students, and their families at local, national, and international school sites and conferences as an invited speaker and consultant. She has an undergraduate degree in special education from Brooklyn College, a master's degree in special education from the College of Staten Island, a supervisory degree from Georgian Court University, and an honorary doctorate from Gratz College. Toby has been recognized by the Council for Exceptional Children and the New Jersey Department of Education as an exemplary educator, receiving two Teacher of the Year awards. Toby has authored and edited more than thirty books and quick reference guides on the topics of disability awareness, co-teaching, and inclusion classrooms. Her interactive professional development and resources offer ways for staff and students to collaboratively focus their eyes, minds, and actions on how inclusion practices connect to educator, learner, and curriculum realities. Toby's ongoing professional goal is to help learners achieve successful inclusion experiences in school and life. To learn more about Toby's work, visit www.inclusionworkshops.com.

To book Toby J. Karten for professional development, contact pd@SolutionTree.com.

Introduction

DATE: Today

OCCASION: Learning

FOR: *All* Professionals, Students, and Families

PLACE: Inclusion Classrooms

TIME: First Option of Service, as Appropriate

RSVP: 1.800.2.INCLUDE

Dear Current and Future Administrators, Educators, and Support Staff,

You are cordially invited to peruse this book, *The ADMIRE Framework for Inclusion*, to increase your knowledge about the inclusion competencies and supports the students you instruct require to make advancements. As architects construct, educators instruct. Architects require time and preparation for proper construction; inclusion classrooms require the same planning, prep, and patience. A building is constructed with step-by-step designs, and so are inclusion classrooms and worlds.

This includes plans, supplies, resources, and qualified individuals to collaborate with as partners and teams. The appropriate weather and climate promote comfortability and growth. That perfect *edifice of inclusion* therefore requires time, continued effort, materials, strategies, and prepared personnel who honor each learner's individualized education program (IEP), with eyes on how the parts connect to the whole. *The ADMIRE Framework for Inclusion* values how individuals capitalize on one another's strength and ability within the dynamics of the inclusion classroom. When exceptionality is perceived as a strength, not a deficit, then the sky is the limit.

One floor of a building is constructed at a time, yet the building stands as a whole. Inclusion classrooms gain their strength from the power generated by each student, respectful peers who comprise that inclusion classroom, and the collaborative dedication of the general and special educators, administrators, and supportive families. You are invited to read *The ADMIRE Framework for Inclusion* to learn more.

Respectfully yours,

Toby J. Karten

Attitudes Toward Inclusion

In theory, inclusion goes hand in hand with preparation for life. Mastery of the prerequisite academic skills for successful postsecondary outcomes is an agenda that general and special educators want for *all* students. As the title suggests, the ADMIRE inclusion framework treats a positive attitude as a prerequisite. If we ADMIRE inclusion and the possibilities it offers, then learner successes are catapulted. However, this is often easier said than done.

Attitudes and actions influence results. Teachers who are openly favorable toward the inclusion of students with a disability may also harbor fears about how that disability impacts their teaching practices (Jury, Perrin, Rohmer, & Desombre, 2021). As a teacher and inclusion coach for elementary through high school grades, I've met consummate professionals who are motivated to ensure success for their students, but they lack prior experiences working with a certain population of students with differences. Teachers need more knowledge and support strategies on what works best for students with intellectual and emotional differences and those with autism (Sharma & Sokal, 2016).

Throughout this book, I invite you to assess, delineate, monitor, instruct, revise, and engage both professionals and students, as well as their families, to activate, decide, model, involve, reflect, and enrich each other with increased knowledge and skills. The curriculum, what is taught, cannot reach each student the same way; therefore, an awareness of individual student differences is imperative to ensure that the inclusion practices are appropriate and implemented with fidelity. If a professional thinks that a student's specific label of disability negates inclusion successes and they do not know what needs to be done differently, then frustration results for the professionals, students, and families. Bottom line: negativity thwarts growth.

Positive attitudes toward inclusion can have a significant impact *and* can be the biggest hurdle to the effective execution of inclusive classroom practices (Carrington, Tangen, & Beutel, 2019; Karten, 2015). As an example, a quantitative research study (Kazmi, Kamran, & Siddiqui, 2023) reveals that teachers' sense of self-efficacy mediates the relationship between behavioral disorders and inclusive settings in schools. The teachers play a pivotal role in accommodating disabilities, as it directly impacts students' learning and development (Raath & Hay, 2016). The study finds that teachers who hold positive attitudes toward including students with disabilities in their classrooms are more likely to provide accommodations and modifications, foster positive relationships, and create a more inclusive classroom environment (Kazmi et al., 2023).

It's with this asset orientation that this book was written. We use the *ADMIRE* acronym as follows to support all students in the inclusion classroom.

A Assess and activate

D Decide and delineate

M Model and monitor

I Instruct and involve

R Reflect and revise

E Engage and enrich

Each chapter of this book includes evidence-based practices with inclusion applications for preservice and current inclusion professionals who are blessed to instruct students with and without exceptionality to create a microcosm for that journey called life.

ADMIRE Inclusion Supports and Actions

The ADMIRE model is the basis for the strategies presented in this book. The acronym summarizes the inclusion supports applied across the grades, exceptionalities, and disciplines in K–12 classrooms. Table I.1 (page 4) lists sixty-five actions, illustrating how they align with the six ADMIRE categories. Each chapter includes a reproducible you can use to take notes about ways to ADMIRE inclusion that stood out to you from that chapter.

About This Book

The ADMIRE Framework for Inclusion propagates that the teachers of students who are taught in inclusion classrooms have high expectations regardless of the challenges students present. Inclusion educators continually assess and progress-monitor the knowledge and skills of individual learners. That data impact the inclusion plans with the appropriately delivered supports that lead toward mastery. With fidelity, planning, and collaborative supports, inclusion educators and families advance the competencies of students to prepare them for successful postsecondary lives.

This book explores student realities along with comprehensive inclusion practices for planning, instruction, and advancements for K–12 students taught within inclusion classrooms. It is not a quick read. It takes a great deal of digestion because it is filled with inclusion supports for students, their families, general and special educators, and

Table I.1: ADMIRE Actions

A **Assess and Activate**	The teacher assesses and activates: 1. Prior successes, student levels, language needs, and culture 2. Interest 3. Motivation 4. IEP goals and 504 plans 5. Learner profiles 6. Emotionally safe learning environments 7. Working memories 8. Ongoing learning 9. Class and student routines
D **Decide and Delineate**	The teacher decides and delineates: 10. Learning targets 11. Formative assessments 12. Evidence-based practices 13. Baseline levels 14. Procedures 15. Learning norms 16. School rules 17. Self-regulation 18. Step-by-step organization 19. Transitions 20. Collaborative staff and student roles 21. Time frames
M **Model and Monitor**	The teacher models and monitors: 22. Learning activities 23. Assessments 24. Respect for differences 25. Evidence of learning: examples and nonexamples 26. Student behavior 27. Rubrics 28. Critical thinking skills 29. Open-ended responses 30. Efforts and progress through portfolios 31. Universal Design for Learning (UDL)
I **Instruct and Involve**	The teacher instructs and involves: 32. All students 33. General education and special education staff 34. Administration 35. Families 36. Coaches 37. Related service providers

	38. Differentiated instruction (DI), multitiered system of supports (MTSS) 39. Understanding by Design (UbD) 40. Project- (problem-) based learning (PBL) 41. Cooperative learning (CL) 42. Visual, auditory, kinesthetic, and tactile (VAKT) elements 43. Whole-part-whole lessons 44. Low-high technology options 45. Learning celebrations
R **Reflect and Revise**	The teacher reflects on and revises: 46. Supports (to help, but not enable), with a plan to reduce and fade assistance 47. Lessons with discrete task analysis 48. Engagements and processes 49. Illustrations and visualizations 50. Timelines 51. Pacing 52. Lesson objectives 53. Instructional models 54. Successful outcome criteria 55. Achievements
E **Engage and Enrich**	The teacher engages with and enriches: 56. Opportunities for advancement, practice, reinforcement, and repetition 57. Revisiting to solidify concepts 58. Creativity 59. Cross-disciplinary connections 60. College and career prep goals 61. Anchor and sponge activities 62. Higher- and lower-level learners 63. Collaborative approaches 64. Metacognition 65. Edutainment

related staff. Its concepts are solidified with activities that you are invited to absorb with multiple representations that include audio, visuals, and both low-tech and high-tech resources and tools that are equally high-impact and evidence based, with neither being better than the other.

This book is intended to be used as a collaborative resource, since many professionals in education work together to make the advancements a reality for students with and without exceptionality. It offers sound practices for classroom teachers at all levels with embedded scaffolding and K–12 models intended for duplication in your grades for students who learn alongside each other as grade-level peers in inclusion classrooms. As the author, my role is to facilitate that process. Fashioned as a suitable guide, this book aims to remove the labor-intensive work teachers fear of most inclusion books to provide students of all ability levels access to and success with the curriculum. Inclusion means that the knowledge and skills learners need to be successful in life are not omitted from their course of study because they receive specialized services under a category of exceptionality.

Chapter 1 (page 9) sets the groundwork by defining inclusion and summarizing current research in the fields of education and inclusion. The premise of special education is that the services are delivered with the appropriate strategies and interventions, whether that instruction occurs within inclusion classrooms or in other settings considered more restrictive on the least restrictive environment (LRE) continuum, which outlines the range of educational placements. The chapter explores the evidence-based practices that are connected to how each student learns.

Chapter 2 (page 29) examines some of the characteristics of exceptionality that allow teachers to view students as individuals, never capped or defined by a label. Some students know more, and some know less; some care more, and some care less. Some have IEPs, some have 504 plans, and some learners are not identified for services, yet they struggle with academics or behaviors. In this chapter, we imagine what it looks like in a real-world context to see student diversity as an asset rather than a deficit.

Chapter 3 (page 49) connects theory with the realities of how educators, students, and families apply the ADMIRE model to K–12 inclusion plans. Whether students are identifying the theme of *The Outsiders* (Hinton, 1967), comparing groups of items to identify greater than and less than in sets, graphing quadratic equations, comparing political systems, or calculating the formula weight of compounds, we ADMIRE inclusion. Given that successful inclusion classrooms require planning with and for students, we examine tools teachers can use to plan at the year, month, and week levels. When we ADMIRE inclusion and commit to collaborating to meet students' needs, families, students, and educators bring out the best in each other.

Chapter 4 (page 75) offers guidance and resources teachers need to practice supportive classroom management. This includes cultivating a positive classroom environment, setting routines and expectations, providing individualized support, and prioritizing ADMIRE inclusion principles.

Chapter 5 (page 95) acknowledges common challenges in inclusion and proposes helpful solutions. While challenges can feel frustrating, they offer amazing opportunities for innovation and invention. Solutions discussed in this chapter include adjusting complexity and delivery, anticipating barriers to inclusion, tapping the diverse strengths found in inclusion classrooms, and adapting instruction to meet students' needs.

Chapter 6 (page 125) explores how to manage inclusion anxiety for inclusion staff, students, and families. The text offers ways to collaboratively help the students who need more or less to reinforce abstract and representational concepts. The solutions need not be complex. As an example, taking a mathematics walk reinforces the geometry vocabulary for concrete learners while it also allows a few inattentive and fidgety learners an acceptable motoric release beyond the fake errand you might set up with a colleague.

Chapter 7 (page 149) calls teachers to ADMIRE wellness for students, teachers, administrators, support staff, and families to create a positive and supportive classroom culture. Topics in this chapter include wellness competencies, tips for ensuring teacher well-being, a ten-step intervention plan to secure student wellness, and reminders for nurturing relationships.

The ADMIRE model connects to each discipline, each student, and each professional. Administrators are vital partners who support students, their families, and educators. The inclusion partnerships facilitate growth. Inclusion teams collaborate to meet the needs of each and every learner. This book provides content-specific strategies and resources to achieve successful inclusion realities for students and staff. It invites staff to reflect on and revise their inclusion supports to engage and enrich all learners. We apply the inclusion frameworks in the templates and activities offered in each of the chapters so they connect to your inclusion realities. Resources for planning, instruction, assessments, and ongoing professional growth across the disciplines are presented in print and digital format.

The ADMIRE Framework for Inclusion offers a fresh perspective on how we help students with and without exceptionality succeed in the classroom and life. Some learners who struggle have lower levels of self-esteem, more or less family support, and both successful and frustrating experiences that influence their ability to learn, remember, and very often care more or less about subjects, concepts, and themselves. Access to and achievement of core academic and functional knowledge and skills is an outcome for students with and without exceptionalities who are taught within K–12 classrooms. School professionals provide the supports that honor the diversity of our student population. Thank you to all the professionals, collaborative partners, students, and families who take on this task.

CHAPTER 1

What Students and Staff Need to Know

Appropriate is a key word in inclusion classrooms. Inclusion acknowledges how evidence-based practices *appropriately* connect to individual learners in the general education classroom. So, how do we as educators determine what *appropriate* means? Professionals, students, and families acknowledge that a student's starting or baseline level defines the *appropriate* behaviors and actions. Whether students are seated in the classroom learning about fractions, political systems, or consonant blends, they need *appropriate* ways to learn the content. Professionals and related staff must be aware of who is learning what and who may need more or less support.

In this chapter, we discuss common myths about inclusion as well as seven questions to guide us to define inclusion for the purposes of this book. Next, we look to research to learn about keys to successful inclusion, including evidence-based practices, collaboration, and professional development. Finally, we zoom in to explore what it means to ADMIRE how students achieve competencies within their inclusion classroom.

Common Myths About Inclusion

Inclusion is the process of providing equal access and opportunities for individuals with disabilities to participate fully in all aspects of society. This can include education, employment, recreation, and social activities (United Nations, n.d.).

The National Center for Education Statistics (NCES, 2023) reports that the amount of time students spend in general education classes increased from 2009 to 2020, with 95 percent of school-age students served under the Individuals With Disabilities Education Improvement Act (IDEA, 2004) in fall 2020 enrolled in regular schools. When students attend a neighborhood school for their education, not a special or private school out of district, their belonging within their community increases as they learn and make friends with peers their age.

Before we clarify what inclusion *is*, it's helpful to recognize what inclusion *is not*. Let's examine five common myths about inclusion.

1. **Myth:** Inclusion is not appropriate for all students with disabilities.

    Fact: Inclusion is a legal right for all students with disabilities under IDEA and should be considered as an option for every student (U.S. Department of Education, n.d.a).

2. **Myth:** Inclusion means that students with disabilities will receive less individualized attention.

    Fact: Inclusion actually provides opportunities for more individualized attention and support, as students with disabilities can receive specialized instruction within the general education classroom (Friend & Bursuck, 2019).

3. **Myth:** Inclusion is too expensive.

    Fact: Inclusion is an efficient use of funds and holds the potential to improve education for all students. Funds are allocated for teacher and staff training and the provision of appropriate learning resources. Making education inclusive is not about cost cutting. Investments in inclusion may eliminate redundancy and the high costs of running parallel programs (Open Society Foundations, 2019).

4. **Myth:** Inclusion places too much burden on teachers.

    Fact: Inclusion can benefit teachers, students, and the community with collaboration to creatively brainstorm and expand ideas to welcome and connect to a diversity of difference (Bill & Melinda Gates Foundation, 2024; Karten, 2021).

5. **Myth:** Inclusion is only beneficial for students with disabilities.

    Fact: Inclusion benefits all students by promoting diversity, fostering empathy and understanding, and preparing students for the real world (Cologon, 2022; Understood Team, n.d.).

Now that we've dispelled these common myths about inclusion, let's turn our attention to what inclusion *is*. As educators, we need to define inclusion beyond a textbook definition by involving a reality-based connection. Consider the following basic facts about students.

- **Students with and without exceptionality have strengths:** Teachers and other staff can ease the classroom struggles a student may have by capitalizing on their stronger skills, interests, and abilities and by valuing who the student is with responsive, appropriate inclusion interventions (Karten, 2017a). The term *exceptionalities* in K–12 schooling refers to both disabilities and giftedness (IRIS Center, n.d.b).

- **Students achieve mastery at different times:** Renowned cognitive psychologist Benjamin S. Bloom (1976) notes the following variables influence achievement levels and learning outcomes.
    - Instruction that is approached sensitively and systematically
    - Delivery when and where students have learning difficulties

- Sufficient time to achieve mastery
- Clear criteria for what constitutes mastery

- **Students are not identical:** Students have unique capacities when it comes to their academic levels, motivation, prior experiences, sensory input and output, behavior, home supports, and more, regardless of if they share a label of identification, as with those under IDEA. Diversity jolts us into cognitive action in ways that homogeneity simply does not (Phillips, 2014).
- **Each student's starting point varies:** Diversity and differences among all individuals should be accepted, respected, and valued as part of inclusion. It also targets the development of school systems for every individual (Ghosh, 2022).
- **Inclusion is not a program or service; it is a way of life (Karten, 2015):** As stated in UNICEF's (2017) overview of the Convention on the Rights of Persons With Disabilities, inclusion education promotes:
  - Participation in public life
  - Exercise of legal capacity
  - Work and employment
  - Adequate standard of living (p. 6)

With these facts about inclusion now at the forefront, let's examine a series of questions to guide us to a working definition of inclusion that lives up to the reality of day-to-day practice in the classroom.

Seven Questions to Guide a Definition

As an inclusion facilitator, I cannot underscore enough the importance of asking questions to generate the inclusion actions. Inclusion inquiry spurs collaborative thought on the next steps of instruction, rather than thinking a student cannot or will not learn a specific concept within the inclusion classroom. The questions posited in the following sections generate inquiry and increase awareness of the inclusion practices.

What Does Inclusion Look Like?

The inclusion classroom can be as soothing as a calm beach day or as hectic as navigating the expeditious flow of air traffic at a busy airport. Inclusion at its best is invisible. We see the whole classroom, never the stigmatization of individual students. Each student is an integral member of that classroom from the early elementary grades and onward in the secondary classrooms across the subjects. Inclusion in schools is the preparation for life (Karten, 2021).

Educators must not approach inclusion with a cookie-cutter mentality; specific student populations educated in that same inclusion classroom may each have a different set of competencies that require a different set of inclusion supports. These populations include, for example, twice-exceptional learners; students with learning differences; learners with attention deficit hyperactivity disorder (ADHD); learners with social and behavioral differences; learners with autism; learners with intellectual or emotional differences; culturally diverse learners; and learners with hearing, visual, or physical impairments.

Inclusion is about peers with and without differences learning together side by side in a grade-level classroom to achieve academic, social, communication, and functional skills. It occurs when communities of learners of the same age are educated together within natural school settings. This is not a policy, place, or service, but rather a way for students with differences to have access to the general education curriculum with the appropriate planning, preparation, and participation as they further benefit from peer modeling and supports. Inclusion education values the strengths of all learners to be accepted in classrooms, schools, and communities, and as adults in inclusive societies.

What Professional Learning Experiences Do Teachers in Inclusion Environments Require to Achieve Successful Outcomes?

Teachers in inclusion classrooms need to be knowledgeable about each student's strengths and unique needs, evidence-based strategies and interventions, grade-level content, types of measurements that assess and progress-monitor student knowledge, and ways to capitalize on family supports.

Professional learning experiences for teachers in inclusion classrooms should focus on supporting teachers to connect to their students. Professional development equips teachers to apply strategies such as emotional check-ins, art, music, movement, visuals, small groups, curriculum videos, and positive reinforcement.

What Are the Most Important Ingredients of an Inclusion Classroom?

You wouldn't bake a cake without first preheating the oven, finding the right-sized pan, gathering the ingredients, and consulting a recipe. In the same way, teachers must gather the materials and strategies needed for inclusion. Although inclusion presents certain complexities, it requires basic ingredients. The most important are:

- A positive *can-do, will-do* attitude
- Time to plan and prepare
- Collaboration with colleagues, students, and families
- Appropriate scaffolding to match individual student and staff levels and competencies
- Emotionally safe environments
- High expectations for all students
- Knowledge about individual students
- Knowledge about the curriculum
- Willingness to grow and learn

Who Are the Collaborative Partners?

Collaborative partners include general and special education administrators, educators, and all staff. Related staff providers are also included; think physical therapists and occupational therapists; speech-language pathologists; mobility trainers; literacy and mathematics interventionists; supervisors; coaches; art, music, and physical education teachers; media and technology specialists; paraprofessionals; and instructional support teams. School bus drivers, secretaries, custodians, lunchroom aides, families, and students themselves also count as collaborative partners.

What Roles Do Family Members Play?

Family members are the ones who multiply each student's academic, social, emotional, and behavioral gains. Home environments that partner with school norms reinforce the learning and communicate a loud and clear message that advocates for and reinforces each student's success. Professionals meet families of students with exceptionalities who experience a variety of emotions at different stages of adjustment. Ann Turnbull, Rud Turnbull, and Michael L. Wehmeyer (2013) outline the emotions that families of students with special needs may experience, with stages of shock, denial, anger, guilt, grief, and acceptance as they come to terms with their child's exceptionality. This happens on different timelines, but professionals who listen without judgment very often impact positive outlooks with step-by-step school-home collaboration. Families of children with intellectual disabilities may experience emotional distress related to the child's behavior and social isolation (Telethon Kids Institute, n.d.). According to Kate Davis and Susana Gavidia-Payne (2009), parents of children with autism spectrum disorder may go through stages of shock, denial, anger, guilt, depression, and acceptance as they adjust to the diagnosis.

Overall, families maximize student competencies. Professionals meet families as they try to sort through a lot of information that they never knew they needed to know and emotions that surface as a result, as they try to figure out how to help their children as they navigate the special education jargon of initials and terms that often overwhelm, rather than soothe. It is important for professionals to understand the emotional experiences of families of students with special needs and to provide appropriate support throughout the stages of adjustment.

How Can Students With Different Ability Levels and Skills Simultaneously Benefit From Being Taught in the Same Inclusion Classroom?

The inclusion classroom is often a microcosm of the world. The goal of education, whether it is labeled under the umbrella of *special* or *general education*, is to prepare students to lead productive, independent adult lives. When the students are given the appropriate scaffolding that matches and advances their present level of performance to achieve academic and social gains within inclusion classrooms, then they are prepared with attainable adult successes. Instructing students with different ability levels within the same classroom requires preparation and planning for the whole class, small groups, and individualized learners. Each student is unique, and each class has its own needs and personalities that must be addressed. Evidence-based and instructionally sound practices such as differentiated instruction, low-high technology, adding VAKT engagements, collaborative instruction (such as co-teaching models), and PBL, along with positive behavioral interventions and supports (PBIS), benefit learners with and without difference.

Instruction within inclusion classrooms needs to think every learner is part of a classroom orchestra, with each contributing their music to simultaneously produce that excellent symphony. As with orchestras, each musician requires training and practice before they are expected to perform their best. The educators are the ones who masterfully conduct that orchestra with the support and collaboration of the administrators, students, and families.

When Would Inclusion Be an Inappropriate Placement?

Inclusion would be an inappropriate placement if the needs of one group of students were sacrificed for another. Inclusion would be an inappropriate placement if a student was physically included but emotionally, socially, or academically excluded. According to the U.S. federal law IDEA, the general education classroom is looked at as the first option of placement if it best meets that student's needs. For example, if a student's disability requires intensive one-to-one attention or specialized instruction, inclusion in a general education classroom may not be appropriate. In such cases, a more restrictive setting, such as a special education classroom, may be necessary. According to IDEA (2004), students with disabilities should be placed in the LRE that is appropriate for their needs. Inclusion may not always be an appropriate placement for a student with a disability if it prevents the student from receiving an education that matches their academic, social, emotional, behavioral, and communicative skill sets. Inclusion, therefore, requires appropriate assessment and instruction for *each* student in the class.

Inclusion is about students achieving success, under the auspices of trained educators who focus on each student's unique strengths and promote the potential of all. If the inclusion environment does not meet that student's needs with the appropriate supports or frustrates that student who fears or notices that they are conspicuously different from their inclusion peers, then they become stigmatized by the inclusion classroom, and the general education classroom negates the development of that learner's competencies.

Given what we've discovered about inclusion so far, figure 1.1 depicts *inclusion* in the form of a Frayer model, a graphic organizer that clarifies a concept via its definition, characteristics, examples, and nonexamples.

Inclusion

Inclusion Definition
Peers with and without differences are learning side by side in grade-level classrooms. Instruction includes academic, social-emotional, behavioral, and functional learning targets based on their individualized needs.

Inclusion Characteristics
Teachers receive professional learning experiences to connect to and maximize:
  a. Students' diverse and unique competencies
  b. Application of evidence-based inclusion strategies and interventions
  c. Knowledge of grade-level content that is connected to baseline knowledge
  d. Measurements that assess and progress-monitor student knowledge and skills

Inclusion Examples
Multiple entry points are offered for student access to and success with grade-level curriculum

Discrete task analysis is employed

Responsive learner engagements, representations, actions, and expressions

High expectations for general and special education students

Accepting attitudes of professionals, families, and peers

Differentiated instruction for content and process to address varying learner levels

Combination of inclusion services

Ongoing communication, collaboration, and reflection

Inclusion Nonexamples
Offering identical strategies and supports to all learners

Considered to be a policy, place, or service

Stigmatization of learners with IEPs within the inclusion classroom

No small-group instruction for repetition, practice, or enrichment

Missing or inappropriate emotional, social, behavioral, and academic supports

Not aligning inclusion supports with the specially designed instruction within a student's IEP

Figure 1.1: Inclusion Frayer model.

Inclusion in the Research

What does research show us about inclusion and how students learn? The following sections explore important aspects uncovered by research into inclusion, specifically evidence-based practices, collaboration, professional development, and benefits and challenges for peers and adults.

Evidence-Based Practices

As teachers, we know from experience that students vary. *Neuroscience*—the study of the nervous system and how it relates to behavior, cognition, and learning—affirms that students learn through a variety of processes such as attention, perception, memory, and problem solving (Howard-Jones, 2014; McCandliss, 2010).

Though teachers are not expected to be neuroscientists, we need to understand there's a limit to what we know. This requires that we approach students with curiosity rather than assumptions. Reflection about neuroscience is imperative. A student's differing behavior and learning aren't random; they arise from a valid reason. As professionals, we need to know that students' brains search for patterns and ways to piece together, process, and remember what they hear, see, and understand. When we seek to understand the reason, we may identify a specific subskill the student needs and the alternate representation or engagement that is required. Evidence-based practices structure the classroom instruction with increased awareness, compassion, collaboration, and reflection. When we assess, delineate, monitor, involve, and reflect, we respond with pedagogy that engages learners' brains with the responsive instruction.

Collaboration

Inclusion is not a solitary task. Inclusion research has implications for students, teachers, support staff, and families who attend the same school in the same community. A successful inclusive classroom requires a collaborative effort among teachers, families, and other professionals to view diversity in a positive light (Ainscow, Dyson, & Weiner, 2013).

Ideally, families partnering with educational systems advocate for their children and have the power to plan for support and catapult their children's growth. That is an ideal scenario, but some learners with and without IEPs do not have supportive home environments. That's when school personnel intervene with home-family supports and interventions (for example, school guidance counselors, social workers, and school psychologists). Just as each student is unique, so is each learner's level of family supports.

The collaborative instructional practice of co-teaching often occurs in inclusion classrooms. That is when two or more professionals, often a general and special education teacher, work together to provide a class of learners with their instruction. This includes a configuration of schedules with roles and responsibilities to co-plan, co-instruct, co-monitor, and co-assess learners. Some co-teachers and support staff may work with multiple grades and teachers in different subject areas in different schools, while other co-teachers are assigned full-time for one classroom or grade. Whether a co-teacher is present 100 percent of the time, the supports are constant. That's why collaborative planning and preparation are essential.

Having two teachers in the room helps address a diversity of academic and student behaviors to offer learners with and without exceptionality shared instruction and increased attention (Karten, 2015). Co-teaching practices include collaborative models with responsibilities that allow for a combination of shared whole-class, small-group, and individualized instruction. Pedagogy includes co-teaching models such as team teaching; alternative teaching; stations, centers, or forums; parallel teaching; lead-assist; and teach-observe. (For example, in lead-assist, one co-teacher can keep data, while the other co-teacher instructs.) Collaboration occurs face-to-face and with online communication, planning, and consultation (Karten & Murawski, 2020).

Administrators are an integral part of the co-teaching process. When it comes to inclusion, they collaborate with teachers in myriad ways. Consider the following ways administrators contribute to co-teaching.

- Providing ongoing professional development with co-teaching supports
- Pairing personnel
- Structuring time parameters
- Facilitating conflict resolution
- Supporting a strength paradigm
- Setting up logistics
- Curriculum—specially designed instruction applications
- Knowing content
- Scheduling
- Propagating growth opportunities
- Knowing student characteristics
- Promoting team mentality
- Building relationships with staff, students, and families
- Following legislation and IEPs
- Framing conversations

Collaboration includes the students, too. Inclusion classrooms comprise students who have diverse levels, skills, and interests. However, the inclusion norms are collaborative ones that apply to all students; they are set up with this diversity in mind (for example, following class routines and procedures, interacting appropriately with teachers and peers, and reflecting on advancements to be a forward learner). Together we learn and together we grow, but we need to collaborate with each other to make inclusion happen and thrive.

Professional Development

Inclusion does not occur spontaneously. Teachers need ongoing professional development and teacher training to effectively support diverse learners (Holmqvist & Lelinge, 2021; Karten, 2021). Inclusion is always a process, never a manufactured product. Just like students in classrooms have differing prior knowledge and skill sets, so do adults. Some general and special education teachers may have learned about research-based practices such as DI, MTSS, PBIS, PBL, UbD, and UDL in their preservice studies, but all is naught if educators do not have professional development training on how to best implement these evidence-based practices in inclusion classrooms. The translation of these evidence-based practices and the research that supports their practice are offered in table 1.1, with application threaded in chapters 2–7 (pages 29, 49, 75, 95, 125, and 149, respectively).

Table 1.1: Evidence-Based Practices Overview

Evidence-Based Practices	Academic Vocabulary
Differentiated instruction (DI) DI is an evidence-based practice that connects the curriculum to student diversity.	☐ Content ☐ Process ☐ Product ☐ Learner strengths, interests, profiles ☐ Prior knowledge ☐ Meaningful tasks
Research supports that differentiation is a way to effectively serve students in heterogeneous classrooms while being responsive to varied learner needs (Wu, 2013).	
Multitiered system of supports (MTSS) MTSS ensures that all students, those with and without IEPs, excel. All students receive solid core curriculum, alongside their peers, during Tier 1. Intervention in Tiers 2–3 offers additional and more intensive supports, which are not scheduled when new learning or the core instruction occurs.	☐ Framework of academic and behavioral interventions ☐ Identification-screening ☐ Progress monitoring ☐ Support and collaboration ☐ Core instruction for all (Tier 1) ☐ Tiers 2–3 for struggling learners with more intensive support
Research supports that MTSS can be an effective approach for promoting inclusion in the school setting. By providing differentiated instruction and support to all students, including those with disabilities, MTSS can help to ensure that all students have access to high-quality education and opportunities for academic and behavioral success (Arway, 2023).	
Positive behavioral interventions and supports (PBIS) PBIS promotes a positive school climate within a data-driven multitiered system of behavioral expectations and supports.	☐ Appropriate positive behavior supports ☐ Schoolwide, class- and learner-specific ☐ Team monitoring ☐ Data based ☐ Incentives ☐ Expectations ☐ Proactive and preventative
Research supports PBIS in promoting positive behavior and reducing problem behavior in inclusive schools with lower suspensions and higher reading and mathematics proficiencies (Pas, Ryoo, Musci, & Bradshaw, 2019).	

Project-based learning (PBL)	☐ Student-centered pedagogy
PBL is a student-centered pedagogy that offers learners access to and exploration of the knowledge, skills, and concepts through active exploration of real-world challenges and problems (driving questions).	☐ Offers access to and exploration of concepts ☐ Active exploration of real-world challenges and problems ☐ Driving questions ☐ Invites inquiry ☐ Collaboration with peers ☐ Critical thinking skills ☐ Constructivist approach
Research supports PBL as an inquiry-based instructional approach that allows students to work together in small groups to solve problem-based questions that have several solutions (Jonassen, 2003). PBL is effective in promoting engagement, motivation, and learning among all students, including those with disabilities and other diverse needs, to promote collaboration and problem-solving skills (Deutscher et al., 2021).	
Understanding by Design (UbD)	☐ Curriculum planning
UbD specifies the desired results of what students will learn (Stage 1), along with the evaluative criteria (Stage 2) and the learning plan that makes that happen (Stage 3).	☐ Outlines the understandings and skills ☐ Prioritizes learning goals and outcomes of a lesson or unit ☐ Evidence and assessment outlined at onset ☐ Collaborative learning plan ☐ Products connected to outcome ☐ Backward design
Research supports UbD and shares that UbD is not a rigid program or prescriptive recipe but a set of helpful tools to purposefully think about curriculum to prioritize the learning goals and outcomes of a lesson or unit, rather than just the content or activities (McTighe & Wiggins, 2012). UbD was developed by Grant Wiggins and Jay McTighe (2005) and is widely used in education.	
Universal Design for Learning (UDL)	☐ Multiple engagements
UDL values multiple means of learner engagement, representation, action, and expression. The affective recognition and strategic networks address the why, what, and how of student learning. UDL connects to learner interests, self-regulation, comprehension, physical actions, perceptions, expressions, communications, and goal setting.	☐ Multiple representations ☐ Multiple actions and expressions ☐ Goals, methods, materials, assessments ☐ Barriers minimized ☐ Recognition (what) ☐ Skills and strategies (how) ☐ Addresses learner variability ☐ Accessible to a variety of learners ☐ Connection to affect
Research supports UDL as an instructional design framework that can be used to address learner variability in the classroom (Rao & Meo, 2016; Rose & Meyer, 2002; Meyer, Rose, & Gordon, 2014). UDL has been found to improve student motivation, engagement, and self-efficacy, as well as academic achievement and retention (Capp, 2017; Dalton, 2017). The Center for Applied Special Technology (CAST; www.cast.org) has resources with UDL guidelines for teachers.	

Benefits and Challenges for Peers and Adults

Inclusion promotes positive social and emotional development for students with disabilities by providing opportunities for social interaction with peers without disabilities (UNICEF, 2017). This can lead to increased self-esteem and social skills. For example, the inclusion classroom offers opportunities for students to work in cooperative groups to explore more knowledge and skills with their peers. Cooperative learning has been found to be a successful teaching strategy for inclusion classrooms. According to researchers Spencer J. Salend and Laurel M. Garrick Duhaney (1999), cooperative learning allows for students with disabilities to work together with their peers in a supportive and inclusive environment, which can lead to increased academic achievement and social skills development.

Cooperative learning has been found to have a positive impact on the attitudes and perceptions of students without disabilities toward their peers with disabilities (Willis, 2021). Cooperative learning includes strategies such as group projects, peer tutoring, and team-building activities. Inclusion teachers provide clear instructions and expectations for each activity and ensure that students of diverse skill sets are productively engaged in the learning process.

Inclusion has both benefits and challenges, but when teachers admire the challenges, they're able to embrace collaborative solutions. Some general and special educators, students, and families require increased structure, awareness, compassion, collaboration, and reflection. Often, this requires a change—in personnel, schedules, instruction, or assessment.

I reference the TTWWADI Syndrome, known as *That's the Way We Always Did It*, in my professional coaching sessions. The TTWWADI Syndrome is a common problem in organizations where people resist change and innovation because they are comfortable with the way things have always been done (Schaaf, n.d.; Kotter & Cohen, 2002). As an inclusion facilitator, I encourage open-mindedness, brainstorming new ideas, capitalizing on one another's prior experiences and strengths, and fostering a culture of continuous improvement, collaboration, and reflection. It's important to remember that change can be difficult, but it's often necessary for growth and success in both personal and professional settings.

ADMIRE the Competencies

Together, we ADMIRE how students achieve competencies within their inclusion classrooms. This cannot occur without the evidence-based practices that include, but are not limited to, UDL, UbD, MTSS, DI, PBL, PBIS, and cooperative learning. As established earlier, staff need to ensure that learners across broad spectrums, who have differing prior knowledge, intellectual levels, IEP classifications, 504 plans, behaviors, social and emotional levels, sensory needs, physical acumens, communication preferences, motivations, interests, strengths, cultures, language proficiencies, and home environments, achieve high levels of performance. This diversity necessitates the planning and preparation of diverse strategies to achieve competencies across the grades and disciplines. Ultimately, student mastery translates to young adults who are ready to go on to college and enter the workforce.

To accomplish this monumental task, staff need to continually meet students at their instructional levels to raise their achievement. ADMIRE is intended to circumvent the existing or perceived barriers by infusing strategies that honor student levels and evidence-based practices. Integral ways to achieve inclusion successes with applications to the students, families, professionals, and the subjects taught follow, with application to the specific numbers (1–65) in the ADMIRE chart, as table I.1 (page 4) illustrates. These ADMIRE numbers are referenced in the next few sections, with ongoing curriculum applications in chapters 2–7 (pages 29, 49, 75, 95, 125, and 149, respectively) to raise the achievements for students and staff.

Assess and Activate

Assessment of prior successes determines student levels (1) and guides instruction. Honoring diversity with high expectations offers responsive instruction (Murata, 2013) that connects to learner interests (2) and activates student motivation (3) to the curriculum to honor IEP goals and 504 plans (4) and cultural diversity. Learner profiles (5) need to be established and then activated in emotionally safe learning environments (6). Student data include basics such as grade level, date of birth, IEP classification, academic and functional levels of performance, annual goals in IEPs and 504 plans, cultural factors, language proficiency, prior content knowledge, and inclusion experiences. Strengths and interests are applicable to subjects, modalities, and learner preferences for reading, writing, mathematics, science, engineering, history, art, music, physical education, technology, working with others, self-evaluation, animals, dance, soccer, and more. The learner profile template resource can act as an informal screening instrument to plan for and monitor strides.

Students are like flowers, with educators as the gardeners who assess and activate growth from the early grades through high school and beyond. Staff and families plant academic, social, behavioral, and emotional seeds. Like flowers that strive to grow in varied climates, students are exposed to different elements with varying academic, behavioral, emotional, social, communicative, physical, and language supports in their homes and schools. The ultimate goal is to provide all learners with the appropriate conditions, regardless of the barriers presented. Schools and homes supply the soil for the seeds to germinate, but like a seed that develops leaves to make its own food through photosynthesis, students need to develop self-sufficiency. Whether flowers grow indoors or outside, all require sunlight, water, and nutrients, but the degrees fluctuate from flower type to flower type. Both humans and flowers thrive within hospitable environments that offer specially designed supports. Respiration occurs with the elements of air or water, and instruction occurs in a variety of settings with a multitude of inclusion interventions, resources, and supports.

There needs to be a yin-yang of cognitive and affective skills. Within the inclusion classroom, achievement involves more than just getting the correct answer. Students need to know why an answer is correct and persevere in solving tasks that require a range of reading, writing, mathematics, and cross-disciplinary critical thinking skills. Therefore, self-management, self-efficacy, self-discovery, and social awareness of self and others impacts academics. Research highlights the impact of social competencies, reflections, and attitudes concerning social and emotional learning (SEL) and the connection to academic achievements (Durlak, Weissberg, Dymnicki, Taylor, & Schellinger, 2011). Self-regulatory student checklists target increased awareness of student initiatives that influence academics.

Student diversity is often deeply rooted, not clearly visible or labeled. Even when student levels are assessed and activated, school staff need to reflect and acknowledge that students' working memories (7) may not hold equal pieces of information. Teachers must infuse evidence-based practices—such as cooperative learning and adding more visuals or movement—to ensure that students retain information to manipulate the concepts as the years progress. Strategies are matched to the data, and results are listed.

Learning is ongoing (8), with no finish line. Assessment and activation also include sharing class and student routines (9) with colleagues, families, related service providers, and all students. Common formative assessments involve the evidence collected, learning intentions, consistency, collaboration, changes in instruction, building bridges between units, and providing ongoing feedback (Ainsworth, 2022; Wisconsin Department of Public Instruction, 2017). Assessment and activation promote student growth within nurturing inclusion environments.

Decide and Delineate

Once teachers have assessed students, they use grade-level baseline levels as the starting point for multitiered instruction to decide and delineate the learning targets (10). Analysis of progress toward mastery of the curriculum is ongoing with embedded formative assessments (11) and the monitoring of response to evidence-based practices (12) to advance baseline levels (13). Collaborative decisions are made to delineate specific procedures (14) that connect to student achievements and IEP goals. Learning norms (15) and school rules (16) are nonnegotiable since they promote self-regulation (17) with step-by-step organization (18) that clarifies student expectations. Norms and rules delineate shared goals while inclusion classrooms respect diverse student levels. Table 1.2 illustrates a sample of classroom norms and corresponding inclusion supports. To create your own, use the template in the reproducible "Creating Classroom Norms" at the end of this chapter (page 27). Invite colleagues and students to contribute learning norms and inclusion supports. This increases buy-in and self-efficacy within structured and pleasant classrooms.

Early learners, as well as learners who prefer visual presentations, benefit from accompanying pictures. The picture sentence shown in figure 1.2 illustrates one example of how to represent abstract text as an image.

Table 1.2: Sample Classroom Norms

Student Learning Norms	Rationale for Inclusion Supports
Have fun!	Brain research affirms that pleasant classroom environments encourage students to feel comfortable and take risks while they learn (Jensen, 2005).
Respect difference. Remember that no one learns the same way! You are you, and that is just who you want to be!	Value learner strengths to compensate for different skill sets. Allow students to learn in different ways, such as song, dance, poetry, visuals, art, videos, games, and so on.
Try your best and ask for help!	It is OK when students make errors, but it is not OK to ignore them, since the curriculum spirals. Value and encourage student queries to solidify concepts.
Value growth and know that learning takes time!	Students learn with curriculum pauses, beyond a skill-and-drill mentality. Infuse time for practice and repetition.

Figure 1.2: Sample visual representation of a concept.

Students are diverse, yet learners are responsive to organizations that lessen the many demands with *too much too soon* that overwhelm learners. The norms and rules allow for transitions (19) across content and from grade to grade with consistency and clearly communicated expectations for academics and behaviors. These are the basics that learners and educators decide and delineate. In addition, educators should delineate ongoing collaborative staff and student roles (20) and desired outcomes within time frames (21) throughout the close of each unit of study and each marking period across the school year.

Model and Monitor

Teachers model and monitor learning activities (22) based on student assessments (23) and a respect for differences (24). Evidence of learning (25) is just as diverse as the learners are in inclusion classrooms, and multiple paths of engagement and representations yield multiple expressions. Staff model and monitor appropriate student behavior (26) with examples and nonexamples for academics and expectations and with rubrics (27) for learners to ensure that the curriculum is understood, and the bar is raised high. Critical thinking skills (28), such as those offered by Bloom's (1956) taxonomy and Norman Webb's (1999) Depth of Knowledge, address the cognitive demand students need beyond recall and comprehension to reproduce, apply, synthesize, and evaluate skills and concepts to become strategic learners who extend their thinking. Higher-order thinking is required in open-ended responses (29) to offer more insights into learning than true or false responses, matching letters to numbers, or reciting definitions. Invite learners to construct viable arguments and critique the reasoning of others in mathematics, science, social studies, and other disciplines to integrate and evaluate information presented in diverse media and formats. Presentations may be formatted visually, quantitatively, and orally for comprehension and collaboration with the reading, writing, speaking, and listening skills. Monitor efforts and progress through portfolios (30), observation, embedded assessments, and more. Educators who prepare multiple ways to model expectations and monitor students' progressions proactively infuse UDL (31) strategies that connect students to the competencies with varying representations, engagements, actions, and expressions. Peers are also valuable inclusion players who model skills, knowledge, and behaviors. Students learn side by side with grade-level peers as models.

Instruct and Involve

All students (32) interact within the inclusion classroom with assists from general education and special education staff (33), administration (34), families (35), coaches (36), and related service providers (37) on the instructional team. A slew of strategies with a slew of initials—DI or MTSS (38), UbD (39), PBL (40), CL (41), and VAKT (42)—are involved. Not everyone learns the same thing at the same time. At first, the teachers introduce the whole class to a concept, then they offer remediation, practice, reinforcement, or enrichment to small groups or individual learners. Afterward, the class gathers as a whole. This approach honors diversity within whole-part-whole lessons (43). Adaptations that involve supplemental instruction, accommodations, and modifications are a part of the instruction. In addition, technology options (44) afford learners many ways to strengthen weaker areas—for instance, a voice typing tool that is activated by a student with dyslexia or a visual impairment; a sound amplification system that is installed in a classroom for a student with a hearing impairment or one who needs help to auditorily process; a digital pen that records and scribes a teacher's lesson for a student with dysgraphia; or an iPad that helps a student with autism to communicate. There are numerous ways to differentiate instruction to achieve inclusive learning celebrations (45).

Reflect and Revise

If a flower is not growing, the gardener reflects on the conditions and revises the horticultural decisions with more or less water, food supplements, degrees of shade or sun, and a combination of other factors until growth is obtained. The same holds true with learning across the curriculum and grades; if a student or students are not achieving progress, educators must reflect and revise instruction and supports.

Supports (46) include reflecting on the learning from prior and succeeding years; mapping out the learning targets for each quarter or marking period, month, and week; providing and communicating the learning objectives in student-friendly language; offering a visual task analysis of expectations; and revisiting instructional decisions based on assessments. Learners with diverse needs and abilities obtain successes in lessons that include discrete task analysis (47) to see which parts of a concept or skill require more or less complexity. Mastery is evolutionary, with fidelity given to evidence-based practices. Documentation of student results yields collaborative reflections that acknowledge revisions are required if the selected interventions are inappropriate, based on the student data. Inclusion engagements and processes (48) activate motivation, creativity, and the desire to explore more. This means that a student revisits or expands on learning individually, with peers, or with the intervention of specialists. Diverse student populations need illustrations and learning visualizations (49) that offer a variety of concrete, representational, and abstract presentations. Timelines (50) are set up to plan for various instructional pacing (51). It is also crucial that the lesson objectives (52) are introduced at the onset of the lesson or unit and then revisited at the close. Instructional models (53) appreciate the value of evaluations, assessments, deliveries, and strategies that honor diverse learner characteristics. The goal is for learners to achieve successful outcomes based on criteria (54) and ongoing life achievements (55).

Engage and Enrich

Learners with exceptionalities need engagements that, on any given day, provide a combination of practice, reinforcement, advancement, and repetition (56). Students with intellectual disabilities often require revisiting the learning to solidify concepts (57), while learners who are twice exceptional appreciate opportunities to express their creativity (58). Many learners with cultural differences, learning disabilities, ADHD, or other diversities excel at subjects other than English or mathematics, which may include music or other fine arts. Cross-curricular connections (59) allow the students a chance to enrich their learning, for instance, in a collage depicting the elements of the periodic table, in music with a rap song about a novel, or maybe in an interpretive dance about a historical period. College and career prep (60) begin in the early grades and onward through purposeful engagements that connect to diverse learners. Inclusion classes simultaneously offer anchor and sponge activities (61) to solidify or enrich the learning for higher- and lower-level learners (62). This includes collaborative approaches (63) with metacognition (64) for professionals, students, and their families. Last but not least, fun activities, edutainment (65), and academic rigor are compatible elements that form strong compounds that bond the learning to student lives.

In the coming chapters, we will explore ADMIRE strategies for K–12 grade levels and disciplines within inclusion classrooms. With this strategic approach, educators can feel confident that they are helping all learners achieve high potentials that value who they are and ADMIRE how to get them to where they need to be.

Conclusion

Inclusion professionals view the whole classroom of students, never the stigmatization of individual students. Students with and without exceptionality have unique strengths. Students and staff who have positive attitudes and actions as delineated in the ADMIRE inclusion framework drive results in a positive direction. Inclusion is never a solitary task, since communication and collaboration catapult practical solutions. Take a moment to reflect on the information and strategies you've read by completing the "Admiring What Students and Staff Need to Know" reproducible at the end of this chapter (page 28).

Creating Classroom Norms

Use the following chart to collaboratively establish and respect the norms, rules, and shared agreements for your classroom as well as inclusion supports aligned with each norm.

Student Learning Norms	Inclusion Rationale for Supports
1.	
2.	
3.	
4.	
5.	

Admiring What Students and Staff Need to Know

Use the following template to ADMIRE the actions that students and staff need to know. In the space provided, note which of the ADMIRE action items stood out to you from this chapter.

A — Assess and Activate	
D — Decide and Delineate	
M — Model and Monitor	
I — Instruct and Involve	
R — Reflect and Revise	
E — Engage and Enrich	

CHAPTER 2

Think Individuals, Not Categories

If you are an avid moviegoer or reader, then you have probably seen a slew of movies and read an abundance of books across many genres. Each movie or book may have similarities to one you've read or seen before, but none are identical. Students also have uniqueness, as they reveal themselves as individual learners.

Students have similar characteristics, but they are never identical to one another, even if they share a label or IDEA classification. Each student, whether they share a category of exceptionality, is unique. Never define learners by a category of difference. Each student enters an inclusion classroom with various ability levels, prior successes, interests, needs, likes, and dislikes. As inclusion professionals, we understand and respond to the individual characteristics each student presents.

We begin this chapter with a focus on functional skills—those daily skills students need to thrive—and ways to make those skills more accessible for all students. Because students come to the inclusion classroom with many diverse needs, we consider what it means to ADMIRE exceptionality as a difference rather than a deficit, definition, or limitation. Inclusion educators succeed when they recognize student diversity as a strength rather than a deficit. Finally, we ADMIRE student realities, striving to imagine what these ideas look like in a real-world context.

Focus on Functional Skills

When we understand students as individuals, not their categories, then we reinforce what legislation requires. IDEA (2004) is so important because it is the legislation that offers a free and appropriate public education to students within their LRE. It first acknowledges that diversity exists, but then offers the protocols, strategies, and timelines for a student's individualized services. An IEP is the written statement of services that includes the measurable academic achievement and functional performance goals for a student with a disability to make progress in the general education curriculum. Under IDEA, *appropriate* education provides aids and services that are designed to meet each student's individual needs.

Progress in inclusion classes includes more than raising a test score from 40 percent to 60 percent or 80 percent achievement; it includes progress toward functional skills. These skills often perplex students with differing cognitive levels, genetic dispositions, and processing speeds. While some students are able to ignore physical and sensory distractions, others are completely sidetracked by them and can't concentrate, no matter how well the teachers teach. Differing skill sets and limited or fractured prior experiences influence what students see, hear, and learn. Therefore, the definition of *appropriate intervention* is student generated.

Daily living skills such as learning how to break down tasks into their components are confusing for students when there are multiple steps or directions. That's when a student who requires executive function skills will benefit from more visual support to reduce verbal reminders. Following and completing skills step by step helps, whether that skill is used for converting a mixed number to an improper fraction, for dressing and grooming, or for managing finances and behavior.

Collaborative input formulates each IEP. General education and special education staff, specialists, and families collaboratively write an IEP for a student who is evaluated and determined to have one of thirteen classifications under IDEA. I like to think of the IDEA classifications as a thirteen-word mnemonic that sends a strong message and values a strength paradigm: *All very determined students deserve infinitely more opportunities than schools have ever offered.*

1. **A**utism
2. **V**isual impairment (including blindness)
3. **D**eafness
4. **S**pecific learning disability
5. **D**eafness-blindness
6. **I**ntellectual disability
7. **M**ultiple disabilities
8. **O**ther health impairment
9. **T**raumatic brain injury
10. **S**peech and language impairment
11. **H**earing impairment
12. **E**motional disturbance
13. **O**rthopedic impairment

While we as educators must think of students as *individuals,* not their categories, as this chapter title suggests, the thirteen IDEA classifications guarantee that the funding, programs, and personnel are available for students to receive a free and appropriate public education in their LRE.

A fourteenth category, *developmental delay*, specifies services for students who evidence significant delays with cognitive development, physical or motor development, communication development, social or emotional development, or adaptive development. In some states, this category serves students who range in age from 3 to 5, 3 to 7, and 3 to 9. These thirteen categories are listed in section 300.8 of IDEA (2004), but across the states, specificity and criteria vary.

Supports sustain buildings and programs. IEPs and 504 plans (ADMIRE model 4, from table I.1, page 4) are not detours but strategic road maps. Thankfully, segregation, exclusion, and resistance are replaced with inclusive mindsets that allow students with disabilities to receive appropriate school services and interventions. Collaborations include families, schools, students, and communities. When all parties empower each other with interactions, strategies, and reflections on who needs what and when, where, and how, the IEPs translate to "It's educationally prudent!"

As professionals, we read and view each student's IEP as the road map that guides the learning. The IEP is implemented with fidelity as the annual script and plot that we must follow; otherwise, the placement in an inclusion classroom does not plan for learner achievement of the goals and objectives delineated. The IEP provides guidance about how the inclusion teacher provides support to meet a student's needs.

Specially designed instruction—instruction tailored to a student's individualized needs—is meant to address the goals in each student's IEP. This includes academic, social, emotional, behavioral, communication, health, and functional considerations. Note that specially designed instruction is specific instruction delivered to the student, *not* differentiated instruction, accommodations, active learning strategies, or other instructional interventions designed to facilitate learning for all students. Specially designed instruction is closely monitored to ensure effectiveness. It does not lower standards or expectations for the student (United Federation of Teachers, n.d.). The goal is for the student to achieve grade-level content standards. Specially designed instruction acknowledges the student's level and then looks at what specific skills a student needs to achieve competencies within the general education curriculum. Specially designed instruction is specific to each student.

Specially designed instruction offers specific adaptations that support the concepts and skills of the general education curriculum to meet the unique needs of a student with a disability. If some students are not achieving at expected levels, staff should change the services, supports, and specialized instruction rather than lower expectations (Quenemoen & Thurlow, 2017).

Consequently, general education staff need to consider what specially designed instruction is possible in that general education setting to offer students with exceptionality the appropriate services and supports that increase their access to the content.

ADMIRE Exceptionality as a Difference, Not a Deficit, Definition, or Limitation

It is a given that differences exist. Whether differences are one or a combination of language-related, cultural, emotional, social, behavioral, physical, sensory, or academic differences, increased knowledge and positive attitudes must prevail.

According to Jing Qi and Amy S. Ha (2012), potentially facilitating factors for student successes in general education classes include professional preparation, perceived competence, previous teaching experiences, and available support from the school. In contrast, potentially inhibiting factors include the lack of in-service training, inadequate preparation, and the type and severity of the disabilities of students.

As brain research affirms, neurodiversity exists (Stenning & Bertilsdotter-Rosqvist, 2021). Viewing students through their abilities, rather than their deficits, is a way to achieve gains and capitalize on student interests and strengths to maximize postsecondary opportunities in a diverse, not deficit-filled, society. How teachers view diversity can influence outcomes. At times, students with differences are perceived as not on par with grade-level peers. Special education has been weighted down with a history that often emphasizes words like *deficit*, *dysfunction*, and *disorder* (Armstrong, 2016). Focusing on what students cannot do keeps them in a holding pattern that limits their potential for future school and postsecondary success. Most important is to remember that, regardless of their classification, each learner responds differently to a given intervention.

In addition, within each disability group, category, and label, heterogeneity exists. Comorbidity occurs as well, meaning that a student with one disability may share the characteristics of another disability label. For example, a student with dyslexia may or may not display characteristics of ADHD or dyscalculia, or a student with an emotional difference may or may not have a learning difference.

Educators should, of course, value academics, but they should *also* think about the applicable competencies that honor each student's strengths without defining each student by their disability. At times, a label exists for funding purposes and to ensure services, but that diagnosis never caps achievement. Consider the following examples general and special educators may employ to ADMIRE diverse reading, writing, language, speaking and listening, and mathematics skills.

- ADMIRE how students read
    - **A**ssess students' interests. **A**ctivate reading choices and levels to IEP goals and learner profiles.
    - **D**ecide on formative assessments to monitor progress. **D**elineate the learning norms to read different types of genres throughout the year.
    - **M**odel critical thinking skills with read-alouds and open-ended responses in addition to factual questions. **M**onitor efforts and progress toward mastery.

- **I**nstruct with technology that supports the written text; utilize online tools. **I**nvolve VAKT elements to make the reading 3-D.
- **R**eflect on pacing to allow wait time. **R**evise instruction based on student outcomes.
- **E**ngage higher- and lower-level learners. **E**nrich with cross-disciplinary connections for both fiction and informational text.

- ADMIRE how students write
  - **A**ssess if writing routines include credible sources. **A**ctivate student motivation with multiple print and digital sources as prompts.
  - **D**ecide on the collaborative writing pieces, with eyes on process as well as product. **D**elineate step-by-step organization with multiple writing planners.
  - **M**odel with writing models, examples, and nonexamples. **M**onitor student behavior to ensure writing is practiced over time.
  - **I**nstruct and involve whole-part-whole lessons, such as adding transitional words. **I**nvolve PBL with products that include cooperative peer writes.
  - **R**eflect on whether writing shows evidence of planning, revising, editing, rewriting, and creativity. **R**evise timelines as needed.
  - **E**ngage college and career readiness skills with writing tasks that tie to life situations. **E**nrich writing with diverse assignments and genres.

- ADMIRE student language and vocabulary
  - **A**ssess student vocabulary levels with context clues and structural analysis. **A**ctivate working memories with repetition of word phrases.
  - **D**ecide on time frames to explore the language content. **D**elineate examples of English grammar, usage, and mechanics.
  - **M**odel respect for differences for students from other cultures. **M**onitor student behavior for language meaning and style.
  - **I**nstruct on figurative language with visual examples. **I**nvolve related service providers, such as speech-language providers.
  - **R**eflect on illustrations and engagements. **R**evise instructional models that clarify the meaning of grade-appropriate words in listening, reading, and media. **R**evise processes and pacing to ensure that the conventions of standard English are applied in writing and speaking.
  - **E**ngage relationships across contexts with reading, writing, and speaking and listening language connections and skills. **E**nrich with both literal and nonliteral meanings.

- ADMIRE how students speak and listen
  - **A**ssess whether content includes words, graphics, images, and videos. **A**ctivate emotionally safe, nonjudgmental environments for open expression.

- **D**ecide on communicative tasks that honor listeners' and speakers' baseline levels and interest. **D**elineate the collaborative range of conversations.
- **M**odel how to integrate and evaluate information from diverse media. **M**onitor that the information is accurate and relevant.
- **I**nstruct with technology with expressions and presentations. **I**nstruct whole class, peers, and small groups. **I**nvolve families to honor cultural differences and the adaptation of speech.
- **R**eflect on processes and engagements to support lesson objectives that organize evidence and logical reasoning in speaking situations. **R**evise and adapt speaking and listening goals as needed.
- **E**ngage collaborative voices that analyze (break down text, words, and the communication of ideas to understand their parts) and synthesize (ability to combine multiple sources to support, disprove, compare, and contrast ideas as well as individual and collective thoughts). **E**nrich with interdisciplinary connections to solidify concepts.

- ADMIRE how students do mathematics
  - **A**ssess whether students have conceptual understandings or are relying too much on procedures without expertise of the concepts. **A**ctivate working memories.
  - **D**ecide on how students will demonstrate mathematics understandings with formative curriculum-based assessments. **D**elineate the mathematics resources.
  - **M**odel how to represent situations symbolically. **M**onitor mathematical processes.
  - **I**nstruct with practical mathematics connections to students' lives. **I**nvolve cooperative learning so the students explain the mathematics to each other. **I**nvolve technology tools, such as virtual manipulatives, interactive step-by-step videos, and tutorials.
  - **R**eflect on illustrations of mathematical concepts. **R**evise pacing to ensure understanding, retention, and application.
  - **E**ngage students in opportunities to consistently explore subject matter to solidify calculations, concepts, and explanations. **E**nrich students with Socratic discussion and fun activities with real-life mathematics applications.

Recognize Student Diversity as Strength

Each student with and without exceptionality is unique. Disabilities themselves, although defined in legislation with IDEA categories, are complex. Students may possess challenges in some areas, but they possess strengths in many others. Inclusion classrooms include students with IEPs or 504 plans, English learners (ELs), learners who are culturally diverse, learners who are twice exceptional, and students who are gifted.

Educators may also misinterpret a cultural difference as a disability. Teachers who reflect on their practices and beliefs mindfully view cultural differences as diversity, not as a deficit (Dray & Wisneski, 2011). Diversity is not the problem; it is often the response of individuals to the diversity that is problematic (Barrera & Corso, 2003). A large achievement gap exists between ELs and their non-EL classmates. According to the NCES (n.d.), in the United States, the achievement gap between ELs and their non-EL classmates is significant and persistent. This achievement gap highlights the need for targeted support and resources to help ELs succeed academically. ELs need assistance with literacy skills, such as fluency, vocabulary, and comprehension, and benefit from frequent assessments and small-group interventions with active student participation (ASCD, 2009). Additionally, if ELs come from low-income families, they may face other barriers to academic success, such as limited access to resources and support.

Included in the diversity mix are students of poverty, those who are homeless, and children of migrant workers. Socioeconomic levels influence children's vocabulary. By age three, children who have had less exposure to adult conversation have a 30-million-word gap from their wealthier age-level peers (Hart & Risley, 2003). This disparity affects achievements since the limited exposure to rich conversations has a negative impact on reading, writing, listening, and speaking skills for comprehension and collaboration. These students enter schools with vocabulary deficits that require more classroom conversations to close this gap.

Overall, achievements are gained when applicable strategies are infused for a combination of learners who all have individualized needs and levels. Staff must know and apply evidence-based practices to help learners at both higher- and lower-ability levels achieve advancements within inclusion classrooms.

Embrace the Strength Paradigm With Appropriate Instruction

The ADMIRE strategies are intended to strengthen student academic levels with literacy, mathematical, and cross-disciplinary skills. As professionals, we enrich students' lives with active and meaningful engagements. Learners with differences require positive experiences that mimic lifelong successes.

The strengths of learners cannot be extracted if their deficits are highlighted by inappropriate instruction that does not match their needs. If skill sets and prior language and comprehension levels differ, then appropriate supports (for instance, hyperlinked definitions, visuals, digital and print glossaries, and extended opportunities for practice and application) are required to ensure ongoing progress for students of all abilities. Appropriate instruction is required for students whether they read or write about a novel, solve word problems, learn about the civil rights movement, or explore double replacement.

As an example, each discipline has vocabulary within the text that needs to be understood. However, before students even delve into the examination of the vocabulary, they must understand the makeup or nature of the text; a poem, instructional procedure, recipe, historical account, mathematics word problem, and scientific process each requires a different reading approach. A student needs to identify the *big text picture* to discern the task they must complete to demonstrate knowledge. Once the nature of the task and the reading genre of the text is established, students can then better sort out the vocabulary.

Interrelated vocabulary is often the foundation for advanced knowledge. World-Class Instructional Design and Assessment (WIDA; www.wida.us), one of the consortiums that a majority of states have adopted for their ELs, points out language functions and topics across the curriculum, such as linguistic complexity at the discourse level, language forms and conventions at the sentence level, and vocabulary usage at the word and phrase level. These topics include, but are not limited to, compound and complex sentences, expanded related ideas, and specific content words and expressions. Learners would need to explore general, academic, and domain-specific vocabulary at different tiers of complexity, such as the following.

- **Tier 1, general vocabulary:** Basic conversational words, usually those without multiple meanings, such as *read*, *notebook*, *big*, *small*, *student*, and *family*
- **Tier 2, academic vocabulary:** Words found across the disciplines, such as *audience*, *calculate*, *discuss*, *describe*, *differentiate*, *explain*, *explore*, *justify*, *opinion*, and *summarize*
- **Tier 3, domain-specific vocabulary:** Words that relate to specific content, such as *hypotenuse*, *latitude*, *constellation*, *plate tectonics*, *democracy*, and *personification*

It is important to note that within inclusion settings, it is sometimes the students with the most abilities who will learn the least since the instruction is not on their level of learning and they are not being challenged. The students in inclusive classes who do not have IEPs or 504 plans are entitled to appropriately leveled instructional activities to achieve successful outcomes from the early grades onward. Whether students are achievers or underachievers, or quiet or more excited, "policymakers and administrators should take the time to critically examine the campus climate(s); a school climate that is inviting to parents, teachers, students, and visitors encourages mutual respect" (Flint, 2010, p. 3). Therefore, it is incumbent upon educators to honor and incorporate individual preferences for curriculum and thinking styles.

Students with differences or classification under IDEA have a variety of strengths and abilities, depending on their individual characteristics, situations, needs, and interest. Some potential strengths of students with difference may include the following.

- **Resilience:** Many students learn how to develop resilience and perseverance at a young age when faced with challenge, which is a trait that assists them as they enter adulthood.
- **Adaptability:** Students with difference may have to adapt to different situations and environments, which can help them develop strong problem-solving and coping skills (Holahan, Ragan, & Moos, 2017).

- **Creativity:** Some students with difference may have unique ways of thinking or approaching tasks, which can lead to creative and innovative products and solutions.
- **Empathy:** Students with difference may have a heightened sense of empathy and understanding for others who face challenges or barriers.
- **Attention to detail:** Some students with difference may have a natural ability to focus and pay close attention to details, which can be a valuable asset in many fields.

It's important to remember that each student is unique, and these strengths may not apply to every student with a specific disability or difference. It's important to approach each student with an open mind and a willingness to understand individual student strengths and needs.

Recognize Both Hidden and Visible Characteristics

A *hidden disability* in inclusion classrooms is a disability that is not immediately visible or physically obvious to others but can still significantly impact a student's ability to learn and participate in the classroom. Examples of hidden disabilities may include the following.

- Learning differences such as dyslexia or dyscalculia
- ADHD
- Autism spectrum disorder
- Anxiety disorders
- Chronic health conditions such as diabetes or epilepsy
- Hearing or vision impairments that are not easily visible
- Emotional difference
    - *Internalizing* (such as withdrawal, depression, and anxiety)
    - *Externalizing* (disruptive and acting-out behaviors, such as aggression, impulsivity)
- Processing difference
- Sensory difference
- Speech-language difference

It is important for teachers and school staff to be aware of hidden disabilities and to provide appropriate accommodations and support to ensure that all students can fully participate in the classroom and reach their full potential. This may include providing assistive technology, offering extra time on assignments and tests, giving a student a reading passage on a different Lexile level, allowing for movement breaks, scheduling emotional check-ins, providing a quiet or low-stimulus environment, and more. As an example, online literacy sites and resources such as CommonLit (www.commonlit.org/en),

Smithsonian magazine (www.smithsonianmag.com/category/teachers), and ReadWorks (www.readworks.org) have passages and tools that offer high-quality content on multiple reading levels with individual adaptations that acknowledge diversity.

Plan for Diverse Skills and Behaviors

When teachers view difference and diversity through a strength paradigm, they are prepared to assist individuals with high-incidence differences that are often presented in an inclusion classroom. These include, but are not limited to, specific learning differences such as dyslexia, dysgraphia, and dyscalculia. Teachers often find that what they say and think impacts their actions, so let's circumvent the limitations from the start to offer more positive connotations of categories of differences to view and treat students as individuals who benefit from differentiated instruction.

Specific learning disability is a disorder in one or more of the basic psychological processes involved in understanding or using spoken or written language, which may manifest itself in an imperfect ability to listen, think, speak, read, write, spell, or do mathematical calculations. The term includes such conditions as perceptual disabilities, brain injury, minimal brain dysfunction, dyslexia, dyscalculia, dysgraphia, and developmental aphasia. The term does not include learning problems that are primarily the result of visual, hearing, or motor disabilities; intellectual disability; emotional disturbance; or environmental, cultural, or economic disadvantage (U.S. Department of Education, 2024). The definition of specific learning disability is taken from IDEA (2004) regulations, specifically 34 CFR §300.8(c)(10).

Specific learning disability is a broad category that includes differences that interfere with reading fluency and comprehension, written and oral expression, and mathematical problem-solving and computational skills. Dyslexia affects students' reading since they do not have automaticity with the different forty-four sounds that the twenty-six letters of the alphabet produce in different combinations. Dysgraphia affects the physical writing and the organization of thoughts, while dyscalculia impacts mathematics concepts and calculations in areas such as computations, telling time, sequencing, and solving word problems. An overlap of characteristics is often presented. Students require step-by-step explanations if prior knowledge differs, along with multisensory approaches—for example, Orton-Gillingham (www.ortonacademy.org) instruction to decode or encode words such as tapping out syllables, using TouchMath (https://touchmath.com) or manipulatives such as number lines, manipulating Unifix cubes or algebra tiles to learn mathematics concepts and perform calculations, writing with a slant board, or using a word prediction program.

Consider the following tips for supporting students' unique needs.

- Embed feedback during instruction with increased modeling, inquiry, and exploration.
- Treat errors as learning opportunities.
- Ensure that strategies not only honor the correct answer but also teach students to explain their reasoning.

- Offer self-regulation and co-regulation to monitor student behavior with more and less supports, respectively.
- Create opportunities for teachers and families to collaborate to shape and guide positive reactions and interactions with others with assistance that leads to increased student independence.

Support Students With Attention Difference and ADHD

ADHD is a neurodevelopmental disorder that affects a significant number of students in classrooms. Although it is not an IDEA (2004) category, students receive services with medical documentation under the category of other health impairment (OHI) or with a 504 plan. The characteristics of ADHD can include difficulty in paying attention, hyperactivity, and impulsivity (American Psychiatric Association, 2013). These characteristics can affect a student's academic performance, social skills, and overall functioning in school and be present in varying degrees. Although challenges are present, with effective strategies, students with ADHD, like students without ADHD, thrive when the appropriate supports are given.

Consider the following tips for supporting students' unique needs.

- Provide students with ADHD with a structured, predictable, and organized environment that clearly states the behavioral expectations. This can involve creating a consistent daily routine, using visual aids, active student involvement, and breaking down tasks into smaller, more manageable pieces (Karten, 2017c).
- Use positive reinforcement to encourage appropriate behaviors and redirect negative behaviors to reward on-target ones. Students with ADHD often have difficulties when the memory demands increase beyond rote memorization and working memory is necessary. Research supports that many students with ADHD learn best when material is repeated and practiced to facilitate the transfer of information from short-term to long-term memory (DuPaul & Stoner, 2014).
- Encourage family collaboration to reinforce skills beyond the inclusion classroom. This can include daily report cards and increased parent-teacher contact, either by phone, via email, in person, in online forums such as Google Classroom, or with a phone app, such as Remind Hub (visit https://remind.com/parentsquare). Structure with consistent communication and direction is essential since ADHD may also run in families (Low, 2023). Assignments, frequent feedback, and parent-teacher collaboration can improve homework completion and behavior management with consistency, structure, and collaboration between home and school environments.
- Provide opportunities for movement. Students have a wide range of needs with degrees of impact. Learners with differing physical stamina require frequent breaks. If students are on medication, be sensitive to the curriculum demands and offer schedule changes for assignments and assessments.

- Offer guidance as needed. Learners with ADHD may require more guidance to filter out external or internal distractions or to develop and improve study skills to circumvent weaker organizational, visual-spatial, or auditory working memory skills. Adaptations include modeling with guided practice and embedded supports such as text callouts; more detailed oral or written notes for directions; and rubrics for academic, behavioral, and social expectations. Adjust pacing and offer timely specific feedback for academics and behavior to promote higher self-efficacy and increased self-regulation.

The Center for Parent Information and Resources (2015) and organizations and resources such as Children and Adults With Attention-Deficit/Hyperactivity Disorder (CHADD; visit https://chadd.org) offer additional insights and information. Overall, research suggests that providing structure, consistency, and support can be effective in helping students with ADHD succeed academically. It is important for teachers and families to work together to develop individualized strategies that meet the specific needs of each student with ADHD.

Offer Adaptations for Students With Autism

Autism spectrum disorder is a neurodevelopmental disorder that affects social interaction, communication, and behavior. It is estimated that 1 in 54 children in the United States are diagnosed with autism (CDC, 2023). Research shows that inclusion can be beneficial for students with autism, as it provides opportunities for social interaction and academic growth (Rea, McLaughlin, & Walther-Thomas, 2002).

General education staff need to be privy to the autism knowledge and strategies to assist individual students with autism who may share a label but are not identical to one another. Students with autism spectrum disorder require individualized education that matches their levels to achieve success. Some students with autism may require a combination of services, such as behavior training in an applied behavior analysis class and then placement in a general education mathematics class, if that is an area of strength. It is imperative to provide each student with maximum opportunities to be included with grade-level peers. These opportunities include, but are not limited to, assemblies and morning meetings, along with special subjects and areas of interest, such as physical education; art; chorus; orchestra; science, technology, engineering, and mathematics (STEM) classes; and more.

It is essential to offer students with autism and other differences adaptations that help but do not enable. Gauge behaviors during guided instruction, independent practice, or cooperative assignments, and then fade support. Applied behavior analysis with structured reinforcement is often used to increase the academic and functional skills of students with autism. This includes gaining incremental skills to read texts aloud, converse while maintaining eye contact, take turns with peers, see things from different perspectives, understand sarcasm, decrease repetitive behaviors, adjust to changes in routines, and respect personal space. Students may require assistance with abstract representations, figurative language, and social cues.

Consider the following tips for supporting students' unique needs.

- Remember that students with autism exist on a spectrum with a variety of academic, communicative, social, and behavioral levels.
- Provide more visuals and guided instruction to increase academic understanding and appropriate social interactions as needed. Some examples include posted schedules, scripted social stories, checklists, visual cues, physical prompts, and technology options from avatars to hyperlinked definitions of academic and domain-specific vocabulary (see table I.1, page 4).
- Offer technology supports as needed, such as iPads, Boardmaker (https://goboardmaker.com), or Proloquo2Go (www.assistiveware.com/products/proloquo2go). Social stories with visuals assist with transitions and often ease anxieties. There are many technology tools and apps available that can help individuals with autism in different areas of life. When considering the following tools, consult with professionals and families to collaboratively determine the appropriate choices for individual students, based on their level of academic achievement and functional performance.
    - **Communication apps:** Nonverbal individuals with autism can communicate their wants and needs by tapping buttons with symbols and typing words. Some popular apps include Proloquo2Go and TouchChat.
    - **Visual scheduling apps:** Visual schedules can be helpful for individuals with autism to understand what tasks they need to complete and what is coming next. Apps like Choiceworks and First Then Visual Schedule can be helpful for students to complete daily routines and to increase their emotional regulation with positive behavior support, as they transition from one activity to the next.
    - **Social skills apps:** Several apps and online sites are available that can help individuals with autism practice social skills through simulated scenarios and communities, such as conversation, turn taking, and empathy. Examples include Do2Learn and Model Me Going Places.
    - **Educational apps:** Some educational apps that can help individuals with autism learn academic skills, such as mathematics, reading, and writing, include Autism Read and Write Pro, Speech Blubs, Toca Boca, Starfall, and Endless Alphabet.
    - **Sensory regulation apps:** Sensory regulation apps, such as GoNoodle, Calm, and Headspace, can assist individuals with autism who may become overwhelmed by sensory input. These apps provide guided meditation and relaxation exercises.
    - **Augmented and alternative communication devices:** For individuals with severe communication difficulties, augmented and alternative

communication devices like Tobii Dynavox (https://us.tobiidynavox.com) and PRC-Saltillo (www.prc-saltillo.com) help with communication.

- Consult with experts and related staff providers such as occupational therapists and behavioral interventionists.
- Be aware of sensory sensitivities and offer a variety of processing strategies and adaptations—for example, sensory table, weighted vest, less clutter on worksheets and classroom charts, study carrels, seating away from a window or door due to glare or distractions, and an opportunity to use headphones.

Explore the life and work of Temple Grandin, a prominent animal researcher, to learn more about one prominent figure with autism. Grandin describes her sensory confusion with scratchy clothes that feel like sandpaper, but her affinity for visuals (Flatow, 2006). She also shares her social awkwardness and advocates for students to learn daily living skills (Grandin & Moore, 2021). Additionally, visit Autism Speaks (www.autismspeaks.org) for more resources and information.

Create Executive Function Assists

Executive function refers to a set of cognitive skills that are important for planning, organizing, initiating, and completing tasks. Students who need assists with executive function skills may have difficulties with time management, organization, working memory, and self-regulation (Dawson & Guare, 2010, 2018; Gathercole et al., 2008).

Executive functioning skills vary in all students. Instruction also needs to have a positive impact on students, with work that is not too slow or too easy if students are gifted (VanTassel-Baska, Feng, Swanson, Quek, & Chandler, 2009). Students who are gifted or considered to be talented have unique educational needs that differ from those of other students, which also include more or less executive functioning skills. These students require varied services and supports to process ideas at a level that matches their higher level of knowledge and skill sets. It is a myth that gifted students require no assistance (National Association for Gifted Children, n.d.). Reinforcements are appreciated at all skill sets, with families and school staff coaching students with academic and emotional needs.

This category becomes even more complicated if students are gifted and also have a learning disability, being twice exceptional. Students may display high degrees of creativity but poor organizational or planning skills (Rosen, n.d.). At times, screening does not recognize both characteristics within the same student and causes either the giftedness or the learning needs to be left unaddressed. Some students who are twice exceptional lack executive skills, which include flexibility, goal-directed persistence, metacognition, organization, planning and prioritizing, response inhibition, sustained attention, task initiation, time management, and working memory (Dawson & Guare, 2018).

Students who have executive dysfunction can become problematic if characteristics are misinterpreted as laziness (Dawson & Guare, 2010; Belsky, n.d.). Difficulties may overshadow student strengths, not allowing learners with both giftedness and weaker areas to maximize their achievements. Joseph S. Renzulli and Sally M. Reis (1997) define *giftedness* as a combination of the three factors of above-average ability, creativity, and task commitment. For gifted education to survive and thrive, the field needs to rethink excellence to raise the levels of underachieving groups, but not by allowing high-performing groups to slip (Plucker & Callahan, 2014).

Consider the following tips for supporting students' unique needs.

- Focus on personalizing supports that connect to student interest.
- Encourage goal setting with interim scheduled student-teacher check-ins.
- Give step-by-step directions in oral and written formats.
- Offer modeling before students engage in tasks.
- Provide individualized supports to help students complete assignments.
- Help students to organize themselves and their work so they are able to plan the next steps needed.

ADMIRE Student Realities

Let's consider an example to imagine how the principles in this chapter apply in a real-world context. A seventh-grade English class has twenty-one students who live in a rural area. Exposure to other cultures is limited. The majority of families are actively involved in their children's education. Most of the class is reading on grade level, but six students are reading at least two grade levels above, while three students are reading two grade levels below, with two of these students having signs of dyslexia. In addition, some students are more motivated than others. The teacher has dual certification in special education and English. The class has recently begun a poetry unit, and the teacher selected seven poems for the class to cooperatively explore: "Still I Rise" by Maya Angelou (1978), "Dream Boogie" by Langston Hughes (n.d.), "My Grandmother Is Waiting for Me to Come Home" by Gwendolyn Brooks (n.d.), "Slam, Dunk, & Hook" by Yusef Komunyakaa (2001), "After Apple-Picking" by Robert Frost (1977), and "City of Glass" by Martín Espada (2006). The following sections explore fictional staff communications and differentiated instruction in more detail.

Staff Communications

DI happens when professionals deliver and assess content with varying levels of complexity and support. General and special education teachers reflect on the challenges presented to generate solutions. Consider how the following seventh-grade inclusion teacher ADMIREs student diversity using responsive lessons.

General education teacher: "Some students get it and run with the reading and writing lessons, and some students labor at everything they read and write. I am glad that I had special education training. I offer the class differentiated lessons with a range of

Lexile levels on the same content and, when possible, connect the assignments to their interests, to increase motivation. I work with small groups for both enrichment and remediation. This poetry unit has been particularly tough for my students with encoding and decoding problems. When they hear a poem read aloud, they understand the concepts, but when they have individual reads, some learners stumble over the longer words and lose the gist of the poem and the symbolism involved."

ADMIRE Differentiated Instruction

Let's imagine what it might look like in this example to ADMIRE differentiated instruction. **A**ctivate class routines that value a whole-part-whole structure. The class is initially together for the introduction of the poetry unit. Next, since students have diverse levels and interests, allow them to work in smaller groups to think-pair-share and jigsaw diverse poems. Keep the learning ongoing by establishing a class poetry book. Require the students to contribute three poems throughout the year, which are revised in writing conferences with peers and teachers before they are published and shared online for families and friends to access. **A**ssess prior knowledge about the selected poets and motivate students to explore more poems also authored by these poets. Walk about to ascertain student understandings of the assignment and to hear oral reads. Also allow students to record passages with online tools and extensions that are listened to at a later date by both the students and teachers. Students can record their reading and post it on an online platform, such as Google Classroom or Canvas. This allows the teacher a way to gauge their fluency level and promotes self-reflection for the student. This recording and listening offers three objectives.

1. Student recordings increase self-awareness of miscues.
2. It is multisensory since it combines the visual with the auditory. If the poem is printed, then students follow along with eyes, pointers, reading screeners, ears, and more tools.
3. The recordings are data used by teachers to guide instruction. Teachers are able to listen to and share the recording in meetings as documentation, the same way fluency with pronunciation or miscues is collected in person and scribed on paper.

It is important for students, professionals, and families to value the error analysis for which letters were pronounced incorrectly, so that instruction remedies the discrepancies; such as *cat versus cut* (medial vowel sound confusion). For a deep dive, check out special projects editor Julie Rawe's (n.d.) article about a structured literacy approach and educator Aaron Davis's (2016) advice on using voice recordings on Google Docs.

Delineate the baseline standards that all students will achieve—for example, understanding how a poem's form and structure contribute to its meaning and the understanding of figurative language. **D**ecide on the collaborative roles during cooperative work: *discussion director, word wizard, researcher, artist,* and so on.

Model how to analyze a poem during whole-class discussion with examples of imagery, mood, and details. **M**onitor students' critical thinking skills. Provide UDL (see table 1.1, page 18) strategies by preparing a range of resources and tools for students to access on a strategy table, such as the following.

- Line readers
- Highlighters
- Graphic organizers
- Low tech and high tech, along with student-specific tools and apps, such as www.merriam-webster.com
- Text-to-speech tools
- Books, games, and apps for students with dyslexia, such as Learning Ally's audiobooks
- Special dyslexia font (see www.dyslexiefont.com)
- Prerecorded poems
- Daily opportunities to express themselves in their writer's notebooks

Instruct with differentiated representations and engagements with VAKT elements, such as illustrated metaphors and similes, PowerPoint or Google Slides presentations; **i**nstruct with a variety of levels, using books and online resources to teach more about figurative language (activate the closed-captioning feature for students with dyslexia). **I**nvolve the families in learning celebrations with a poetry-reading day. Share the poems with seniors in local nursing homes. **I**nvolve related staff providers and specialists to collaborate and offer ideas on figurative language, and invite the reading teacher to intervene with structured lessons to raise the levels of students with dyslexia.

Reflect on lesson objectives with pacing that includes appropriate instructional models—high interest but lower reading level for students with dyslexia if grade-level texts are used and more visuals with cultural references for students with English language needs. **R**eflect on timelines to offer different pacing for students who are reading above or below grade level, with an increase of analytic and persuasive essay requirements for students at higher levels. **R**evise lesson objectives based on student products.

Engage with creativity and **e**nrich concepts by inviting the students to mirror the style of a favorite poet. Employ collaborative approaches with history, mathematics, science, physical education, art, and music teachers by inviting these educators to ask their students to write a poem in their respective disciplines. **E**nrich your knowledge of specific learning differences by visiting sites such as these.

- Dyscalculia.org (www.dyscalculia.org)
- International Dyslexia Association (https://dyslexiaida.org)
- Learning Disabilities Association of America (https://ldaamerica.org)
- National Center for Learning Disabilities (www.ncld.org)

- Understanding Dysgraphia (https://dyslexiaida.org/understanding-dysgraphia)
- The Yale Center for Dyslexia and Creativity (http://dyslexia.yale.edu/whatisdyslexia.html)

The following quote is attributed to King Solomon (well before *differentiated instruction* became a buzzword): "Educate each child according to his own way, and even when he is old, he will not depart from it" (*ESV*, 2016, Proverbs 22:6).

Success is an ongoing personal quest, journey, and challenge. Students possess a wide range of knowledge, personal experiences, interests, and motivation. The academic topics presented in the classroom may or may not interest them. However, professionalism is critical. The learning for students, families, and school staff is ongoing. Knowledge has no finish line, but many peaks to climb, using a multitude of instructional strategies, tools, and resources, according to the way each individual learns and smiles.

Conclusion

Each student in the inclusion classroom is unique—regardless of any label used to categorize their academic abilities. The definition of *appropriate intervention* is therefore student generated in inclusion classes. The specially designed instruction in the IEP is specific to each student. Professionals ADMIRE exceptionality and respond to it with interventions that never view a difference as a deficit, definition, or limitation. Take a moment to reflect on the information and strategies you've read by completing the "Admiring Individuals, Not Categories" reproducible at the end of this chapter.

Admiring Individuals, Not Categories

Use the following template to ADMIRE the actions to think individuals, not categories. In the space provided, note which of the ADMIRE action items stood out to you from this chapter.

A — Assess and Activate	
D — Decide and Delineate	
M — Model and Monitor	
I — Instruct and Involve	
R — Reflect and Revise	
E — Engage and Enrich	

The ADMIRE Framework for Inclusion © 2024 Solution Tree Press • SolutionTree.com
Visit **go.SolutionTree.com/specialneeds** to download this free reproducible.

CHAPTER 3

Connect to the Realities That Teachers, Students, and Families Face

Teacher, student, and family dynamics are complex. Realities are defined and refined by communications, interactions, and relationships. When teachers, students, and families are a collaborative team, then knowledge, respect, and understanding increase. The expression "walk a mile in someone else's shoes" encourages empathy and understanding of another's perspective. Students exist beyond the classroom walls. Teachers and families are collaborative partners who share realities to catapult successes.

In this chapter, we take a closer look at some of the practices that successful inclusion educators rely on. Teachers *assess and activate* awareness as a first step to getting to know students with the help of a learner profile. They *decide on and delineate* inclusion structures with help from various online resources. They leverage tools to plan with and for learners at the year, month, and week levels. Finally, successful inclusion teachers collaborate with families through consistent communication and check-ins.

Assess and Activate Awareness

It is essential that educational professionals know their students' skills, behaviors, and prior histories. That way, they connect learner interests and strengths to concepts and subjects. The goal is for educators to effectively deliver the adaptations stated in a student's IEP, but without assessment and awareness, which becomes a much more difficult, if not impossible, task.

When I think about this, the song "Getting to Know You" from the 1951 Richard Rodgers and Oscar Hammerstein musical *The King and I* comes to mind. Anna, a British schoolteacher who has been hired as a governess, sings the song as she strikes up a relationship with the children and the wives of the King of Siam. The song's lyrics highlight the importance of getting to know someone and building relationships. The song's message is particularly relevant today, where students are often more connected to their gadgets than their interactions with others.

The song is a reminder that connections—those that prioritize listening, learning, and appreciating interactions—lead to mutual understanding and respect.

Getting to know your students is something you can work on in a multitude of ways throughout the school year. Consider the following examples.

- Make time for face-to-face conversations and interactions with students.
- Use Google Forms (www.google.com/forms/about/) to facilitate family communications, messages, or emotional check-ins, such as those at Do2Learn (https://do2learn.com/activities/SocialSkills/EmotionCheckIn-Checkout/index.html).
- Create a survey, such as *Tell About Yourself* (TAY), created with Google Forms. Scan the QR code to access this survey. Also, consider using the reproducible "Interest Survey" at the end of this chapter (page 71) with your students to better connect. Consider completing the survey and sharing it with students as a way to build connections and create opportunities for conversation.

In addition to connecting to each student as a member of the class, sometimes teachers need more comprehensive information about a learner, especially one with more specialized needs. In such cases, consider creating a learner profile for the student. *Learner profiles* are a way to describe each student's likes, dislikes, ways of knowing, preferences, and more. They share who students are as learners with information teachers can use to support lesson delivery and content as appropriate.

Figure 3.1 provides a sample learner profile for a first-grade student. The learner profiles were generated by extracting information from students' IEPs, along with educator, student, and family conversation, observation, and communication. A learner profile offers a fuller picture of a student, beyond their standardized test grades, into the core of who the student is and what the student needs. This information is then connected to instructional choices for your students to ensure that what you teach highlights how your students learn best.

In this example, it is important to know that Amir is a hands-on learner to then provide manipulatives for number identification and to solve mathematics word problems. Tactile associations are also offered when he is learning sound-letter combinations. Tactile practice helps to imprint the correct sizing and formation of letters, such as writing letters in sand, salt trays, shaving cream, or sand to "feel" the letters. Amir needs changes and transitions preannounced. If the readings or word problems relate to farming or fishing, then his attention and interest are increased. Co-regulation with modeling and feedback is required to increase Amir's positive relations with peers.

Figure 3.2 (page 53) provides a sample learner profile for a seventh-grade student.

Learner Profile	
Student: Amir	**Grade level:** 1
Strengths and Challenges (Includes VAKT preferences)	Strengths: • mathematics skills are strong; good one-to-one correspondence; difficulty with retrieval and number identification • Helps peers but often wants to lead or direct • memory is stronger with association Challenges: • Lacks social reciprocity • Fine motor skills difficult; labors at writing within given spaces
Interests and Likes (Includes in school or outside)	Likes: • Tractors • Fishing • Farming • Army
IEP Goals and Objectives (For example, academic, social, emotional, behavioral, physical, communication)	• Literacy-phonemic awareness • Social turn taking • Attention seeking • Handling frustration
Accommodations and Modifications	• Behavioral plan to assist with transitions and interactions with peers • Empowerment under auspices, such as voice-choice assignments • Bibliotherapy to gain social skills • Small group • Frequent positive praise • Sticker chart • Configuration boxes for handwriting within given parameters • Extra time • Provide a highly structured, predictable learning environment • Frequently check for understanding • Repeat, clarify, or reword directions • Allow wait time for processing before calling on student for response; provide short breaks when refocusing is needed
Current Performance Level	Reading: Kindergarten level • Amir has memorized the Fundations sound card and sayings and can produce letter sounds. However, Amir has a harder time identifying initial letter sounds in words presented. On the unit 1 benchmark assessment, Amir scored 8/10 (80%) on letter names and phonics unprompted. Mathematics: First-grade level • Amir counts with manipulatives (cross-counting) and shows a word problem with manipulatives. • Amir needs help to process auditory information with more length and complexity.

Figure 3.1: Sample learner profile for a first-grade student.

Learner Profile	
Student: Levi	**Grade level:** 7
Strengths and Challenges *(Includes VAKT preferences)*	Strengths: • Imagination • Building • Good academic and expressive vocabulary • Decoding skills are strong • Learns with visuals Challenges: • Social cues • Self-confidence • Verbal and written expression • Problem solving • Multiple-step directions • Sensory input and overload, such as loud noises • Decision making • Concentration • Processing speed
Interests and Likes *(Includes in school or outside)*	Likes: • Building • Video games • LEGO bricks • Animals and pets • Friends • Movement • Writing • Mathematics • Music • Graphic novels Dislikes: • Fire and evacuation drills • Loud noises in assemblies • Changes in schedule and routines • When not given a voice
IEP Goals and Objectives *(For example, academic, social, emotional, behavioral, physical, communication)*	• Capitalize on strengths and interests for reading comprehension, such as including animals and pets in mathematics word problems and text passages • Gamify reading and mathematics practice skills • Pragmatic language • Emotional regulation • Impulse control • Manage anxiety and depression • Positive teacher and peer experiences • Social skills with reciprocity and interpreting cues

	• Focusing • Offer curriculum-related comics, such as political cartoons
Accommodations and Modifications	In school: • Understand Levi's point of view • Pace accordingly to honor his processing speed • Verbal and gestural prompts • Consistent praise • Intermittent checks • Conferencing • Emotional check-ins, such as online Google Form using a 5-point scale • Review classroom rules at the onset of a lesson • Facilitate problem solving • Clear expectations • Reinforcement for on-task behaviors, such as hand raising • Self-monitoring (for example, "Think it, don't say it!") • Frequent breaks • Behavioral data At home: • Understand Levi's point of view • Cool-down time • Tent therapy • Meditation • Reinforce classroom rules with family discussion • Facilitate problem solving • Clear expectations • Reflection with support
Current Performance Level	Literacy: • Vocabulary-word meaning • Inferential clues are more difficult Mathematics: • Approximately fifth grade • Zone of proximal development = fifth grade Sources of frustration: • Multistep word problems with extraneous information • Picking up social cues

Figure 3.2: Sample learner profile for a seventh-grade student.

In this example, Levi needs assistance with his behavior with social skills that include co-regulation. Since he likes videos, the teacher offers one that is appropriate for his age group. Support also includes emotional check-ins and consistent reinforcement for Levi.

Inclusion professionals who know their students can better advance skills with connections to self, others, and the curriculum. See the "Learner Profile" reproducible at the end of this chapter (page 73) for a template.

Decide and Delineate Inclusion Structures

Inclusion teachers plan, organize, and individualize the learning for their students in the general education class. It is a given that inclusion educators will instruct students who possess varying levels of prior knowledge and experiences with words, numbers, and concepts across the curriculum and grade levels. In addition, there are multiple proficiencies that will be evidenced with social, emotional, and behavioral interactions during instructional and noninstructional time—for example, whole-class and small-group instruction (ADMIRE model 43, from table I.1, page 4), lunchroom, hallways, transitions, and more.

Remember the importance of involving families (ADMIRE model 35) and other support systems in the student's education. Regular communication with home environments can help teachers understand students' needs and develop an effective plan for academic success (DuPaul, Weyandt, O'Dell, & Varejao, 2009). A practice such as mindfulness is important for students and adults in both school and home environments to address inclusion anxieties and apprehensions.

Consider the following benefits *students* may gain from mindfulness practices (Karten, 2019).

- Learners with and without disabilities learn best within a nonthreatening school and classroom climate.
- Students become more resilient to internal and external distractions that block the learning paths in their minds.
- Students gain time and space to reflect on and process their feelings about related services and activities, which may place heavy demands on their time.
- Students learn increased coping strategies for handling anxiety and other stressors that may overshadow the brain's ability to process information.

Consider the following benefits that *educators and family members* may gain from mindfulness practices (Karten, 2019).

- Increased ability to be present and process daily stressors
- Increased ability to recognize students' needs and pace instruction accordingly
- Increased capacity and skills for dealing with challenging emotions

To gain access to the benefits in the preceding lists, consider accessing the following mindfulness activities and resources.

- Body Scan (www.mindful.org/body-scan-kids)
- Calm (www.calm.com/schools)
- Calm-Down Bottles (https://rhythmsofplay.com/calm-down-sensory-bottles-101)
- Child Mind Institute (https://childmind.org)
- Transformative Life Skills and Dynamic Mindfulness (https://pg.casel.org/transformative-life-skills-dynamic-mindfulness)
- DIY Stress Balls (www.naturalbeachliving.commake-stress-balls-kids-will-love)

- GoNoodle (https://support.gonoodle.com/article/321-recommendation-calming-mindfulness)
- MindUP Curriculum, Grades PreK–12 (https://mindup.org/core-curriculum)
- Healthy Brain Network (https://healthybrainnetwork.org)
- Meditation Apps (www.commonsensemedia.org/lists/meditation-apps-for-kids)
- Mindful Breathing Using Shapes (https://calmahoykids.co.uk/2021/02/05/teach-mindful-breathing-using-shapes)
- Mindfulness Practices for Kids With Autism (http://blog.stageslearning.com/blog/six-simple-mindfulness-practices-for-kids-with-autism)
- Mindful Walking (www.mindful.org/6-ways-to-engage-kids-and-teens-in-mindful-walking)
- A Network for Grateful Living (https://gratefulness.org/resource/three-ways-to-cultivate-gratitude-at-school)
- The Raisin Meditation (https://mindfulnessbox.com/raisin-mindfulness-exercise)

Finally, the definition of mindfulness varies from person to person, but the ultimate goal is to achieve a sense of well-being in the classroom and community. Model and monitor positive behaviors (ADMIRE model 26) to replace student anxieties and apprehensions with increased self-efficacy. Learners who stretch and breathe while they learn focus better with increased awareness of their emotions. Mindfulness connects to learners of all ability levels to spin challenges into improvements in relationships with oneself and others.

Consider how involved parties might ADMIRE mindfulness.

A **A**ssess and **a**ctivate mindful practices, whether that's taking a minute to wiggle or letting out a deep cleansing sigh.

D **D**ecide on and **d**elineate the importance of reflection and self-care, being mindful of how self-confidence influences performance.

M **M**odel and **m**onitor a classroom culture that values each learner's skill set.

I **I**nstruct and **i**nvolve learners with activities and discussions that promote awareness of actions.

R **R**eflect and **r**evise based on social-emotional functioning and academic performance. *ADDitude* magazine (www.additudemag.com/slideshows/youtube-videos-for-kids) and PBS Kids (https://www.pbs.org/parents/learn-grow/all-ages/social-skills) offer a few videos and ways to teach social skills.

E **E**ngage and **e**nrich with breathing exercises, body scans, and visualization.

Mindfulness-based interventions have been shown to improve social-emotional functioning and academic performance in students with diverse backgrounds, including those in inclusion classrooms (Karten, 2019; Ridderinkhof, de Bruin, Blom, & Bögels, 2018; Semple, Reid, & Miller, 2005). Mindfulness practices, such as breathing exercises and body scans, can help students regulate their emotions and reduce stress, which can lead to better behavior and academic outcomes (Felver, Celis-de Hoyos, Tezanos, & Singh, 2016; Schonert-Reichl et al., 2015).

Plan With and for Learners

Taking a proactive UDL approach (see table 1.1, page 18) means providing lessons and resources that honor students' diverse ways of learning. Individual knowledge and skill sets should guide a teacher's adaptations. Inclusion plans that have visuals, auditory presentations, tactile learning, and ways for students to move about value classroom diversity. Planning with and for learners means that students know what and how they'll learn, and inclusion teachers connect their interests and modalities within units of study for motivation, instruction, and assessment.

Students with and without exceptionality who have different levels respond to multiple modalities. Multiple modalities or paths to the learning, such as VAKT instruction (see table I.1, page 4), offer students different ways to process and engage with the learning. According to a review by researchers Tamara van Gog and John Sweller (2015), the use of multiple modalities can reduce cognitive load, which can improve learning outcomes, especially for novice learners.

Daily lessons, therefore, need to include ways to reinforce academic concepts for students in the ways they learn best. Getting to know students ensures we have the relevant information to differentiate instruction according to their needs, strengths, and challenges. For students in primary grades, consider sites like Vidtionary (www.vidtionary.com), which has engaging and brief visual explanations of vocabulary, or Storyline Online (https://storylineonline.net), which features actors reading stories. Some students may write letters in salt trays before they write on paper or hop on numbers to remember their multiples. Secondary students like PhET's (https://phet.colorado.edu) platform with interactive online science and mathematics simulations. CommonLit (www.commonlit.org) has resources across the grades that invite differentiated instruction with multimodal ways to teach literacy to students who respond better to other modalities. To learn more, access CommonLit's article "4 Ways to Use CommonLit to Support Differentiation" (Riddle, 2022). Planning with and for learners means that inclusion professionals include multiple modalities to reach multiple students' needs in the inclusion classroom!

This is no small task. Organization is essential to success. According to research by the National Center on Accessible Educational Materials (2023), well-planned and -organized lessons can support the success of students with disabilities in inclusive classrooms. That does not exclusively mean the day-by-day planning, but if the year is divided into sections such as each term or marking period, month, and week, then that prepares for better days. The frontloading occurs at the onset of the year, with continuous supports that include how to deliver the curriculum, along with how to include a continuum of skills attained at different levels and times for individual students throughout the school year.

A helpful way to achieve this planning—and to ensure inclusion of evidence-based practices outlined in chapter 1 (page 18), such as UDL, UbD, DI, MTSS, PBL, and PBIS, throughout the year—is to create mega, macro, and micro inclusion plans. Teachers use *mega* and *macro planning* at the onset of the school year, while *micro planning* occurs at the beginning of each month to ensure that the weekly instruction does not sacrifice the learning targets or the diversity of the inclusion class population.

Time for repetition, enrichment, and practice is proactively slated because it is a given that students with and without IEPs exhibit a combination of proficiencies before, during, and after instruction with their understanding, retention, and application. It is also a given that the same concept taught within the inclusion classroom will be learned with varying levels of complexity and retention. It is a further given that students have more or less home support, motivation, and interest.

Mega, macro, and micro planning help inclusion collaborators to *expect the unexpected*, such as evacuation drills, snow days, school closures, more and less attentive students, and peer dynamics. Of course, deviations from the plans occur due to the nature of the inclusion classroom and education in general, but teachers and administration who continually have their eyes on their inclusion plans can better ADMIRE their students' knowledge and skills.

Lesson planning is essential to ensure that all students, regardless of their abilities, have access to the same curriculum and learning opportunities. The easy-to-read mega, macro, and micro inclusion lessons offer planning formats to outline the school year's subjects, concepts, and objectives juxtapositioned. The year is shown at a glance, subdivided into terms or marking periods for the mega planning, then months for the macro planning, and then weeks for the micro planning. The mega and macro planning offer the overall picture. The plans decide and delineate the adaptations and how the specially designed instruction will be implemented to meet the needs of the diverse students in an inclusion classroom. More detail is included in the weekly plans and then each day, based on observation, anecdotal notes, and curriculum-based assessment. The rationale is multifold to offer approximate time frames before the year begins and then to easily make the adjustments during the months, weeks, and days that follow.

This approach to lesson mapping offers proactive *flight plans* that know *each student will soar on their schedule, not ours*. This allows the teacher to keep track of who knows what, at what level. Inclusion teachers require both subject knowledge and awareness of the levels of the diversified classroom members. Effective lesson planning involves deciding and delineating learning targets (ADMIRE model 10), selecting appropriate materials, and modeling and monitoring learning activities (ADMIRE model 22) that are accessible and engaging for all learners (ADMIRE model 32). This organization sets up the classroom in a way that promotes inclusivity and accessibility, managing materials and resources efficiently, and establishing clear expectations for behavior and participation (Center for Parent Information and Resources, 2022).

The following sections explore each of these stages (mega, macro, and micro) in more detail.

Mega Planning: The Year at a Glance

The mega planning outlines the year at the onset, with the concepts and skills slated in each quarter, each trimester, or set marking periods for given units of study. Teachers plan with the curriculum in mind while *also* recognizing that students who have varying executive functioning levels, social-emotional-behavioral skills, and academic levels will learn at their pace and level of competency. This does not always correspond with the date of a scheduled assessment or lesson observation, so it is important to consider the content along with nonacademic objectives.

Social-emotional, behavioral, emotional, and functional proficiencies often impact academic knowledge and skills. The content remains the same for all students, but the long-range objectives have eyes on how students respond, with multiple deliveries, entry points, and follow-ups that are student-specific. Inclusion values how the learners respond to the content based on factors such as interest, literacy and mathematics levels, prior experiences, and how they intake, process, and apply information. Figure 3.3 illustrates a fifth-grade teacher's sample mega planner. Notice how it allows the teacher to see the year at a glance, including both academic and nonacademic essential objectives offered for each quarter.

Macro Planning: Month by Month

During macro planning, the teacher outlines essential objectives for the upcoming months and units. Like mega planning, macro planning values both academic and functional objectives. Macro planning invites the big picture without the day-to-day specific details, narrowing down the quarterly topics into specific months. Figure 3.4 (page 61) illustrates the same fifth-grade teacher's sample macro planner.

Note that the topics—along with pre-, inter-, and post-assessments—drive the weekly (micro) plans for each day's lesson. All three planners slate time for small-group and individualized instruction to hone and advance student skills with the differentiation that reaches students where they are at the time of instruction. The instructional delivery is given on a level that is aligned with each student's zone of proximal development with help from a more knowledgeable other (MKO). The *zone of proximal development* is a theoretical framework developed by Lev S. Vygotsky (1978) that describes the difference between what a learner can do independently and what they can achieve with guidance and support from an MKO, who might be a peer tutor, school teacher, instructional assistant, or family member.

Quarterly Lesson Plan Units
(for each marking period) aka *The Big Picture*
First-Quarter Goals and Objectives
Mathematics: To increase fluency with whole numbers for addition, subtraction, multiplication, and division facts and place value to billions
Language arts: To express written thoughts in a coherent paragraph for intended audience on topic of choice, using online tools and writer's notebook
Reading: To identify the story elements of character traits, setting, plot, climax, and resolution in a short story of choice
Science: To learn about ecosystems and the food chain; VAKT tactile demos of producers, consumers, and decomposers
Social studies: To create a timeline of U.S. history events; begin unit on exploration and European imperialism; include cooperative kinesthetic debate
Perceptual or physical: To attend to teachers and peers, filtering out distracting stimuli; introduce transitional movement break choices
Social or behavioral: To follow all classroom and school norms established for academics and behavior; homework, completion of tasks, working in groups, and so on
Executive skills: To organize upcoming school assignments and personal events in handheld trackers, online calendars, and tools
Second-Quarter Goals and Objectives
Mathematics: To apply computational skills to solve one- and two-step word problems with whole numbers using all four operations; continue computational drills; include Touchmath assessments
Language arts: To improve writing with descriptive vocabulary, transitional words, and *wh-* expanders in a three-paragraph personal narrative
Technology: To explore differentiated tools, extensions, and online sites (for example, Chrome extensions—Read&Write, Immersive Reader); word prediction, speech recognition, graphic organizers, visual dictionaries, summarization tools, and artificial intelligence (AI)
Reading: To work cooperatively in literature circles with a choice of genres in fiction and nonfiction text with assigned roles of passage pickers, artists, word wizards, discussion leaders, and connectors
Science: To identify the needs of plants and animals; classification unit on vertebrates includes UDL principles with varying representation, engagement, and expression offered during instruction and for assessment
Social studies: To explore local, national, and global events in What's Going On in this Picture? (access this book's webpage via **go.SolutionTree.com/specialneeds** for a link), Time for Kids, and CommonLit articles; jigsaw the students into centers to explore the different colonies with peers to learn about the NE, middle, and southern colonies

Figure 3.3: Sample mega planner.

continued →

Social or behavioral: To exhibit social reciprocity with peers in class and nonacademic times; norms revisited; emotional check-ins
Executive skills: To outline information in social studies and science using text headings, cloze notes, study guides, and recorded video tutorials as tools
Third-Quarter Goals and Objectives
Mathematics: To solve computations and word problems with decimals, fractions, and whole numbers in whole-class, small-group, and individual instruction
Language arts: To proofread writings for descriptive essays, using rubrics, auditory or visual models, and input from peer and teacher conferencing
Reading: To understand the motives of characters and the sequencing of events; share author videos
Science: To observe, record, and graph daily weather; investigate the water cycle, erosion, and weathering in the community; use PhET
Social studies: To outline events leading to the American Revolution and Civil War; explore primary documents
Communication or global perspectives: To communicate with pen pals overseas within supervised digital platforms
Social or behavioral: To increase self-awareness by tallying on-task behavior to support PBIS
Executive skills: To create mnemonics and acrostic sentences for concepts in English, social studies, mathematics, and science
Fourth-Quarter Goals and Objectives
Mathematics: To apply geometric principles and solve ratio, proportion, and probability with real-life application in PBL unit; include school sensory walks
Language arts: To apply figurative language in writings; to complete poetry unit with published class poems donated to the school media center
Reading: To accurately answer oral and written cause-and-effect and inferential questions in fiction and nonfiction genres; offer self-checks
Science: To explore plate tectonics of convergent, divergent, and transform plate boundaries with global identifications
Social studies: To explore early U.S. government, westward expansion, and immigration in the early 19th and 20th centuries
Technology: To collaboratively complete hyperlinked Think-Tac-Toe choice boards for prior science, mathematics, and social studies units
Social or behavioral: To practice mindfulness at set times each week in school and at home
Executive skills: To self-assess achievement in content areas by reviewing digital portfolios and classwork

*Visit **go.SolutionTree.com/specialneeds** for a free reproducible of this figure.*

	Long Range Monthly Plans
August	Review IEPs and 504 plans with teams and share specially designed instruction adaptations with all staff; personal interest survey sent to students; family survey sent to establish connections and increase awareness for both environments
September	Class norms and organizational tools for whole-class, small-group, and individualized instruction; mathematics: computational drills; preassessment; language arts: vocabulary tools, graphic organizers; writer's notebook; social studies: government unit; science: biome; mindfulness
October	Introduction to movement breaks, cooperative and small-group centers; mathematics: two-step word problems; reading, language arts: literature circles; structural analysis; dystopia, monster unit; social studies: outlining with and without online tools; emotional check-ins
November	Mathematics: intro to fractions-decimals in computations with real-life application; social studies: colonial projects; science, study skills: how we remember best—brain basics; PBIS incentives; reading, language arts: author's purpose, writing for an audience
December	Reading, language arts: persuasive essays; community holiday projects—letters, poems, songs, and food collections for older individuals and veterans; mathematics: holiday budgets; science: vocabulary picture books; technology: defining accessibility; cultural preferences
January	Mathematics: class graphs of favorites, logic boxes; social studies: centers on geographic regions; reading, language arts: literature groups, persuasive essays; student-teacher progress conferences with next steps outlined; science: water cycles, erosion
February	Language arts, reading: writing for an audience, figurative language, idioms, analogies across the subjects; science: heart facts bulletin board; social studies: plays based on information from primary documents (for example, Declaration of Independence, Bill of Rights)
March	Mathematics: tessellations, probability, graphs; social studies: women in history, branches of government; science: weathering—PhET simulations; language arts, reading: character perspectives; Black Beauty unit; SEL, behavior: self-regulation tools, digital etiquette
April	Science: inquiry and inventions; social studies: Civil War, westward expansion; language arts, reading: cause-effect, author's voice, Holocaust unit; SEL: acceptance of self and others—unit on differences; mathematics: checkups; science PBL centers
May	Language arts, reading: classroom newspaper, editorials, book reviews; mathematics: hands-on algebraic equations, reinforcement, practice, and check-ins; science, physical education: exercise logs, light and shadows; visualization tools
June	That's a Wrap: Here's What We Learned, Think-Tac-Toe choice boards, self-assessment; next steps; review of class assignments and digital portfolios; language arts, reading: poetry unit; mathematics: sports, art mathematics centers
July	Breathe, rejuvenate, and reflect on collaboration with input as appropriate from inclusion educators, related service providers, families, and administration

Figure 3.4: Sample macro planner.

Visit **go.SolutionTree.com/specialneeds** *for a free reproducible of this figure.*

Micro Planning: The Weeks and Days

Teachers may use the next two micro-inclusion planners—(1) Daily Agenda and Schedule Highlights (DASH) and (2) By the End of the Week Inclusion Strategies Educate (BE WISE)—to delineate the weekly interventions with the objectives, materials, and goals, along with the procedures, strategies, and steps; the curriculum-based assessments; and the collaboration required. Digital versions of these and additional inclusion planners are available online at the QR code on this page.

Figure 3.5 provides a sample of the DASH planner and figure 3.6 (page 65) contains a sample of the BE WISE planner. Notice that the DASH and BE WISE micro-planning tools outline the objectives, instructional plans, and monitoring for each week, with as much detail as teachers need to guide their instruction, yet they make it responsive and prescriptive. Apply UDL (ADMIRE model 31) to the weekly lessons to offer multiple representations, engagements, actions, and expressions to invite mastery at each student's pace. Additionally, introduce the essential learning targets and monitor student progress with observation, along with both formal and informal curriculum-based assessments (ADMIRE model 23).

Since inclusion has no template, reflections from inclusion teachers' observations are imperative. These notes assist to ensure that the learning is retained beyond a string of lessons and that the professional roles are shared. Consider the following inclusion reminders.

- Keep data in guided reading, offering minilessons with syllabification, medial vowels, vocabulary, and fluency.
- Alternate which co-teacher instructs smaller groups requiring more advanced work and those who need remediation to avoid stigmatization.
- Offer praise for time on task and efforts, as well as achievements.
- Send home a mathematics packet with practice for those students who require remediation and those students needing higher-level work.
- Ensure all students engage in daily critical thinking skills.
- Post websites for practice weekly in an online platform such as Google Classroom.
- Make weekly contact with families to boost collaboration and mutual support.
- Cue study groups to quiz each other with outlines or graphic organizers for main idea and details.
- Schedule individual conferencing to provide emotional check-ins, and review work samples and portfolios to encourage metacognition and self-efficacy.
- Model study skills for student organization, interpreting directions, and note-taking.
- Monitor specific students for their time on task during whole-class instruction.
- Continue podcast and presentation slide for the project (ADMIRE model 40).
- Notice which students need writing frames to begin and organize their thoughts.

Connect to the Realities That Teachers, Students, and Families Face   63

DASH: Daily Agenda and Schedule Highlights

Teachers: Mary Monitor   **Grade or Subject:** 5   **Week of:** 1/15

Monday: Breanne's and Zachary's birthday. Timed fluency exercise in the a.m. Class discussion and kinesthetic activity of the solar system. Library lesson at 12:00. Introduction to structural analysis charts, figurative language, and idioms. Time for kids distributed and discussed. Mathematics, science, and social studies objectives and vocabulary introduced.

Tuesday: Computer lab time: 10:00. Student Tm's re-evaluation meeting (10:15–11:00). Writing rubrics given to students. Class geography bee. Planet art activity. Individual writing conferences. Time for kids comprehension quiz. Discuss civil rights and contributions of Martin Luther King.

Wednesday: Peer editing and teacher writing conferences. Social studies discussion and debate. Guidance counselor character education lesson at 1:35. Mathematics ratio exit cards. Continue mathematics scaling project, science PowerPoints, and social studies debates.

Thursday: Send students (groups of 5) to the nurse for physicals in the a.m., beginning at 9:45. Independent practice with www.studyisland.com. Ratio quiz. Reading review of "Don't Give Up" Literature Unit; structural word lists shared. Send family email updates.

Friday: Science PowerPoints shared. Grade-level professional learning community meeting to reflect upon this week's activities and to plan for next week's theme: balance. Deadline for school essay contest today. Mathematics chapter test. Class meeting to discuss daily living connections with human or capital resources, astronomy, proportion, and other weekly assignments.

Inclusion Strategies

Weekly Class Interventions		
☐ Alternate materials	☐ Enrichment activities	☑ Praise increased
☑ Assignments modified	☑ Family involvement	☑ Pre-teaching and prior knowledge
☑ Assistive technology	☑ Graphic organizers	☐ Private signals
☐ Auditory cues and options	☑ Guided practice	☑ Repetition or reteaching
☐ Behavior interventions	☑ High expectations	☐ Role playing
	☑ Interdisciplinary lessons	☑ Scaffolding
	☑ Intervention groups	☐ Seating and teacher proximity

Class Monitoring and Curriculum-Based Assessments		
☑ Advance notice for quizzes or tests	☑ Interpersonal	☐ Open-book tests
☐ Alternate assessments	☑ Intrapersonal	☐ Participation graded
☑ Attention and behavior checks	☑ Logical-mathematical	☐ Portfolios
☑ Baseline level established	☐ Musical-rhythmic	☐ Posttests given
☑ Benchmarks given	☑ Naturalistic	☐ Pretests given
☑ Chapter test	☑ Verbal-linguistic	☑ Progress recorded
	☑ Visual-spatial	☐ Retest offered
		☑ Rubrics distributed

continued →

***Figure 3.5:** Sample DASH micro planner.*

The ADMIRE Framework for Inclusion

- ☑ Classwide peer tutoring or mentoring
- ☐ Collaborative projects
- ☑ Concrete presentations
- ☑ Cooperative learning groups
- ☑ Co-teaching
  - ☐ Bouncing ideas
  - ☐ Parallel teaching
  - ☐ One lead, one assist
  - ☐ Small groups or one-to-one
  - ☐ Stations or centers
  - ☑ Team, staff consultation, and services
- ☑ Debates
- ☐ Differentiation of objectives
- ☑ Discussion
- ☑ Empowerment of students

- ☑ Literature circles
- ☑ Modeling
- ☑ Multiple intelligences
  - ☑ Bodily-kinesthetic
  - ☐ Existentialist
  - ☑ Interpersonal
  - ☑ Intrapersonal
  - ☑ Logical-mathematical
  - ☑ Musical-rhythmic
  - ☐ Naturalistic
  - ☑ Verbal-linguistic
  - ☑ Visual-spatial
- ☑ Note-taking modified

- ☐ Simulations
- ☑ Sponge activities
- ☑ Study skill support
- ☑ Tactile activities and materials
- ☐ Thematic lessons
- ☐ Time extended for responses
- ☑ UbD
- ☑ UDL
- ☑ Visuals
- ☑ Writing reduced

- ☐ Collaborative assignments
- ☑ Efforts monitored
- ☑ Exit cards
- ☐ Extra credit or bonus questions offered
- ☐ Functional behavioral assessments
- ☐ Grading or homework modified
- ☑ Homework graded
- ☑ Individual assignments or learning contracts
- ☑ Informal checks
- ☑ Journals and logs checked
- ☑ Know-want to know-learned charts
- ☑ Long-term projects
- ☑ Multiple intelligences
  - ☑ Bodily-kinesthetic
  - ☐ Existentialist

- ☑ Multiple test formats and deliveries
- ☐ Answers recorded
- ☑ Clutter reduced
- ☐ Fewer or simplified concepts
- ☐ Fewer choices
- ☐ Fewer questions
- ☐ Questions read
- ☐ Quieter setting
- ☐ Verbal responses
- ☑ Vocabulary simplified or explained
- ☑ Notebook checks
- ☑ Observations

- ☑ Self-assessments
- ☑ Self-regulation or learning journals
- ☑ Student conferencing
- ☐ Study guides
- ☑ Quizzes
- ☐ Take-home test
- ☐ Time extended or pacing varied
- ☐ Unit test
- ☐ UbD
- ☑ Weekly test
- ☑ Work lesson samples

Other Interventions: Class word wall, small groups twice a week (no co-teacher)

Other Monitoring and Assessments: Visual tracking exercises

Visit go.SolutionTree.com/specialneeds for a free reproducible of this figure.

BE WISE Lesson Plans

Theme: Yes ✓ No ___ If Yes __Technology and Nutrition__
Teachers: __Gettum Going, Art Praise__ Grade: __7–8__
Week Beginning __3/14__
Revisitation Date: __3/21, 5/20__

Academic Achievements (AA): Students demonstrate literacy and mathematics skills with technology.

Functional Performances (FP): Students identify how technology can help us in everyday activities and keep food and exercise diaries and listen to podcasts.

Baseline knowledge: Students define technology, giving low-tech and high-tech examples.

More advanced: Students investigate how technology works (for example, cars, clocks, cell phones, iPods, podcasts, laptops, calculators, elliptical machines, SMART Boards).

Knowing beyond: Students cooperatively design an innovative technological device (ongoing enrichment station or activity).

Objectives, Materials, and Goals (OMG)	Procedures, Strategies, and Steps (PSS)	Curriculum-Based Assessment (CBA)	Inclusive Collaborative Strategies
			Weekly co-teaching options: 1. Bouncing ideas off each other 2. Parallel teaching 3. One leading, one assisting 4. Small groups or one-to-one 5. Stations or centers 6. Consultation team
			Related Services IA: Instructional Assistant SLP: Speech-Language Pathology OT: Occupational Therapy PT: Physical Therapy CS: Counseling Services M: Mobility ORS: Other Related Services
READING To read books online (http://bookbuilder.cast.org/library.php, www.readinga-z.com) and books on tape in the class library. Co-teaching option 6 (computer teacher).	Students choose a book (with teacher direction) on appropriate reading grade level to summarize and outline plot, characterization, resolution, and theme.	Completed summary in class and for homework. IA: Student LG	**Classroom or Student Considerations** Students monitored in computer lab to ensure time on task and attention to directions. Co-teachers and instructional assistant circulate at stations to take observational notes.
LANGUAGE ARTS AND WRITING To write a chapter book with computer software tools and online sites (http://bookbuilder.cast.org/create.php, http://plasq.com/comiclife). Word processing tools Co-teaching options 1–4.	Students write their own books in a word document or graphic novel format, using computer tools, keyboarding, clip art, and electronic dictionaries.	Completed work samples and teacher observation.	

continued →

***Figure 3.6:** BE WISE micro planning template.*

Objectives, Materials, and Goals (OMG)	Procedures, Strategies, and Steps (PSS)	Curriculum-Based Assessment (CBA)	
MATHEMATICS Students choose recipes at different food stations to halve and double ingredients in algebraic problems and keep exercise and food logs. Podcasts selected from http://allrecipes.com. Materials: Calculators to check computations with whole numbers and fractions. Co-teaching option 5.	Sample problems on SMART Board modeled to practice calculator tools: www.aplusmath.com Students circulate to different nutrition food pyramid stations or centers around the room.	Doubled and halved recipes with equations. Collaborative behavior monitored; food and exercise logs or podcasts.	
SCIENCE AND TECHNOLOGY Investigate how technological devices work. Materials: invention list, graphic organizers, writing and presentation rubrics designed from http://rubistar.4teachers.org, mP3 players for podcasts.	Students choose a product from invention list and record information in a wh– graphic organizer to present. Sites include www.greatachievements.org, www.howstuffworks.com/cell-phone.htm.	Presentation options: Songs, collages, graphs, poems, podcasts, screenplays graded with student rubric. Speech-language pathologist: Students WC and TT	SG: Small Groups (use student initials) SG BK, WC, TT
SOCIAL STUDIES AND GLOBAL STUDIES Conduct research to compare and contrast technology from 100 years ago to the present time.	Students cooperatively research and outline how technology has globally changed over the past century by responding to a webQuest.	Completed webQuest.	One-to-one (use student initials) IT, LG
STUDY OR PERCEPTUAL SKILLS To transfer notes to flashcards.	Flashcards available at https://teachables.scholastic.com/teachables/type/flash-cards.html.	Online flashcards.	
SOCIAL SKILLS Compare and contrast technology to face-to-face interactions as forms of communication. Co-teaching option 1.	Class discussion to create survey questions for students to solicit responses from peers and adults.	Shared survey answers. IA: Student IT	
WISE TIP Value inquiry, allowing students the opportunities for self-discovery and elaboration rather than just practice and repetition.			

Visit go.SolutionTree.com/specialneeds for a free reproducible of this figure.

Figure 3.7 illustrates one way of sharing observational notes with students' learning consultants, school, psychologists, and families to increase collaboration.

- Co-teachers and instructional assistants will continue to circulate to record students' progress, inconspicuously offering minilessons with syllabification rules, vowels in medial positions, more difficult vocabulary, and fluency during guided reading times.
- Give ongoing praise for time on task and efforts as well as achievements.
- Make a home mathematics packet with extra practice available to those students who require remediation or those students needing higher-level work.
- Post academic websites for more practice on the class's weekly website for family collaboration and support.
- Student study groups will quiz each other with Inspiration outlines (www.inspiration-at.com), columned graphic organizers, main idea and details sheets, extra practice problems, and cloze science and social studies notes and vocabulary flashcards.
- Consider individual conferencing about work samples in portfolios to encourage metacognition and self-regulated learners.
- Alternate which co-teacher instructs smaller groups requiring more advanced work and those students needing remediation.
- Offer whole-class study skills for student organization, interpreting written directions, and note-taking.
- Offer one-to-one monitoring for student time on task during science, social studies, reading, writing, and mathematics instruction.
- Continue podcast and PowerPoint projects.
- A few of the students need writing frames to begin and organize their screenplays.
- Some students need extra help to find information to answer *wh-* questions in invention assignment.
- Will investigate other techno ideas at www.edtechroundup.org/ed-tech-sites.html.
- Communicate observational notes to share as feedback with students, learning consultant, school psychologist, and families.
- Collaborate with music, art, and physical education teachers, and speech-language pathologists about themes to extend lessons across rooms and disciplines.

Figure 3.7: *Inclusion observations, notes, and future plans.*

Tracking student progress over time provides useful data for the inclusion teacher. The teacher or assistant keeps the data for a given lesson or a unit of study to note academic and behavioral patterns. This allows them to monitor student participation and provide supports appropriately matched to a learner's level of performance. These data drive the adaptations required (that is, the setting, complexity of content, resources, and supports).

Figure 3.8 (page 68) illustrates a tool teachers can use to track these data. This example shows how inclusion professionals might keep track of four fictional students' participation in a unit of study to note patterns and triggers and to drive instructional decisions.

Hierarchy of Inclusion Classroom Participation

Teachers: Genny Ed, Sara Special

Directions: Check off appropriate columns to keep track of inclusion participation progress for one student over time, or for eight different students in the class. Duplicate as needed.

Student (name or initials) or dates	Able to fully participate in the same lesson as peers	Needs modified expectations and extra materials to accomplish lesson's objective	Can independently participate in a different but related assignment in the room	Requires supervision or assistance to complete or attend to assignments	Cannot proficiently complete task in classroom, even with support	Brief comments, observations, needs, interventions, modifications, notes, VAKT concerns, future plans
AC	✓					AC completes the tasks with intermittent monitoring.
LM		✓				LM is reading below grade level; requires simplified text.
ZK					✓	ZK shuts down if concepts are not within her prior knowledge.
YS				✓		YS has difficulties attending and requires gestural prompts.

Source: © 2010 by Corwin Press. From Inclusion Strategies That Work! Research-Based Methods for the Classroom (2nd ed.) by Toby J. Karten. Used with permission.

Figure 3.8: Hierarchy of inclusion classroom sample participation data collection form.

Visit **go.SolutionTree.com/specialneeds** for a free reproducible of this figure.

Inclusion planning ensures that progress monitoring is an integral part of instruction for content, application, and behavior. Inclusion lessons require appropriate anticipatory sets that assess and activate student interest to increase motivation and retention. Inclusion classes value whole-class instruction and group configurations with guided instruction, practice, and application to pave the path for independence.

Collaborate With Families

School-home communication and collaboration include ongoing and respectful interactions that catapult a student forward. Inclusion is successful when the students, their families, and the staff collaboratively listen to, trust, and support one another to provide the services within inclusion environments. School-home communications are conducted face-to-face, by phone, via email, with handheld school-home weekly logs, through online meets, and with platforms such as ParentSquare (formerly Remind.com) using two-way text messaging.

Communication includes letting families know the content of upcoming lessons and how they can prepare for and support the learning with the application of evidence-based practices. As an example, as an inclusion support teacher faced with a parent asking how they can help their child, I often shared ideas for home practice. Some include Orton-Gillingham word study (www.orton-gillingham.com/approach) and a weekly schedule with online sites for home practice with mathematics to increase automaticity and fluency of number facts or science or social studies curriculum planning guides a week ahead of a unit. This allows the student to become familiar with the academic language and concepts before they hear them during whole-class instruction.

Research indicates that partnerships between schools and their communities support student learning, improve schools, and strengthen families and neighborhoods (Stefanski, Valli, & Jacobson, 2016). Delineated roles and responsibilities increase inclusion successes in schools, homes, and communities. Professionals and families can partner as advocates, collaborators, and providers who exchange information to support, encourage, and reassure each other during often frustrating and difficult times.

Families are challenged when they hear their child's diagnosis and experience emotions like denial, fear, anger, guilt, confusion, powerlessness, and disappointment (McGill Smith, n.d.). An impactful part of my special education journey occurred in a graduate class at Brooklyn College when I attended a panel discussion where family members spoke about how having a child with an intellectual disability impacted the family. The year was 1976, and I still see their faces and hear their voices. Siblings told how a brother or sister with a cognitive difference *stole time away* from their parents, while parents spoke about financial and emotional impact.

Emily Perl Kingsley (1987), a former screenwriter for *Sesame Street*, shares in her poignant essay, "Welcome to Holland," how her dreams changed when she gave birth to a child with Down syndrome. She likens the experience to planning a fabulous trip to Italy, only to find out that the plane landed in Holland. Although the *trip itinerary* changed, and she will not encounter Michelangelo's masterpieces and the gondolas of Venice, if she mourns that loss, she will never experience the beautiful and rewarding things about Holland. Continuing with Kingsley's poignant metaphorical essay, a professional's role and responsibility is to assist parents and families to notice beautiful tulips, windmills, van Gogh's brilliance, and Rembrandt's ageless masterpieces. Side note: Kingsley's son, Jason, lives independently and is gainfully employed as a productive member of society.

Conclusion

Effective lesson planning in inclusion classrooms involves differentiating learning objectives, selecting appropriate materials, and designing activities that are accessible and engaging for students with and without IEPs. Given that the inclusion classroom is diverse, the instruction and assessment should be too. Tracking student progress provides useful data to guide instructional steps. Inclusion teachers can take mindful actions such as including weekly slated time periods for repetition, enrichment, and practice. Learning happens with smiles, collaboration, and connections to the everyday realities students and their families face. Take a moment to reflect on the information and strategies you've read by completing the "Admiring the Realities of the Teachers, Students, and Families" reproducible at the end of this chapter (page 74).

Interest Survey

Interest inventories build relationships between teachers and peers to increase relevancy, learner engagement, and motivation to learn and listen. Learners with and without IEPs are individuals. Build personal connections with your students by inviting input through an interests and strengths questionnaire.

What I like about myself:

What I like about others:

What I would change about myself and why:

What I would change about others and why:

Favorite subjects and activities:

Least favorite subjects and activities:

Best friends:

Songs, books, movies, apps, and websites I like:
A job or career I might like to do one day:
Skills that would help me to do that job or career:
What might stop me from doing what I want (for example, other people, my weaknesses):
Who could help me achieve my goals:
Other things I think about:

Source: Adapted from Karten, T. J. (2021). Inclusion strategies and interventions (2nd ed.). Bloomington, IN: Solution Tree Press.

Learner Profile

Use the learner profile to note a learner's strengths, challenges, likes, and dislikes to allow you to connect with the student. Reach out to the student, the student's family, or prior teachers to gather input for the profile. Revisit the profile throughout the year and use it to adapt lessons as needed.

Student: _____	Date of birth: _____	Grade level: _____
Strengths and Challenges *(includes VAKT preferences)*		
Interests and Likes *(Includes in school or outside)*		
IEP Goals and Objectives *(For example, academic, social, emotional, behavioral, physical, communication)*		
Accommodations and Modifications		
Current Performance Level **Progress Monitoring Timeline to Review Results**		

The ADMIRE Framework for Inclusion © 2024 Solution Tree Press • SolutionTree.com
Visit **go.SolutionTree.com/specialneeds** to download this free reproducible.

Admiring the Realities of the Teachers, Students, and Families

Use the following template to ADMIRE the actions to connect to the realities that teachers, students, and families face. In the space provided, note which of the ADMIRE action items stood out to you from this chapter.

A **Assess and Activate**	
D **Decide and Delineate**	
M **Model and Monitor**	
I **Instruct and Involve**	
R **Reflect and Revise**	
E **Engage and Enrich**	

The ADMIRE Framework for Inclusion © 2024 Solution Tree Press • SolutionTree.com
Visit **go.SolutionTree.com/specialneeds** to download this free reproducible.

CHAPTER 4

Practice Supportive Classroom Management

Without effective classroom management, inclusion mastery is elusive. Classroom management provides positive and proactive support for academics and behavior. It plans for the diversity of levels, interests, strengths, and challenges that the students evidence. Although these management practices need to be standard procedures, what works for one student with a specific learning difference, ADHD, or autism will not be the same support given for each student with that label.

Diversity is why we infuse learner profiles and interest inventories into our practice (chapter 3, page 49). Therefore, inclusion teachers must look at how students respond to interventions and then visually, physically, academically, and kindly organize the classroom and school environment accordingly. As professionals, we must tweak the inclusion structures and management practices for whole-class instruction, small groups of learners, and individual students. Proactive coordination of roles supports diverse populations of learners and the behaviors exhibited beyond special education classifications and preconceived stereotypes.

The effective use of space, time, resources, and personnel ensures that inclusion teachers optimally connect to all students—not sacrificing either the general or special education learners. The foundational premise of inclusion, which is to have students productively learn side by side in an inclusion classroom, cannot occur without supportive classroom management. Supportive classroom management advances knowledge and smiles for students, families, and staff. Let's explore how.

In this chapter, we ADMIRE classroom management as a commitment to creating an environment where *all* students can experience belonging and growth. We examine how cultural responsiveness, classroom rules, routines and expectations, and individualized support contribute to a positive environment. At the end of the chapter, we ADMIRE inclusion principles and consider student realities in a real-world context to consider how ideals of classroom management translate to practice.

ADMIRE Classroom Management

Classroom management in inclusion refers to creating and maintaining a positive and supportive learning environment that meets the needs of all students, including those with disabilities or other special needs (CAST, n.d.; Kauffman, Hallahan, Pullen, & Badar, 2018). Without classroom management, the best inclusion plans will not reach the students who need the most help.

In an inclusion classroom, classroom management focuses on collaboratively establishing and reinforcing class expectations and norms (ADMIRE models 9, 14–16, from table I.1, page 4) with student input. Learners need support to prioritize and organize tasks, follow directions, and cooperatively work with others (ADMIRE model 41). Proactive teachers set up ongoing centers for the times when students need practice, repetition, and enrichment (ADMIRE model 56). That's the UDL approach (ADMIRE model 31) that acknowledges that students need different representation, engagement, and action and expression.

Inclusion classroom management strategies include establishing a positive classroom environment, outlining and reinforcing routines and expectations, and providing individualized support for students with disabilities (Polirstok, 2015). While educators are practiced at establishing routines and expectations, they may have less experience with including individualized support. Individualized support (ADMIRE model 46) might look like providing a learner with headphones and a seat away from a door or window to filter out distractions and increase their attention. Or it might mean color coding visual spaces in the room for easy access to resources and materials, scheduling movement or calming breaks for students who experience anxiety, and using bouncy balls in the classroom in place of standard seating for select learners. These are just a few examples of supports learners might require to better attend and learn. Classroom management includes the establishment and communication of clear expectations and rules for behavior, participation, and interactions with others.

Collaboration and communication with families and other professionals, such as behavior analysts, guidance counselors, and school psychologists (ADMIRE models 33–37), ensures that we capitalize on each other's strengths, with behavioral expectations that are reality-based, supported, understood, and reinforced in all environments. Remember to keep families and caregivers informed of their child's progress. Do not limit communications to *the bad stuff*; make positive contacts to share behavioral and academic celebrations, *the good stuff*, too! This can help build a strong partnership between home and school.

Positive Classroom Environment

Creating a positive classroom and school environment is essential for effective classroom management. That includes a range of resources and methodologies to recognize and celebrate student achievements, both big and small learning celebrations (ADMIRE model 45). A positive classroom establishes, communicates, and reinforces clear expectations, rather than emphasizing restrictions. Verbal praise, written notes, and small rewards are just a few ways teachers promote a positive atmosphere.

The ongoing application of evidence-based practices, such as UDL, UbD, PBIS, DI, and MTSS (see table 1.1, page 18) organizes the students and teachers. These evidence-based practices, which are threaded throughout this book, are also key to this chapter since they are integral components of classroom management. PBIS, with its three-tiered framework, values how SEL catapults everyone forward within a positive school climate (see www.pbis.org).

Research shows that schools that implemented PBIS have lower rates of problem behavior and higher rates of academic achievement (Bradshaw, Mitchell, & Leaf, 2010; Bradshaw, Reinke, Brown, Bevans, & Leaf, 2008; Center on PBIS, www.pbis.org). For example, when implemented with fidelity, PBIS is associated with improvements in school climate, behavior, and attendance and reductions in suspensions and expulsions (Center on PBIS, www.pbis.org).

Students who experience trauma in their personal lives may look to the classroom to be their safe haven. It's a place to learn and develop positive relationships. We, as inclusion professionals, must commit to *reach before we teach*. This means that teachers connect to a student beyond their exceptionality (ADMIRE model 24).

Figure 4.1 depicts "REACH before you TEACH" as an acronym promoting supportive teacher-student connections that facilitate the positive environment students need.

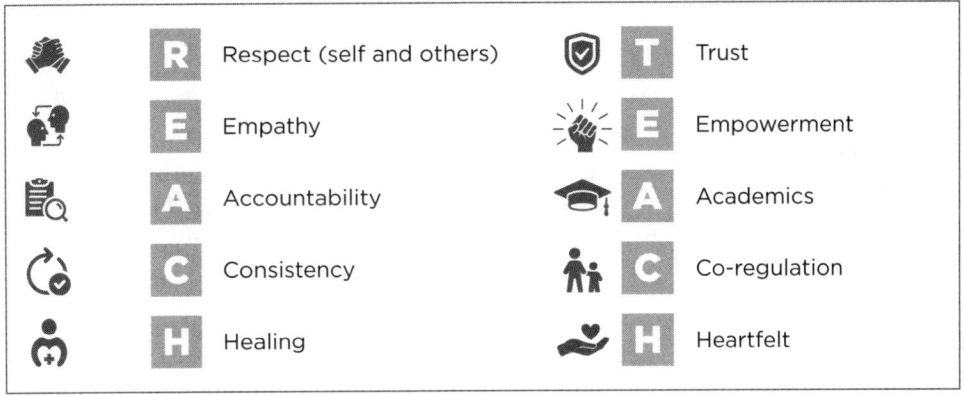

Figure 4.1: REACH before you TEACH.

REACH before you TEACH emphasizes the non-negotiable elements of respect, empathy, accountability, consistency, and healing to nurture trust in the classroom and empower both student and teacher to learn. Professionals, peers, and families co-regulate a student's academic and functional performance. Unfortunately, too many special education students shut down before the lesson begins. A positive classroom climate consistently teaches a student that it's OK not to know something, but it's not OK to keep quiet about it. Classrooms invite students to ask questions within inquiry-based environments that promote student participation with no fear of criticism.

Students need to trust that their teachers care more about them than the subjects they teach. Often, students respond to different incentives, whether that's a smile, a gold star, or a visit to the prize box. When I transitioned from my full-time classroom position as a special education teacher to become an inclusion facilitator, I left a rectangular cardboard treasure box behind. My students knew that they earned a visit to the prize box with their positive actions. Co-regulation was accomplished when they argued why. Ultimately, the prizes mattered less than the positive attention internalized by the student.

Heartfelt positive practices and affirmations are essential. Some students may be open to a teacher's well-intended affirmations, while others reject them in front of peers, viewing them as negative attention. Older learners may prefer more candid communications through a digital platform such as a Google Form. That's why it's important to schedule weekly face-to-face or online emotional check-ins with your students. One way to honor students' preferences is to keep observational data to note patterns of behavior and to uncover and record behavioral antecedents to then tweak and address environmental triggers. If a co-teacher or teacher assistant is present, together they divide and conquer to conduct the check-ins, offer affirmations, and keep the data.

The way you organize the classroom makes a big difference too. Have resources available, like mood dudes, magnetic emotional meters, fidget toys, and academic planners. Organize the space with sensory corners and quieter areas for *learner downtime*, since students, like adults, lead hectic lives and may be frustrated or overwhelmed at times. Consider partitioning a small corner of the room with a tentlike structure or place a tablecloth over a desk as a curtain to block out unwanted visuals and noise. Position beanbag chairs by the classroom library to invite students to grab books to read. Areas designed to offer quieter spaces and sensory tables circumvent stimuli overloads. These types of proactive classroom supports assist a student with specific internalizing or externalizing emotional difference as well as help a student decrease anxiety. Sometimes, professionals do not know what a student needs until the learner communicates displeasure with aversive behaviors and actions. The crux of classroom management is for students to identify and learn more about their emotions and what they need to help themselves.

As you will discover in this chapter's scenarios, diversity never caps mastery. The ADMIRE strategies are modeled for an elementary physical education class, a middle school science class, and a high school history class. Collaborative teacher-student-family actions and coordinated instructional and behavioral plans respond to inclusion challenges. If trust is missing, then students are not empowered to regulate their actions, nor are parents likely to support teachers and school staff. Professionals activate, delineate, model, instruct, reinforce, and enrich positive actions in all environments.

Sometimes, that means that students, peers, professionals, and families require co-regulation before self-regulation occurs with automaticity. As with everything we learn, mastery is a process that requires step-by-step organization, discrete task analysis, and pacing (ADMIRE models 18, 47, 51). It's not that students can't learn or do something, but the bottom line is that successes occur with effective and affective classroom management practices. Let's explore two applications of responsive management practices in the following sections: culturally responsive teaching and classroom rules.

Culturally Responsive Teaching

Ensuring all students feel they belong in the classroom is essential for maintaining a positive environment. One key way of accomplishing this is to practice culturally responsive teaching. *Culturally responsive teaching* is an approach that recognizes and values the diversity of students who are educated in the classroom. It involves understanding and respecting the cultural backgrounds, experiences, and identities of students and using this understanding to create a supportive and inclusive learning environment. Culturally responsive teaching also involves promoting inclusion by ensuring that all students feel welcomed and valued. It supports intellectual growth and can help students solve real-life problems in the classroom. Culturally responsive pedagogy promotes social identity, with cultures and perspectives not only acknowledged but nurtured to empower students to comfortably learn and grow (Will & Najarro, 2022).

Culturally responsive inclusion practices can have a positive impact on student outcomes when classrooms promote the belief that no one group or culture is better than the next. Responsive cultural practices include respect and understanding for one another. TESOL (Teachers of English to Speakers of Other Languages) International Association author Judie Haynes (n.d.) shares uncomplicated yet imperative strategies for ELs. Consider the following practices to value.

- Learn how to pronounce student and family names correctly.
- Explicitly teach content-related vocabulary.
- Scaffold language into manageable chunks.
- Communicate and collaborate with families.

Culturally responsive teachers differentiate instruction by including multiple modalities in their lessons. That includes VAKT connections (see table I.1, page 4) as students interact with the concepts and the academic vocabulary. A student who does not speak English as their primary language requires supports if their speaking and listening skills differ. Differentiated instruction may connect to diverse cultures in multiple ways. For example, recognizing that several students' home cultures value group dynamics over independence, a teacher might favor small-group work over independent work.

For more information about culturally responsive strategies, consider the following resources.

- Learning for Justice's website (www.learningforjustice.org)
- Colorín Colorado's (n.d.) article on creating a welcoming classroom environment (www.colorincolorado.org/article/how-create-welcoming-classroom-environment)
- TESOL's online blog (Haynes, n.d.; http://ftp.everythingesl.net)

I'll share an example of what culturally responsive teaching looked like in one of my classes. One day during small-group instruction, my student Malik (not his real name) gazed at the *Hello in Different Languages* poster that faced him on the opposite wall in the resource room where they sat for reading and language arts instruction five days a week. Malik was from Sudan, and for the first time in this school, his culture was validated with a greeting in Arabic that welcomed him.

His smile sparked the literacy instruction that followed as we read *The Sign of the Beaver* by Elizabeth George Speare (2011). We compared Sudan's wilderness to the 18th-century American frontier in Speare's novel. The other students were in awe as Malik described how elephants roamed the landscape where he lived in Sudan. Malik was fascinated by the stories about life in the United States then and now. These cultural exchanges allowed us to expand our world as we read, wrote, listened, and spoke with one another. Two years later, Malik and I, and a few of the other students who received reading and writing instruction in the resource room, left that setting and moved to a less restrictive environment, an inclusion classroom.

That experience reminds me of Henry David Thoreau's (2004) words: "Could a greater miracle take place than for us to look through each other's eyes for an instant?" (p. 6).

Classroom Rules

Establishing and reinforcing classroom rules (ADMIRE model 16) is another key aspect of cultivating a positive environment. As an example, students need to learn how to regulate their voices to use acceptable volumes or know that they need to raise their hands to respond to a question, while those same voices and hands never disrespect a person or their belongings. Proactive classroom rules prevent challenging behaviors from occurring. Increased adherence to classroom rules increases in-class cohesion and inclusion (Demir, Sener, Karaboga, & Basal, 2023).

The two most important characteristics of effective classroom rules are teaching the rules to students and tying these rules to positive or negative consequences (Alter & Haydon, 2017). These rules can be reinforced with the whole class, in small groups, and through individual discussions (ADMIRE model 43) during a morning meeting, online forums, posters with visual reminders, exploring a protagonist's behavior in fictional text, biography study in nonfiction genre, slide presentations, curriculum videos, and more.

Keep the rules short and to the point. Provide visuals to help students keep rules top of mind, and use language that is easy to understand and follow. Charts and diagrams help students understand rules and expectations. Make sure that these expectations are consistently implemented and enforced. As per age and skill set, allow student voice to create the class rules to increase buy-in and application. Praise and reward based on target behavior with positive reinforcement. This includes verbal praise, stickers, and other small incentives, such as smiles and class celebrations, along with redirection and offering replacement behaviors. Technology (ADMIRE model 44) can support learning and engagement, such as interactive whiteboards with positive messages, age-appropriate emojis, game-based educational apps with incentives given, or ClassDojo (www.classdojo.com)—a website that assigns avatars who provide feedback on behavior to educators, students, and families

Reinforcement is as diverse as our students, with positive feedback having multiple definitions and opportunities for individualization. Some learners prefer journaling, game-based connections, or relatable characters. The website Free Printable Behavior Charts (www.freeprintablebehaviorcharts.com) offers behavioral tools to explore for students from preK to secondary, such as gratitude journals, self-compassion charts, and incentive charts.

Routines and Expectations

The rules and routines of each inclusion classroom are unique and adapted to the individuals present, but an ideal inclusion environment consistently promotes and reinforces inclusivity and respect. It is a positive learning atmosphere that embraces the diversity of its student population. A supportive classroom environment is one where all students feel safe, valued, and comfortable to learn and grow alongside their peers (ADMIRE models 6, 24). The Student Realities section of this chapter (page 86) offers ways to respond to the behaviors of learners with a diversity of challenges, such as ADHD or visual, emotional, physical, learning, and developmental differences. The elementary, middle school, and high school scenarios use the ADMIRE strategy to assess, delineate, model, instruct, reflect, and appropriately engage students. Reinforcement of routines and expectations is imperative to ensure that the focus is on learning and never derailed by students who need more attention and are not shy about letting that be known through their words, actions, and behaviors. Appropriate student behaviors to reinforce include respect for themselves, others, and the classroom property.

The PBIS website (www.pbis.org) offers a proactive schoolwide approach to behavior management. The premise of PBIS is that students receive positive incentives when they understand, follow, and reinforce the rules and expectations. That means that inclusion professionals keep accurate data and are privy to who needs more or less support and when, where, and how those supports will be given, monitored, and faded so they are internalized by the student (ADMIRE models 22, 23, 30, 46–57). PBIS emphasizes positive reinforcement and teaches students how to increase positive behavior.

PBIS includes several tiers of support, with increasingly intensive interventions provided to students who need them. PBIS identifies the root causes, develops goals, creates an action plan, and has indicators to track progress. Data monitors the fidelity of implementation and tracks progress to determine what adjustments, if any, are needed. PBIS is typically implemented through a three-tiered system of support.

- **Tier 1 Universal Interventions (Primary Prevention):** The primary focus of Tier 1 is to establish the positive and proactive school and classroom environments to prevent challenging behaviors.
- **Tier 2 Targeted Interventions (Secondary Prevention):** The primary focus of Tier 2 is to provide additional targeted intervention and supports for students with more behavioral need.
- **Tier 3 Intensive Interventions (Tertiary Prevention):** The primary focus of Tier 3 is to assist students with significant, persistent, and more challenging behaviors.

Teachers reinforce student behaviors in inclusion using clear and positive behavior expectations, actions, and supports. Behavior involves the four Cs—(1) climate, (2) communication, (3) curriculum, and (4) culture—to be in place with evidence in order for a classroom to support and maintain positive relationships (Hannigan, Hannigan, Mattos, & Buffum, 2021). Positive supports might look like greetings at the door, music, rehearsal cards, self-monitoring sheets, positive affirmation chips, and avatars.

Individualized Support

Each student with an IEP has individualized adaptations of their specially designed instruction outlined. Some students need more support, and some need less, but the premise is that each student has unique strengths and challenges. Specially designed instruction is linked to the student's performance and allows students to engage with and understand academic material or behavioral procedures that often are not within their prior knowledge.

Some students require increased definition, modeling, and reinforcement to ensure they respect and follow classroom expectations, not just with words but with ongoing actions and behaviors. Specially designed instruction is accomplished when the professionals offer interventions such as PBIS and DI. That includes having alternative ways to present the content and assess learning products within a positive classroom culture (accommodations and modifications). An inclusion teacher may offer less or more complexity or time, as per student level. Inclusion principles such as discrete task analysis (ADMIRE model 47), which breaks the learning into manageable parts, are an integral part of the classroom management framework.

Accommodations and Modifications

According to Jean Piaget's theory of cognitive development (Fischer, 1964), adaptation occurs when a child or adult develops new schema or modifies existing ones to accommodate new information different from what they already know. Inclusion succeeds when educators adapt their teaching methods to meet the needs of diverse learners by providing accommodations and modifications to support students with and without

IEPs and special needs while fostering positive relationships and interactions among students of different backgrounds.

Accommodation and modifications for students with disabilities or other special needs may include the following.

- Scheduling extra time to complete assignments
- Giving a student preferential seating
- Creating opportunities for students to work together
- Providing visual and written instructions to accompany verbal ones
- Allowing the use of technology, such as screen readers or speech-text
- Simplifying the reading level of a text

It is vital to note the difference between an accommodation and modification. Although both support learning in an inclusion classroom, accommodations offer access to the same content, while modifications alter the learning goals. For example, a student does not have the stamina to complete a mathematics assignment or exam in one sitting and needs that time broken up into morning and afternoon sessions; because the requirements remain the same, the student receives an accommodation. Now imagine a class multiplies two-digit multipliers by three-digit multiplicands while one student multiplies single-digit numbers; because the student works at a different level of complexity, they receive a modification.

Discrete Task Analysis

Discrete task analysis is a process that breaks down complex activities into smaller, discrete steps (Szidon & Franzone, 2009). These steps can be very helpful in creating a structured and systematic way to teach new skills. When planning or implementing discrete task analysis, it is important to consider inclusivity to ensure that everyone can participate and benefit from the task. Teachers achieve this by modifying the task or environment so that students with different abilities and interests can participate (Autism Speaks, n.d.). Discrete task analysis creates a positive learning environment that promotes the success and participation of students with different abilities and interests. It also highlights the importance of adapting tasks to meet the needs of individual learners as it leads toward mastery, one step at a time.

Two prominent educators and researchers, John Dewey and Jerome Bruner, emphasized hands-on learning and the benefits of discovery. Dewey (1916, 1938) believed that students learn best through experiences that are meaningful and relevant to them, while Bruner (1961) advocated for a constructivist approach to education, in which students actively build their own understanding of the world through interaction with it. *The Cambridge Handbook of the Learning Sciences* (Sawyer, 2006) illustrates crucial insights for teaching and learning. These include the importance of scaffolding, metacognition, cognitive apprenticeship, and learning in action.

Discrete task analysis occurs with concrete experiences set up by the inclusion educators. *Experiential learning*, as advocated by the research (Dewey, 1938; Kolb, 1984), is a process by which individuals acquire knowledge and develop skills through direct involvement in a particular activity or situation. Dewey (1938) argues that learning through experience is longer-lasting than knowledge gained through abstract concepts.

As an example, the learning is understood and retained though authentic experiences, such as project-based learning, field trips, service learning, and simulations. A physics class learns about energy and motion by building a model of a roller coaster, students learn about dinosaurs through a field trip to a museum, students take sensory walks to learn about plants, or students set up a school store to gain skills with money and how to interact with others.

David A. Kolb's (1984) experiential learning theory is another influential framework in this area. According to Kolb, learning involves a cycle of four stages: concrete experience, reflective observation, abstract conceptualization, and active experimentation.

Overall, experiential learning has been shown to be an effective approach to learning and development in various contexts. It offers a more engaging and interactive way of learning that can lead to meaningful and lasting outcomes. Let's put the concept of discrete task analysis, one of the inclusion principles, into practice with an activity.

I want you to make an origami pinwheel.

Ready, set, go!

Notice what's happening in your body as you read these words. If you are an *origami aficionado*, you're probably excited, and you know exactly how to complete this task. If you've never done origami in your life, you might feel anxious or confused or irritated. You have no idea how to begin.

Don't worry, I'm going to help you. Scan the QR code on this page to access detailed information about how to complete this task. There you'll find the materials you need, instructions for completing the activity, and even videos illustrating the step-by-step process.

After viewing these materials, check in with your body again. Are you feeling more relaxed and confident?

This is how students often feel in the inclusion classroom. Imagine they're told to diagram a sentence, apply the formula for the slope of a line, analyze a poem's meaning, or distinguish an ionic from a covalent bond. Some students will feel confident in managing these tasks, while others will be at a complete loss. In order to make the learning accessible for all students, teachers draw on scaffolding, modeling, and collaborative learning.

ADMIRE Inclusion Principles

Let's take a look at inclusion principles with rationale and application. Supportive classroom management values these inclusion principles. These are a *must-do anytime and anywhere*. Inclusion principles, as denoted in table 4.1 and detailed in the next sections, are ones to ADMIRE. The expectation is that *all* learners can achieve academic success with these inclusion principles.

Table 4.1: *Inclusion Principles*

1.	Establish prior knowledge of each student's *zone of proximal development* (ZPD).
2.	*Plan for outcomes* (UbD) and *structure* the classroom environment accordingly.
3.	Subdivide concepts into their steps and tasks, valuing *discrete task analysis*.
4.	Offer *practice for social skills*.
5.	Show *concrete, representational, abstract*, and *virtual* examples.
6.	Provide *academic accommodations* and *modifications* that help, but do not enable.
7.	Infuse *VAKT* sensory elements.
8.	Tap into strengths of students and staff by communicating a *growth mindset*: "I can't *yet!*"
9.	Concentrate on students, not their label; *have high expectations*; acknowledge the challenges but focus on the solutions.
10.	Increase student *self-efficacy* and *self-regulation*.
11.	Offer positives before negatives to learners with *affirmation* and *validation*.
12.	Model and demonstrate desired outcomes for students, such as work samples, video clips, *social narratives, adaptations, visual cues*, and *rubrics*.
13.	Vary instruction and assessments, and let the *data guide your next steps*.
14.	Relate to students' lives, such as *culture, ethnicity, gender, abilities*, and *families*.
15.	Teach basics and three Rs (reading, writing, and arithmetic) across curricula with evidence-based *UDL practices*.
16.	Set up a *pleasant, fun atmosphere* with active learning opportunities and connections.
17.	Increase student and staff self-awareness and reflection to advance *social skills* with data collection for *PBIS*.
18.	*Communicate and collaborate* with colleagues, students, families, and related service providers.

Source: © 2015 by Corwin Press. *Adapted from* Inclusion Strategies That Work! Research-Based Methods for the Classroom *(3rd ed.) by Toby J. Karten. Used with permission.*

Consider the following ways to ADMIRE the inclusion principles.

A **A**ssess and **a**ctivate prior knowledge. (Principle 1)
Rationale: Inappropriately leveled work frustrates students. Lessons connect to each learner's independent and instructional levels.

D **D**ecide and **d**elineate how to structure your lessons and environments. (Principle 2)
Rationale: We honor each learner's specially designed instruction when the appropriate classroom management is present.

M **M**odel and **m**onitor accommodations that help, but do not enable your learners. (Principle 6)
Rationale: We want our learners to increase their levels of independence.

I **I**nstruct and **i**nvolve VAKT elements to honor preferred learner modalities. (Principle 7)
Rationale: Each student processes information differently.

R **R**eflect and **r**evise how the learning is applied to student lives and interests. (Principle 14)
Rationale: Student connections increase attention, retention, and mastery.

E **E**ngage and **e**nrich collaborative practices with students, their families, and colleagues. (Principle 18)
Rationale: Together we learn and together we grow, with the inclusion classroom as a microcosm of our society.

Student Realities

Now that we've explored some of the key elements that support classroom management, let's look at a few examples of how these elements might play out in diverse contexts. The examples in the following sections explore student realities, staff communications, and strategies to ADMIRE for elementary, middle school, and high school classes for physical education, science, and U.S. history students who receive their education in an inclusion classroom. Difference exists, but the goal is to ensure that the inclusion principles are applied with fidelity to students of varying levels within the general education classroom.

Physical Education Class

A physical education class includes students who exhibit a variety of cognitive, perceptual, neurological, physical, communicative, social, emotional, behavioral, and sensory levels. The teacher has worked with students with specific learning differences but is unsure of the appropriate adaptations for students with significant emotional and behavior differences. This class includes students with classifications such as intellectual disability, ADHD, emotional disturbance, autism, specific learning disability, traumatic brain injury, visual impairment, blindness, hearing impairment, deafness, and orthopedic disabilities, as well as students who may have multiple disabilities. Specific accommodations are offered for a physical education and health lesson for students with and without academic, social-emotional, behavioral, physical, and language differences.

Staff Communications

Physical education teacher: "After getting to know this year's students, I understand why physical education teachers need knowledge of adapted physical education. We also need to know ahead of time what the students' IEPs state. The adaptations for the students with atypical motor behavior, differing intellectual levels, and varying physical needs are easy to make, compared to the adaptations I have to consider for the students with social and emotional differences. One student seems to set the next one off, and the rest of the class then collapses like dominoes. One student's instructional assistant is helpful; the other assistant needs reminders of where to stand, who to help, and how. My main concern is for the students' safety."

Strategies to ADMIRE

Assess the educational and functional IEP goals for the students that will be most useful for them to master, such as social reciprocity, pragmatic language, and presenting a range of motion and flexibility. **A**ssess safety risks to students for themselves or others and then respond with appropriate expectations with supports that include, but are not limited to, signals, posted rules, visuals, and gestural prompts for individual and class procedures to foster a classroom community. **A**ctivate student strengths (see table I.1, page 4), beyond the classification or label, to motivate and connect to learners' interests. For example, if a student likes digital animations, offer instruction that way, or if students excel in that area, offer them opportunities to create their own animations in health assignments to attach to the technology.

Decide on appropriate yet modified evidence of performance, breaking skills into substeps; allow partial participation to achieve successes from baseline levels with reinforcement for partial mastery. **D**ecide how to offer learners more challenges to raise their baseline levels through multitiered instruction. Schedule a paraeducator or instructional assistant during the physical education class to help the students and teacher. **D**elineate the specific roles for students as peer mentors and the specific goals in shared lesson plans that instructional assistants use to safely engage students in practice tasks and game-based activities to promote functional, physical, social-emotional, and behavioral goals.

Model non-negotiable respect for differences with appropriate student behavior and critical thinking skills for the students with and without IEPs. **M**onitor the knowledge and training that the instructional assistants and peer mentors require to successfully include students. **M**onitor the behavior of students with autism during game-based learning activities and teach them to increase their self-regulation with informal graphing, tallying of positive interactions, and social stories (see table I.1, page 4).

Instruct with functional communication training and a picture board for students who are nonverbal. **I**nvolve related staff—occupational therapist, physical therapist, speech-language pathologist, and mobility and orientation services. **I**nstruct with differentiated approaches to value the varying student levels.

Reflect on ways to use assistive technology and how to include students without creating overdependence on the instructional assistant; be certain to clarify shared roles and responsibilities. **R**evise lessons to include whole-class support and time for mixed-ability grouping along with one-to-one instruction. For instance, while the class is engaged in typical warm-up activities for a basketball game, some combination of general education teacher, instructional assistant, and trained peer mentor assists students with therapeutic or leisure goals such as keeping their heads raised and rolling a ball up and down a ramp to a peer to follow voice command if vision is limited.

Engage students in repeated practice to reinforce educational, therapeutic, and leisure goals; improve muscle tone; and hold head upright. **E**nrich with peer supports—peers with and without disabilities converse with appropriate social interactions during cooperative assignments and help students in modified activities such as wheelchair basketball. **E**ngage all students in fun activities that offer both enrichment and repetition based on individual physical education levels, targeted practice, and the specially designed instruction in their IEPs.

Science Class

A middle school class of twenty-five students has seven students with IEPs. Three of these students have a specific learning disability, two of the students have autism, and two students have a classification of other health impairment with behaviors that include inattention, hyperactivity, and impulsivity. There are also several students in the class who perform tasks above grade-level expectations. This is a co-taught science class with a general education teacher and special education teacher who are working together for the first time.

Staff Communications

General education teacher: "I am responsible for getting the students to master the science curriculum, but the class is so diverse. I am afraid that if we turn around for a second, the students will spill the chemicals or set their hair on fire with the burners. I remind them to keep their goggles on during lab time and to tie their hair back, but some of the students are so impulsive. I never worked with this in-class support teacher before, but she seems to know the students. I like the autism resource sheet she handed me. Seems the more I learn, the more I want to know—because each student with autism is so unique!"

Strategies to ADMIRE

Assess student knowledge of the density properties, melting point, boiling point, solubility, flammability, and odor with 3-D models and videos of the science steps and vocabulary in labs. **A**ctivate prior knowledge on the law of conservation of matter with functional connections, such as how a recipe's ingredients or water's form changes, but that the molecules are never destroyed. When teaching the law of conservation of matter to a student with intellectual disability, it's important to use the appropriate language and visual aids to help them understand the concept (see table I.1, page 4). Start by introducing the concept of matter, explaining how everything around us is made up of matter, and emphasizing that this matter can change form but cannot be created or destroyed. You could use examples such as water evaporating or ice melting, but emphasize that the total amount of matter in the system remains the same even though the form has changed.

Activate emotionally safe environments with positive emotions, realistic risks, and mood management to deal with stress, using, for example, mental rehearsal, visualization of success, yoga, verbalization, and *I can and will* statements (inclusion principle 11). Encouragement and positive reinforcement can also go a long way in building confidence and promoting understanding.

Activate each co-teacher's strengths with parity of roles for planning, instruction, and assessments (inclusion principle 18). Share responsibilities for behavior management and progress monitoring.

Decide how students will determine if a chemical reaction has occurred. **D**elineate specific reactions with concrete examples—for example, mixing zinc with hydrogen chloride, burning sugar or steel wool. **D**elineate and share co-teaching responsibilities by offering students lessons in parallel groups, with the general education teacher instructing one group of students and the special education teacher instructing the other group to lower the teacher-to-student ratio to increase student attention—for instance, one group analyzes and interprets data on the properties of substances before a chemical reaction, and the other group analyzes data on the properties of substances after a chemical reaction. Always think of cross-disciplinary connections to mathematics, technology, literacy, history, and art.

Model chemical reactions between candle wax and oxygen in the air, as accessed at the American Chemical Society's lesson plans (visit www.acs.org/middleschoolchemistry/lessonplans/chapter6/lesson1.html).

Monitor students to be sure they are consistently following lab safety rules. **M**onitor student understanding about how some chemical reactions release energy and some store energy. **M**odel with drawings and digital forms that include atoms; emphasize core ideas and crosscutting concepts to delineate that the total number of each type of atom is conserved, while the mass does not change. Visual aids like pictures, diagrams, or hands-on activities can also be helpful in making the concept more concrete and accessible.

Instruct with atom model cutouts to depict reactants and products. **I**nvolve appropriate online tools; visit Chem4Kids (www.chem4kids.com), American Chemical Society (www.acs.org), and PhET (https://phet.colorado.edu) for ideas. **I**nvolve learners in exploring similarities and differences in findings to learn how matter is conserved in physical and chemical processes. It's important to be patient and flexible in your teaching approach, understanding that different students may learn at different paces and in different ways.

Reflect on how the students will carry out experiments—for instance, will they follow multiple-step procedures and perform technical tasks? Offer kinesthetic releases to decrease impulsivity by working at classroom stations instead of sitting for a full period at desks with excessive note-taking, such as scavenger hunts and people searches. **R**evise designs to highlight the criteria for amount, time, and temperature of the substance.

Engage students in research projects to answer questions that allow for multiple predictions, observations, and reflections. **E**nrich higher-level learners with the exploration of the symbols used in chemical equations using Quizlet flashcards (https://quizlet.com/19234073/chemical-symbols-flash-cards) and games like Blooket (www.blooket.com) and Kahoot! (https://kahoot.com).

U.S. History Class

This U.S. History II high school class of twenty-six students has twelve students with IEPs. Many of these students, although classified with a specific learning disability, also have attention and behavioral issues. Only eight of the students have an in-class support teacher listed as a service in their IEP. One student has a visual impairment and is considered legally blind. There are two teachers co-teaching, but the push-in special education support teacher is not there for the full history period each day, since she also supports students in a science class during this scheduling block. The class is learning about World War II. The general education teacher knows his subject area well and is concerned that the time taken to teach reading and writing will subtract from needed time to expand student knowledge in the history.

Staff Communications

General education teacher: "There is only so much time in the day to teach what I have to teach in social studies, let alone now teaching English as well. The administration pats me on the back for my organization and then places more kids with IEPs in my class. I like the support that I get from the special education teacher, but it is just not enough. Sometimes, I think that I have to be as entertaining as one of the latest apps, music videos, or video games to hold student attention. How can I get them to read and write about World War II, when half of them do not even care enough about themselves or what is happening today?"

Strategies to ADMIRE

Activate class and student routines that value, first, the study of history and, second, the reading and writing involved. **A**ssess students' prior knowledge about WWII and research skills with primary and secondary documents and oral questions, know–want to know–learned (KWL) charts, and informal quizzes. **A**ssess which tools will help differentiate the content, yet not sacrifice the underlying history concepts, such as Rewordify (https://rewordify.com) to define more difficult vocabulary. Offer cloze notes, Text Compactor (www.textcompactor.com) to summarize and simplify more difficult passages, and Immersive Reader (access this book's webpage via **go.SolutionTree.com /specialneeds** for a link to a comprehensive guide) to break words into their syllables, add images, and read the text aloud to the student with visual impairment.

Delineate the formative assessments that are given during the unit. **D**ecide on the evidence required and provide a rubric (ADMIRE model 27) on how to analyze primary sources.

Monitor student behavior and attention with ClassDojo (www.classdojo.com). **M**odel how to avoid plagiarism by citing sources, and offer examples and nonexamples (ADMIRE model 25) with text and online applications. Provide online tools to use for research, from Fact Monster (www.factmonster.com) to Google Scholar.

Involve problem-based learning (ADMIRE model 40) to explore how the political, social, and economic conditions in Europe, Asia, and the world affected the thinking about the war: Should the United States have entered the war on Germany earlier? How did economic conditions in Germany lead to Adolf Hitler's power? Was the United States justified in its decision to drop the atomic bomb? Explore historical novels and events such as *Anne Frank: The Diary of a Young Girl* (Frank, 1952), Bataan Death March, D-Day, *I Never Saw Another Butterfly* (Volavková, 1993), and *Sadako and the Thousand Paper Cranes* (Coerr, 1999). Relate this learning to present-day conditions in the world and ask the students to create a portfolio (ADMIRE model 30) with their responses to document-based questions of primary documents from this conflict. Schedule group time when the special education support teacher is present, with each co-teacher instructing parallel lessons or working with smaller groups or individual students. Circulate to reinforce positive behaviors with closer proximity and to offer positive feedback or redirection to clarify understandings. **I**nstruct with a variety of resources and approaches, such as VAKT, DI, CL, Socratic discussion, kinesthetic debates, mnemonics, study guides, World War II propaganda posters, editorials, ration books, video clips, digital flashcards, transitional word lists, and writing frames (ADMIRE models 38, 41, 42).

Reflect on instructional models and the steps to achieve mastery. Provide audio materials to the student who is legally blind through resources such as Bookshare (www.bookshare.org) and Learning Ally (www.learningally.org). **R**evise processes based on observations and embedded assessments that are shared with the students to increase self-regulation (ADMIRE model 17).

Engage appropriate collaborative approaches with a range of co-teaching models that maximize the time that the special education teacher is in the room to divide and conquer with the parallel lessons—for instance, one teacher offers a lesson about domain-specific vocabulary while another group creates a World War II timeline or analyzes quotations and facts from primary and secondary sources. Be certain to plan and share lessons together. **E**nrich the reading and writing skills required by writing articles for a class or grade-level history newspaper.

ADMIRE Inclusion Principles, Revisited

As seen with the student and class scenarios, we as professionals ensure that our actions connect to the subject matter, the classroom environment, and, most important, the prior successes, student levels, language needs, and culture (see table I.1, page 4). The eighteen inclusion principles (table 4.1, page 85) are nonnegotiable, but in the midst of an instructional moment, they are sometimes forgotten. Table 4.2 provides connections to the eighteen principles, a reminder to us as professionals to apply evidence-based practice. Not every principle is pertinent in each lesson on each given day, but they are all valuable and applicable things to do in classrooms to advance knowledge and skill sets. As you and your colleagues plan and reflect on units of study, discuss and highlight which inclusion principles are implemented. For a blank version of this chart, see the "Admiring Supportive Classroom Management Practices" reproducible at the end of this chapter (page 94).

Table 4.2: ADMIRE Inclusion Principles

ADMIRE Inclusion Principles	
A **Assess and Activate**	Prior knowledge ZPD (zone of proximal development) Discrete task analysis Working memories
D **Decide and Delineate**	High expectations Organization Time frames Desired outcomes
M **Model and Monitor**	Student strength UDL Growth mindset
I **Instruct and Involve**	Self-efficacy DI PBIS UbD VAKT Affirmations Validations

R **Reflect and Revise**	Data-driven academic, social-emotional, physical, and behavioral accommodations and modifications
E **Engage and Enrich**	Communication Collaboration Concrete, abstract, virtual connections Positives before negatives Pleasant class environment

Conclusion

Successful inclusion requires patience, flexibility, and a commitment to meeting the diverse needs of all students. Inclusion professionals must continually assess and activate their classroom management strategies to ensure that they are effectively supporting the learning and well-being of every student. That includes offering role models and encouraging peer acceptance. Seeking professional development for additional teaching strategies and classroom management intervention is ongoing. Remember to approach classroom management with the goal of encouraging positive behavior and providing support. Take a moment to reflect on the information and strategies you've read by completing the "Admiring Supportive Classroom Management Practices" reproducible at the end of this chapter (page 94).

Admiring Supportive Classroom Management Practices

Use the following template to ADMIRE the actions to practice supportive classroom management. In the space provided, note which of the ADMIRE action items stood out to you from this chapter.

A Assess and Activate	
D Decide and Delineate	
M Model and Monitor	
I Instruct and Involve	
R Reflect and Revise	
E Engage and Enrich	

CHAPTER 5

Inclusion Challenges Generate Solutions

When I attended my first yoga class, I looked at the limber attendees, who performed the poses with ease, as I experienced challenge with balance, stance, form, and endurance. It was a challenge for me at first, but with encouragement, instruction, practice, strategy (finding a focal point), and feedback, several weeks later, I improved. A few months after that, with more practice, the gains were even higher. If I abandoned or was expelled from this yoga class, then my challenges would have remained. If my program of study lacked the interventions I required, such as step-by-step direction, guidance from an instructor who circulated and monitored student progress, and peer modeling, then I'd master *yoga stagnation*.

Inclusion obstacles are a given, often presented at the onset. Barriers teachers, students, and families face in creating an inclusive learning environment need to be spun into solutions that accommodate students with diverse needs and abilities toward successful outcomes, rather than ones that impede advancement. As with practicing yoga or any other new activity, improvements occur with observation, instruction, and reflective practices over time. Obstacles cannot overshadow and impede better results. Enough stated, positive actions address the challenges and generate solutions. Namaste.

In this chapter, we discuss that while we may feel frustrated by challenges, they present opportunities for innovations, inventions, and solutions. One of the consistent challenges teachers face in the inclusion classroom is adjusting instruction for complexity and delivery to meet students' diverse needs. Teachers successfully meet and overcome roadblocks when they practice proactive inclusion by anticipating and addressing potential challenges in advance, rather than living in a state of chronic reactivity. Ultimately, approaching challenges in the inclusion classroom begins with educators' attitudes and beliefs about diversity, so this chapter includes a reminder to approach challenges with acceptance and a willingness to provide adaptations. The chapter ends with a look at collaborative, high-tech, individualized, low-tech, and data-driven approaches teachers can draw on for solutions.

Innovations, Inventions, and Solutions

Challenges often lead to innovations, inventions, and solutions. As an example, John Holter, a neurosurgeon who practiced in the mid-20th century, invented the Holter valve, which is a type of shunt used in the treatment of hydrocephalus, since his own son had this condition (Baru, Bloom, Muraszko, & Koop, 2001). This personal experience is said to have motivated him to develop a valve that is used to remove the excessive accumulation of fluid on the brain that results from hydrocephalus, which can cause pressure and lead to neurological problems (Baru et al., 2001).

Often, teachers of students in inclusion classes, their families, and the students are faced with challenges that require solutions and different mindsets that result in inventions or new products driven by necessity, "the mother of invention" as Plato is often attributed to have said.

Challenges evidenced by varying levels of mobility, communication, and performance have led to the development of better technologies for students. These include, but are not limited to, stand-up wheelchairs or ones that are made of materials that offer easier navigation in a school hallway or on the beach, allowing students who are nonverbal to use iPads to communicate, word-prediction programs to ease fine motor skills for a student who may have dysgraphia, and text read aloud to circumvent phonological challenges from impacting literacy requirements to understand mathematics, science, or history assignments.

The implementation of artificial intelligence (AI) in the classroom encompasses a broad definition with both benefits and challenges (Ferlazzo, 2023). AI allows some students to more candidly *speak to* a thought-generated avatar about anxiety and social-emotional needs, rather than expressing emotions in a face-to-face session that may be viewed as more intimidating. Teachers and students can use an AI tool such as ChatGPT in a variety of ways as they respectively plan for and participate in the learning. With the appropriate prompts, ChatGPT can offer ideas to a teacher on how to incorporate movement into a third-grade lesson on friction or how to set up a high school class into stations to learn about the French Revolution. Magic School 3.0 (www.magicschool.ai) generates differentiated lessons and resources, with *mild*, *medium*, and *spicy* tags produced with the click of a mouse. AI tools offer feedback on pronunciation, help students to write essays, research topics, change the readability level of a text, speak aloud, create doodles, compose subject-related songs in the style of their favorite artist, and more.

As with all adaptations and assistive technology, AI requires careful consideration and monitoring for appropriate use and customization to match the goals and objectives in a student's IEP. Educators need to make effective use of the AI tools to adapt to student strengths, not just their deficits (Office of Educational Technology, 2023). Professionals and students need to be certain that AI offers accuracy, not misinformation or bias. Figure 5.1 includes a song written by an AI tool, rhyme.cool (2023). It demonstrates how AI's innovation can be individualized with human interaction and how it encourages individualization, creativity, voice and choice, and cognitive thought.

> **Prompt given to rhyme.cool:** Write a song about inclusion in the style of Billy Joel that uses the words *accommodate, strengths, content, process, engagement, collaboration, awareness, reflection,* and *compassion*.
>
> **Product:**
> [CHORUS]
> Inclusion makes us all stronger
> It's a process we can't ignore
> It helps us understand each other
> And reach for a common goal
>
> [VERSE 1]
> We need to accommodate strengths of all types
> And foster contentment and joy
> By engaging in collaboration
> We will find a way to employ
>
> [VERSE 2]
> Awareness and reflection are key in finding a path
> That's right—compassion is the cornerstone
> It sets our course alight
>
> [VERSE 3]
> Inclusion is a process that's wise
> It's something that we all need
> When we come together in unity
> It gives us something to heed.

Source: *rhyme.cool*, 2023.
Figure 5.1: *An AI-generated song.*

Inclusion requires preparation for known challenges and the need for specialized instruction and support for students with differences. The curriculum and assessment methods used in classrooms may not be accessible or appropriate for students with diverse needs and abilities, leading to exclusion and underachievement (George, 2005). Teachers and school staff require training in inclusion practices, including how to adapt the instructional materials and strategies to meet the needs of all students (Friend, 2020). The necessary resources and support allow the professionals to provide accommodations and modifications for students with disabilities and other special needs.

Another challenge is the need for physical accommodations to ensure equal access for students with disabilities, which may include modifications to facilities, such as ramps and accessible restrooms, as well as assistive technology and equipment (IDEA, 2004). As an example, a building may be compliant with one exit or an accessible bathroom stall, but it might not be the one in a location that benefits a student when they enter, exit, and travel through the building. Even if the media center, mathematics classroom, or science lab is equipped with excellent resources, we need to ensure someone of short stature or someone who has limited vision or mobility also has access.

Teachers and students may have negative attitudes and biases toward students with disabilities or other differences, leading to social isolation and discrimination

(Wearmouth, 2023). Teachers may lack the training and support needed to effectively teach students with diverse needs and abilities, such as training in differentiated instruction or positive behavior support (McGregor & Vogelsberg, 1998). Parents and community members may not be involved in the inclusion process, leading to a lack of support and understanding for students with diverse needs and abilities (Lindsay, 2007).

Inclusion requires a shift in attitudes and beliefs about disability, as well as a commitment to creating a welcoming and inclusive school culture. This can be achieved through professional development for teachers and staff, as well as programs that promote positive attitudes and relationships among students (Giangreco, Shogren, & Dymond, 2020). Teachers can support these efforts by providing resources and accommodations, such as assistive technology and peer support networks, to help all students participate and connect with each other (Galla et al., 2014).

Successful inclusion implementation is contingent upon several factors, such as attitudes, beliefs, biases, acceptances, knowledge, resources, supports, and training. Barriers, whether related to the students, educators, curriculum, assessment, or community, must be removed. Knowledge and collaboration allow teachers to implement evidence-based practices and address the challenges. This includes increased awareness for educational professionals, families, peers, and students. That may translate to a schoolwide program on diversity and exceptionality, along with professional training on specific multisensory approaches to teach reading, mathematics, science, and history, or parents speaking to their son's general education class to help peers understand that his physical impairment of spinal muscular atrophy does not affect his ability to learn or to be a friend.

Awareness is ongoing; whether the student has a label or diagnosis of autism, selective mutism, dyscalculia, or Turner syndrome, they are foremost children who want to be just like their peers—maybe sometimes better, but never less or different.

Inclusion teachers, both special and general educators, can promote positive behaviors with inclusion classroom management. Teachers also need to generate relationships with students to know them better to assist them to attend to, remember, and apply the knowledge and skills. This may require weekly emotional check-ins, training in positive behavior supports, and coordination with an applied behavior analyst or interventionist to learn how to better collect and evaluate the data to then guide the next steps with discrete task analysis for both academics and behavior.

Often, *we didn't know we needed to until we found out we had to*! Hence, the inclusion challenges generate solutions. Thank you to John Holter and other innovators who think outside the box to include learners with exceptionality to succeed (Baru et al., 2001). Creative solutions dictate the outcomes, not the challenges.

Adjust Complexity and Delivery

One of the challenges educators may encounter is designing lessons that target the needs and abilities of all students in the inclusion classroom. This is especially true when some students are struggling to keep up with the pace of the curriculum while others are already excelling at the same pace. Another challenge educators may encounter is balancing the needs of the individual student with those of the larger group. Teachers may need to adjust their teaching styles based on the learning needs and abilities of individual students while still maintaining the larger classroom goals.

For students, one of the challenges may be adapting to the pace of the curriculum and the level of instruction. This is especially true when students have different learning styles, abilities, and behaviors. Students with disabilities may require additional support and accommodations to ensure their success in the classroom. Ongoing assessment and data collection inform classroom management for instructional decisions (Fox, 2000; Karten, 2021).

Overall, a diverse classroom can be a rewarding experience, but it can also be challenging for both the teachers and the students. It is important for educators to stay informed about best practices and strategies for working with students of different abilities and backgrounds. The goal is to adjust the complexity and delivery rather than dilute or delete concepts for any one student or group of learners. Let's look at an example of how an inclusion challenge generates a solution.

- **Challenge:** A student has limited attention and focus during reading and mathematics instruction.
- **Solution:** The student's learner profile lists horseback riding as an interest. As appropriate, the reading and mathematics instruction connects to the student's like of horses (for example, a series of word problems reference horses, measurements of a horse's anatomy, reading selections such as *Black Beauty* [Sewell, 2011], *The Midnight Ride of Paul Revere* [Longfellow, 2001], and more). Figure 5.2 (page 100) models how a perceived challenge is addressed with literacy and mathematics connections to a student's interest, specifically for this student—horses.

Discussion spins a challenge into a learning opportunity. A proactive approach honors the inclusion principles and cross-curricular connection (ADMIRE model 59, from table I.1, page 4). *Cross-curricular instruction* is a way for students to apply the skills they learn throughout their scheduled-subject day with connection to real-world experiences (Lickteig, 2023).

Cross-curricular connections help students in inclusion classes link concepts to multiple contexts and themselves. The subjects are interconnected, rather than locked inside a specific room or time of the day and unavailable for use until the students transition back to that subject or classroom. That applies to phonemic instruction, English, mathematics, Spanish, Mandarin, chemistry, world history, art, music, technology, and more. This permits the learning to be reinforced, often by multiple teachers who add their subject-specific knowledge, voice, and perspective. Cross-curricular learning develops critical thinking skills and deeper understanding in more than one context with diverse peers (Kerry, 2015; van Gog & Sweller, 2015).

In an elementary context, this could look like second graders learning about circles in geometry reading *Sir Cumference and the First Round Table* by Cindy Neuschwander (1997).

Interdisciplinary Thematic Planner
Topic or concept: Collaborative unit on animals to gain academic skills or character traits (for example, perspective, empathy).
Academic goal: To provide written and verbal expression of the main idea and supporting text details and to access credible online sources across the curricula; to compare and contrast genres, syntactic structure.
Functional goal: To connect to student interest and community. For example, the student likes to ride horses; therefore, *Black Beauty* and *The Midnight Ride of Paul Revere* were selected for this unit.
Baseline knowledge: CORE Knowledge   All students answer *wh-* questions about the book and poem and write a three- to five-sentence paragraph for each genre.
More advanced: Conduct research on one of these people or topics: Anna Sewell, Henry Wadsworth Longfellow, American Revolution, horses, freedom; identify the parts of speech.
Knowing beyond: Write poems and short stories that mirror either Longfellow or Sewell's style.
Reading or writing objective: Compare and contrast fiction and nonfiction; investigate why Anna Sewell chose to write the story from a horse's perspective; write author or poet bio for either Sewell or Longfellow or a bio for Paul Revere.
Mathematics objective: Calculate the distance Paul Revere traveled; solve word problems connected to horses; research and graph the total number of *Black Beauty* novels printed; use a scale of miles to measure.
Science or STEAM (science, technology, engineering, the arts, and mathematics) objective: Anatomy of a horse; compare and contrast technology during the colonial period to today's options.
Social studies objective: Investigate life during colonial times; identify cities, states, and countries referenced in text on maps; compare and contrast freedom in the United States to another country's steps toward freedom.
Perceptual, visual arts, musical, or physical education objectives: Sketching a horse; researching songs with *horse* in the title; playing charades with academic vocabulary; creating a step-by-step visual or infographic on how to care for a horse; online resources.
Study skills objective: Increase self-regulation; use different curriculum graphic organizers to collect or review notes; ask for help to clarify understandings; use feedback to adjust initial response (for example, increase responses to full sentences).
Other objectives: Compare and contrast the Disney version of *Black Beauty* to the book; study symbolism in passages, poems, books, and songs; attend to the center of instruction; offer on-topic responses in one-to-one and small groups.
Accommodations or modifications: The student requires at minimum one 1- to 3-minute break (for example, virtual calming, movement, music, specific written and verbal feedback); increase visuals; keep data on progress to then increase or fade support.

Source: Adapted from Karten, 2021.

Figure 5.2: Sample cross-curricular student connection.

They engage in circle games, and the students talk about "circles of relationships" in physical education and health class. A unit on ecosystems includes a musical connection with Elton John's song "Circle of Life" (Rosenthal, 2001).

On a secondary level, when a high school English class reads the Charles Dickens (2012) classic *A Tale of Two Cities*, the chemistry class explores Lavoisier's discovery of the role of oxygen in combustion, with world history class connections to industrialization and imperialism, while in art the students explore neoclassicism. Subject connections are appropriate, never mandatory. The bottom line is that if the students are reading *The Lion, the Witch, and the Wardrobe* by C. S. Lewis (1994), learning about and from the Narnian characters, they're also investigating World War II and the winter solstice. It may even lead them to create fictional magical kingdoms in their own writings. Therefore, subjects connect to each other and our learners through multiple contexts.

While some learners may prefer learning about characters who create video games, play baseball, or are excellent dancers or chefs, the takeaway is that instruction is connected to student interest and that it delineates effort and progress toward a baseline or core level of knowledge (ADMIRE model 13). A portfolio, a purposeful collection of a learner's work, is a tool students can use to provide evidence of their interests, efforts, progress, and areas of need to facilitate more informed decisions about accommodations and supports (ADMIRE model 30). Portfolios showcase students' work and progress to demonstrate understanding and skill. They assist students to become more self-aware and engaged learners, and they are useful tools for both instruction and assessment in language learning (Wang & He, 2020). Teachers review students' progress over time to determine what needs to be added, deleted, and tweaked and at what pace, based on evidence. Inclusion supports are faded as per progress monitoring and student data, the outcome criteria (ADMIRE models 46–55).

Proactive Inclusion

Proactive inclusion aims to create an inclusive environment by anticipating and addressing potential barriers to inclusion beforehand. This approach involves engaging diverse perspectives in ongoing dialogue to ensure that everyone feels valued and included. Inclusion can promote social identification, empathy, and learning from each other's identities (Roberge & Alokha, 2022). By proactively addressing potential barriers to inclusion, professionals can create a more equitable and welcoming environment for all individuals.

As an inclusion facilitator and coach, my role is to ensure that students receive their instruction from qualified general and special education teachers. The goal is to engage and enrich learners (ADMIRE models 56–65), but that cannot happen without discussion of how the inclusion classrooms are designed with *proactive* opportunities for advancement, practice, reinforcement, and repetition. That includes times to revisit concepts, along with ways to increase metacognition through real-life applications and specific feedback. Inclusion facilitation occurs with administrative input, class observation, discussion among general education and special education teachers, planned conferences, inclusion coaching notes, and both in-person and online meets with staff, students, and families.

Proactive inclusion plans for students with academic, executive, and behavior differences. As Sterling K. Brown shares, "Empathy begins with understanding life from another person's perspective. Nobody has an objective experience of reality. It's all through our own individual prisms" (as cited in Birnbaum & Ryan, 2016). Empathy and honest communication increase understandings that transform the challenges into viable and planned solutions.

Proactive inclusion also features classroom management that includes differentiated and collaborative strategies for instruction and assessment. That includes concrete, representational, abstract, and virtual engagement.

In this next scenario, the challenges present in a middle school mathematics class generate an inclusion plan. The setting is a suburban school district with highly involved parents and a teacher who chose teaching as his second career. His prior work experience was with private industry. He transitioned into teaching during a time when instruction, along with student teaching, happened online. The challenges include an inexperienced teacher who has excellent mathematics skills but lacks preservice training on how to adjust instructional pacing for students with academic and behavioral difference. There was a student in this seventh-grade class who loved attention, whether it was negative or positive. The principal received parent phone calls and emails complaining that the teacher couldn't control the class and that their children were not learning the content.

As that teacher, you might consider the following inclusion solutions.

- The teacher attends professional development with coaching sessions to assist with lesson adaptations. That includes discussion and application of positive behavior supports. The teacher also visits other middle school mathematics classes to gain insights on effective classroom management. Mathematics lessons are planned together with colleagues.
- The teacher consults with the school psychologist to develop a plan of action on how to offer positive incentives to the whole class, small groups, and individual students (for example, planned ignoring and positive reinforcement and feedback).
- The students select one to three of the eighteen descriptors in figure 5.3 as target areas of improvement to increase self-regulation. The ratings are Always (A), Becoming Better (B), Can With Reminders (C), and Doesn't Display Behavior (D). These are revisited during conference times each marking period and shared with families.
- The teacher sets up predetermined signals with individual students who seek attention or distraction, with eyes on self-regulation.
- The teacher, students, and families collaboratively acknowledge, promote, and support the steps taken toward mastery of mathematics skills.
- The teacher offers the appropriate instructional scaffolding that aligns with student learning modalities, attention, and stamina for the mathematics involved.

Student Documentation (duplicate as needed)				
ABCD* Quarterly Checklist of Functional Objectives *(denote codes for each marking period)* **Student:** _____	**A**	**B**	**C**	**D**
1. Establishes eye contact with teachers and peers				
2. Uses proper conversational tones				
3. Follows classroom and school rules				
4. Respects authority				
5. Exhibits social reciprocity				
6. Appropriately communicates needs				
7. Demonstrates consistent attention in classroom lessons				
8. Completes all classroom assignments				
9. Finishes all homework and long-range assignments				
10. Able to independently take class notes				
11. Writes legibly				
12. Has an organized work area				
13. Respects the property of others				
14. Works well with groups				
15. Adjusts to changes in routines				
16. Asks for clarification when needed				
17. Takes pride in achievements				
18. Displays enthusiasm about learning				
* Use these codes (+ or − can be added) A = Always B = Becoming better C = Can with reminders D = Doesn't display behavior	Comments:			

Source: © *2007 by Corwin Press. From* More Inclusion Strategies That Work! Aligning Student Strengths With Standards *by Toby J. Karten. Used with permission.*

Figure 5.3: Student documentation tool.

- The teacher gives discrete task analysis with step-by-step instruction for learners who lack prior knowledge (for example, mathematics curriculum videos or tip sheets).
- Learners who require automaticity with fact fluency practice skills during cooperative groups and gamified learning (for example, Factor Football, online computational drills, Think-Tac-Toe).

- Exit cards are given at each lesson close to plan for whole-class, small-group, and individual mathematics instruction with time slated each week for remediation, enrichment, and practice.

- Adaptive tools, such as Immersive Reader (access this book's webpage via **go.SolutionTree.com/specialneeds** for a link to a comprehensive guide), and visuals are available for learners with reading differences who require less text, a word problem or directions read aloud, different complexity, and more explanation (www.mathsisfun.com/definitions).

- Critical thinking activities include WebQuests (www.bookwidgets.com/blog/2016/09/the-ultimate-webquest-creator), Sudoku (https://sudoku.com), Plexers (www.worksheetworks.com/puzzles/word-plexers.html), and Would You Rather? (www.wouldyourathermath.com/would-you-rather-74).

- Administration supports the teacher with regularly scheduled weekly planning times and inclusion coaching.

The curriculum and assessment methods used in classrooms may not be accessible or appropriate for students with diverse needs and abilities, leading to exclusion and underachievement. Proactive inclusion prepares for differences, noting that they make professionals think more deeply about how subject matter reaches diverse learners in the inclusion classroom. Inclusion has barriers, but they never overshadow the interventions. Teachers adjust their teaching styles based on the learning needs and abilities of individual students, while still maintaining the larger classroom goals.

Climate for Inclusion Acceptance

Attitudes and beliefs about inclusion and diversity play a significant role in the success of students with diverse learning needs. Additionally, both teachers and students may face challenges such as communication barriers, cultural differences, and a diversity of attitudes toward inclusion and the competencies of students and educational professionals. Proactive inclusion strategies require the imperative frontloading, as shown with the mega, macro, and micro planning in Plan With and for Learners (page 56 in chapter 3). Analogously speaking, pilots don't fly the plane without a flight plan and contingency protocols in place for turbulence and other unexpected events. Chefs prepare a gourmet meal with a recipe, gathering the ingredients and resources required that perhaps include a preheated oven, a stovetop, a mixer, measuring cups, and more as they follow each step. However, the sky is wide, filled with diverse planes and destinations, and there are a multitude of tastes and recipes. As with flight plans and cookbooks, inclusion challenges and solutions connect to individual people, cultures, likes, dislikes, complexities, and both physical and human resources and practices.

Negative attitudes toward disability disempower individuals with disabilities and lead to their social exclusion and isolation (Babik & Gardner, 2021). By contrast, positive attitudes in inclusion classrooms toward individuals with disabilities promote social inclusion. A welcoming inclusion classroom climate says that all individuals are respected, valued, and looked upon as integral contributors to the class and community.

The following are some key facts to ADMIRE to build an accepting inclusion climate.

- Respect the individual choices of students with and without difference.
- Offer confidence-building activities to build self-esteem.
- Embrace differences through movies and books with fiction and nonfiction genres.
- Promote a classroom environment for students to understand that accomplishments are achieved with perseverance and supports, both human and physical ones.
- Model appropriate inclusion etiquette in language, behaviors, and assignments.
- Incorporate opportunities for students to understand people with differences (for example, guest speakers who talk about their challenges and activities to confront misconceptions and dissolve biases).

Teachers, as inclusion facilitators, value how to teach students and adults to accept people at the level they are at, without comparison to others or preconceived limitations based on a label of exceptionality. The activities in the following sections offer experiential learning to embrace the value of one another. They promote the development of an emotionally safe learning environment (ADMIRE model 6) and, within that inclusion environment, the respect for differences (ADMIRE model 24). Consider the following three disABILITY activities teachers can use with students.

What Is "Normal"?

Introduce to the class the idea that "normal" is subjective. Students should realize that people have different backgrounds, abilities, interests, and experiences. Ultimately, professionals should encourage students to view diversity as a way to broaden their perspectives and promote acceptance and creativity within themselves and others. Teachers can use figure 5.4 to facilitate a discussion with students about differences.

---

1. *What is "normal"?* Invite the students to define "normal" and "different" food, clothes, songs, books, games, and so on.

---

1. Normal food _____   Different food _____
2. Normal clothes _____   Different clothes _____
3. Normal songs _____   Different songs _____
4. Normal books _____   Different books _____
5. Normal games _____   Different games _____

Normal student?
Things to think about:
Why does everyone have different answers?
Can the word *normal* really be defined?

Source: © 2008 by Corwin Press. Adapted from Inclusion Activities That Work! Grades 6–8 by Toby J. Karten. Adapted with permission.

Figure 5.4: "What is normal?" worksheet.

We All Have Value

Humans have a tendency to value people differently based on perception and purpose. The following activity uses money as an analogy, inviting students to see that, though their external traits may differ, all people are equally valuable. To complete the activity, gather the following resources.

- Three empty coffee cans with lids
- Fake or real money (1 one-dollar bill, 4 quarters, 100 pennies)
- Bag or box of uncooked rice
- Small paper lunch bag
- Empty opaque plastic juice container

Consider the various ways to complete this activity and discuss the takeaway with students (Karten, 2008a).

- The students shake three individual coffee cans filled with varying amounts of money (for example, 10 pennies, 1 quarter, and 1 one-dollar bill) to decide which one is worth more.

  Takeaway: Valuable things are not always easily identifiable. Often what we see and hear on the outside does not tell the whole story!

- These same three coffee cans are filled with equal monetary amounts, with different compositions (for example, one has 1 one-dollar bill, one has 4 quarters, and one has 100 pennies). Learners decide which can is worth more.

  Takeaway: The lesson is that sometimes we do not know what's on the inside by what we see or hear on the outside. The contents of each can is equal, but in different ways. People are equal in different ways too!

- Equal amounts of rice are placed in a coffee can, an opaque juice container, and a small paper bag. The students shake each one individually and are asked to identify their contents.

  Takeaway: Even though something may appear different on the outside, what's on the inside is the same. That holds true for each person who may look different on the outside, but all have identical worth.

- Whole-class instruction directs students to break up into small groups to collaboratively respond to this question: "What do you think is worth more, rice or money?"

  Takeaway: The concept of value is as diverse as trying to define the word *normal*. It is important to note that the rice is worth more to a person who is starving on a desert island. That person would have no use for the money. Each person has different needs, thoughts, and circumstances, but each person's thoughts, voice, and choice have value.

Perception Versus Reality

As educators, we need to understand certain things about how a student's brain works. Sometimes there is confusion between the left and right sides of the brain that could make simple activities seem difficult. For example, imagine a student is looking at a collection of shapes with accurate and inaccurate labels listed. The right part of the brain might recognize a shape or color, but the left side of the brain wants to read the name of the shape even if it's not the correct one.

To complete this activity with upper elementary and secondary students, draw a few shapes and write incorrect names inside, as illustrated in figure 5.5. Ask learners to tell you what they see. After the activity, facilitate a discussion with students about misperceptions and misinterpretations.

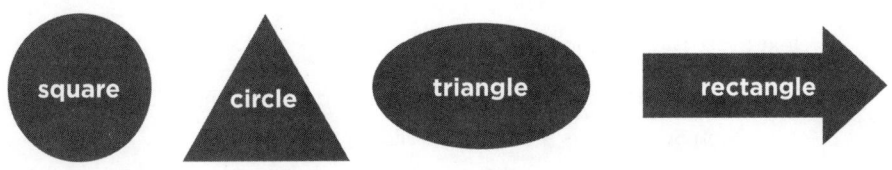

Figure 5.5: What do you see?

This activity reminds us that students see things differently. Therefore, perceptions interfere with the learning. These difficulties were created to experience that confusion, but some students and people encounter these kinds of difficulties every day of their lives. They do not perceive and understand things the same way as everyone else because their brains are wired differently.

Adaptations

Classroom cultures value adaptations and strategies. Challenges to inclusion in classrooms are related to the people, the ones who provide and receive services, and the things in place in the community, such as state or province and district interpretation of policies or providing a ramp at all exits for wheelchair accessibility. At a classroom level, this might include instructing with Unifix cubes to learn about place value with three-digit addends. Funding, adaptations, and the professional training are imperative, but at the core are the people, places, and things used for implementation. The following sections offer visual explanations to solidify abstract concepts for learners with diverse skill sets.

Visual Supports

Some students need to see and know things ahead of time, before they are immersed in the situation, so the elements of surprise and discomfort in *doing a new thing* are removed. Visual supports facilitate organization and comprehension, and can complement verbal or written instructions. As an example, a student with autism becomes less overwhelmed by a change in routine or schedule when a social story or narrative is prepared. To become familiar with expectations before they hear it in whole-class instruction, a student views narration with either realistic or representative visuals and photos that explain the new procedures. Such social stories assist learners who do not easily or positively respond to change by offering a chance to understand and prepare for the expectations without being overwhelmed.

Visuals are often the solution to circumvent inappropriate behaviors in front of peers. Figure 5.6 shows an example of a social story for a student with autism who is beginning high school.

Next Stop, High School!

In September, I will be a ninth-grade student at James Madison High School. It is a different building than eighth grade, but that's OK; I'm different, too.

I can ask my teachers and paraprofessional for breaks when I need it by saying **"I need a break."** These breaks last a few minutes and will be timed. My para will remind me to follow the rules and support me in my classes. I am excited to see the other students and my teachers! MOST IMPORTANT, I will adapt, even if there are changes, such as meeting a new friend or teacher.

If I feel anxious, confused, or worried, or experience other emotions, I will **ask for help** by saying **"I need _____."** I will try to be in the green zone most days.

I will talk about how I am feeling to my mom and dad, and my teachers, who support me. The goal for ninth grade is to learn and smile. YAY! I will soon be starting ninth grade. I can't wait to have a successful year!

Figure 5.6: Sample social story for visual support.

Visuals such as infographics, icons, graphic organizers, real-life photos, and more invite us to learn, without what some people perceive as labor-intensive reading. Visuals and curriculum-related pictures assist students who may have dyslexia and other reading differences, students with varying cognition and processing speeds, and students with and without what is labeled *exceptionality* to better process and remember concepts and unfamiliar vocabulary. Visuals assist ELs and students who may do things more impulsively, without following or taking the time to read directions or reread a sentence if they were not familiar with the vocabulary. Visuals help to concretize abstract concepts.

Figure 5.7 shows how a third-grade inclusion science teacher used visuals to engage the students with the academic vocabulary for a unit on weather.

Topic: Weather

#1: Summer ice storm

Thoughtful question: What is an ice storm?

Define the vocabulary words:

1. Hail: _____
   Check out this video: Mystery Science WW Lesson 1 Have you ever watched a storm (youtu.be/watch?v=Pkl6mf0AO9Y)
2. Ice storm: _____

#2: Clouds and water cycle

Explore clouds here: Earth Science for Kids: Weather - Clouds (https://www.ducksters.com/science/earth_science/clouds.php)

Thoughtful question: Where do clouds come from?

Learn more about the water cycle: The Water Cycle for Kids - How it Works - Diagram & Facts (www.sciencekids.co.nz/sciencefacts/weather/thewatercycle.html)

Define the vocabulary words:

1. Evaporation: _____
   See evaporation: evaporate | Vidtionary: A Video Dictionary (www.vidtionary.com/words/evaporate)
2. Clouds: _____

#3: Local weather patterns and weather prediction

Explore weather patterns here: storm | Vidtionary: A Video Dictionary (www.vidtionary.com/words/storm)

Thoughtful question: How can we predict when it is going to storm?

Define the vocabulary words:

1. Predict: _____
2. Observation: _____

Figure 5.7: *Sample visual tool for third-grade science students.*

Visuals often support students to better understand unfamiliar concepts. This may be especially helpful in providing step-by-step instructions.

Figure 5.8 (page 110) shows one example of how teachers can use visuals to supplement text instructions—in this case, step-by-step directions to solve mathematics word problems. While some students do not require pictures and can respond to text as it is,

Directions: Word Problem Strategies

1. Read the word problem once.

2. Now read the word problem again for more understanding.

3. Write down necessary information in the data box.

4. Write the question you need to answer in the question box.

5. Highlight the strategy box you have chosen.

6. Using a step-by-step approach, figure out the answer to the question.

7. Go back to the question box. Does your answer make sense?

Source: © 2015 by Corwin Press. From Inclusion Strategies That Work! Research-Based Methods for the Classroom *(3rd ed.) by Toby J. Karten. Used with permission.*

Figure 5.8: *Visuals for mathematics problem-solving strategies.*

the extra visuals may motivate another learner and offer the clarification that the words alone lack. If you think along the perspective of a student doing mathematics, which version of the strategies to solve the word problem is more inviting?

Additional resources to incorporate visuals across exceptionalities, ages, subjects, and grades include the following.

- Photos for Class (www.photosforclass.com)
- Visual Dictionary Online (www.visualdictionaryonline.com)
- Vidtionary (www.vidtionary.com)
- Pics4Learning (www.pics4learning.com)

Project-Based Learning

Project-based learning and *problem-based learning* are similarly denoted by the three initials PBL (ADMIRE model 40), but they have minor distinctions. *Problem-based learning* is an inquiry-based instructional approach that allows students to work together in small groups to solve ill-structured problems that have several solutions (Jonassen, 2003). *Project-based learning* is similar to problem-based learning but may include the creation of a product or performance through authentic tasks over a longer period of time (Larmer, 2015). Both have well-constructed driving questions that stimulate student thought and the desire to dig deeper into the facts to yield concrete solutions or products that are connected to real-world situations.

Both PBL approaches allow students to self-regulate their learning in a collaborative environment to critically think along self-directed and collaborative paths to solve open-ended problems. Students with advanced skills benefit from the challenges offered, while students with disabilities receive both affective and academic benefits as they support one another to increase motivation and self-confidence (Belland, Glazewski, & Ertmer, 2009).

Consider the following examples of leading or driving questions across the K–12 curriculum.

- What will happen if humans increase their burning of fossil fuels?
- How can we stay healthy?
- How can students safely use digital tools?
- How does the government affect my family's life?
- How is sound produced?
- What would the world be like if dogs could read, write, and speak?
- How does art or music help people?
- How can our class have an impact on the community?
- What steps can our school take to erase bullying?
- How does inclusion assist students, families, and professionals?

Both PBL approaches invite inquiry with applications across the curriculum that appeal to diverse learners. A diversity of engagements and representations then yields a diversity of critical thinking skills that benefit students who have learning differences, who are culturally diverse, who are gifted or twice-exceptional, and more. Let's answer the next driving question. How do we ADMIRE both forms of PBL?

Consider the following tips.

- **A**ssess needs and **a**ctivate prior knowledge with inquiry.
- **D**ecide on driving questions and **d**elineate organization for project-based learning groups.
- **M**odel project-based learning examples and **m**onitor interim steps.
- **I**nstruct with scaffolding in place and **i**nvolve technology options.
- **R**eflect on when to fade supports and **r**evise pacing.
- **E**ngage metacognition with multiple modalities, such as movement and visuals, and **e**nrich with cross-disciplinary connections.

Understanding by Design

The UbD framework (Wiggins & McTighe, 2005; see ADMIRE model 39, table I.1, page 4) is set up to increase student understandings through three stages. Staff begin the first stage by outlining the desired results with essential questions and the knowledge and skills to be acquired. The questions are to be investigated and explored from different points of view. They are not factual in nature with a right or wrong response but are intended to motivate and engage students to explore the facts. As an example, if a class is reading the novel *Wonder* by R. J. Palacio (2012), an essential question may be, How do school experiences influence self-esteem? In mathematics, an essential question may be, Why do we need to divide?

In the second stage, students think about the evidence for the desired results or products or performances and apply the learning to different contexts—the actual works to be assessed. In the *Wonder* example, the students then go back to the book and offer text-based evidence about Auggie's interactions with other characters to support their responses. For the mathematics example, students generate real-world examples that encourage them to use division to "live the math" in a kitchen, store, restaurant, sports arena, and so on.

Stage three is the learning plan with the activities, experiences, and actual lessons. This stage needs to be responsive to learner differences with consideration to readiness, interests, and preferred ways of learning. McTighe & Wiggins (2012) emphasize that UbD is not a rigid program or prescriptive recipe but a set of helpful tools to purposefully think about curriculum. UbD ties to the desired outcomes and is intertwined with the learning targets. Staff using UbD plan the evidence and learning activities to offer increased access for a diversity of learners. UbD frames the learning with engaging student exploration and well-organized plans.

Consider the following tips to ADMIRE UbD:

- **A**ssess student understandings and baseline skills and **a**ctivate outcomes with engagements.
- **D**ecide on the evidence at the onset and **d**elineate essential questions.
- **M**odel flexibility and **m**onitor the diversity of learners.
- **I**nstruct with scaffolding in place and **i**nvolve all modalities.
- **R**eflect on the learning targets in the UbD framework and **r**evise small-group instruction.
- **E**ngage timelines and **e**nrich higher and lower levels.

Critical Thinking Skills

The inclusion teacher's job in providing adaptations is never to give students the answers but to provide students with the information that leads them to develop the schema. That process of self-exploration promotes higher-level thinking skills.

Let's consider an exercise to illustrate the point (see figure 5.9). The objective of this exercise is to have students think about what they are doing while they use logical sequencing and the tactile elements of the toothpick manipulatives to invite cognitive thought to imprint the learning. Skills like these are then transferred to inferential reading comprehension and all kinds of cognitive thought across the curriculum.

Critical thinking skills are essential and can be promoted in inclusion classrooms. Developing thinking skills can be accomplished through various mediums, whether it's playing I Spy, rhyming games, solving daily Sudoku puzzles, identifying the variables in an algebraic equation, or writing an argumentative essay with credible sources and citations. Mathematics manipulatives can include toothpicks, tangrams, fraction circles, candy hearts, abacuses, flashcards, Cuisenaire rods, algebra tiles, the ones on virtual sites, and more.

> **Toothpick Exercises**
>
> Follow directions to meet written toothpick requirements, always returning to this original position, using 12 toothpicks.
>
> *Note: There's a difference between the words* move *and* remove.
>
>
>
> For the starting position, begin each step with the following setup.
>
> 1. Move 2 toothpicks to make 7 squares.
> 2. Move 4 toothpicks to make 10 squares.
> 3. Remove 2 toothpicks to make 2 squares.
> 4. Move 3 toothpicks to make 3 squares.
>
> Resources needed: Flat toothpicks or craft sticks
>
> Check out this site for more ideas: www.education.com/activity/Toothpick_Math
>
> *The answer key to this exercise appears at the end of this chapter (page 121).*

Source: © *2015 by Corwin Press. Adapted from* Inclusion Strategies That Work! Research-Based Methods for the Classroom *(3rd ed.) by Toby J. Karten. Adapted with permission.*

Figure 5.9: *Toothpick exercise.*

Co-regulation and direct skill instruction can help students to develop the skills that lead to more learning. We were each born with specific traits that are nurtured or shelved at different times of our lives. Educational psychology professors John Dunlosky, Katherine A. Rawson, Elizabeth J. Marsh, Mitchell J. Nathan, and Daniel T. Willingham (2013) share that cognitive education needs to offer ways to help students to better regulate their learning through the use of effective learning techniques. Recommendations from their research reviewed factors such as learning conditions, student characteristics, materials, and educational context.

Easy-to-use techniques, such as elaborative interrogation (generating an explanation for why an explicitly stated fact is true), self-explanation (knowing discrete steps), summarization, highlighting (or underlining), the key word mnemonic, imagery use for text learning, rereading, practice testing, distributed practice (scheduled at intervals), and interleaved practice (mixing of different learning material at the same time) assist students (Dunlosky et al., 2013).

Collaborative, High-Tech, Individualized, Low-Tech, Data-Driven Approaches

As teachers seek to address the unique challenges presented in their inclusion classrooms, they must hold themselves and their students to high expectations. As professionals, we must ensure that our inclusion practices are CHILD-based:

- **Collaborative:** Inclusion classes require collaboration among school professionals, families, and students with diverse abilities, knowledge, and prior experiences. Collaborative practices seek input from general and special education staff, along with related service providers. Inclusion classrooms encourage students to work together on projects, assignments, and activities. This approach promotes the exchange of ideas and mutual support among professionals, families, and students, fostering a more inclusive and supportive learning environment.
- **High-tech:** High-tech inclusion classes incorporate advanced technology tools and resources to support students with exceptionalities. This may include assistive technology devices, specialized software, communication apps, and adaptive hardware. These technologies can help students with diverse ability levels access and engage with educational content more effectively.
- **Individualized:** Inclusion classes aim to provide the appropriate supports for students' unique needs. This involves creating IEPs that outline the specially designed instruction. Specific academic and functional goals and accommodations are collaboratively determined with school and family input.
- **Low-tech:** While high-tech solutions have their place, low-tech approaches are also valuable in inclusion classes. These may include simple modifications, such as providing tactile materials, using visual aids, or implementing multisensory teaching techniques. Low-tech strategies ensure that students with a wide range of abilities can access and engage with the curriculum.
- **Data-driven:** Inclusion classes benefit from data-driven approaches to monitor student progress and make informed instructional decisions. Educators use data to assess the effectiveness of accommodations and interventions. Professionals identify areas where students need additional support, and adjust the teaching strategies accordingly. Technology often facilitates data collection, analysis, and reporting to improve the overall quality of inclusive education.

Please note that whether a practice is high-tech, like an AI platform, or low-tech, like masking tape that helps paper stay steady for a student with dysgraphia, its choice is based on effectiveness with optimally low burden to implement. A consistent challenge in all inclusion classrooms is that no two students learn the same depth and breadth of knowledge at the same pace or complexity. The following four students—*Ima Included*, *Lucas Learns*, *Bill B. Hayve*, and *Cara Can*—show how to support the specially designed instruction in each student's IEP with collaborative, high-tech, individualized, low-tech, and data-driven approaches.

To complete a specially designed instruction documentation chart for students in your class, see the reproducible "Documenting Specially Designed Instruction" at the end of this chapter (page 122). Figure 5.10 provides an example of specially designed instruction documentation for a fictional student with attention, learning, and visual needs.

Specially Designed Instruction Documentation	
 **Student:** Ima Included *Ima has attention, learning, and visual needs.*	**IEP states** • Preteach vocabulary • Redirection and repetition • Increased proximity • More breaks • Larger font • Provide study guides

Specially designed instruction provided:
- Audio notes of class lessons and worksheet directions were given on 5/18, 20, 22, 26, 28, 6/3. Digital files are in Ima's online portfolio that she reviews with read-aloud tool.
- Biweekly one-to-one conferencing with Ima. With family permission, each fifteen-minute session is recorded for Ima's reflection.
- Social studies vocabulary on ancient Egypt and science vocabulary on plate tectonics were provided three days before the lessons with handheld and digital flashcards.
- Ima was provided with step-by-step video instruction on how to enlarge font on websites, PDFs, and Word documents. Worksheets and resources are also emailed and provided on a Padlet with a 16-point font and bolded text.
- Due dates for assignments are modified, with interim checks for longer assignments.
- Ima accesses weekly and monthly Google Calendars in addition to a handheld planner. Ima's daily schedule is dependent on her stamina and attention as communicated by her parents and in-class observation and performance.
- Ima takes daily movement breaks, such as mindfulness, GoNoodle, and music.
- Study guides follow the same format with graphic organizers that compartmentalize the main ideas and subtopics. Study guides are ongoing for the whole class at the onset of each new unit. The content of Ima's study guides is reviewed and checked for accuracy during her biweekly conference time.
- Ima uses handheld devices and annotation tools to highlight the main ideas from online PDFs and websites. She uses Evernote to bookmark and access certain sections for later review.

Figure 5.10: Sample specially designed instruction documentation for a student with attention, learning, and visual needs.

Ima Included's adaptations of advanced planning, conferencing, and audio notes take time, but it's time well spent. Differentiation is thinking about the technology before delivery, whether it's low-tech like a handheld highlighter or high-tech like Evernote. Remember to offer the movement breaks as scheduled classroom management.

Figure 5.11 (page 116) provides an example of specially designed instruction documentation for a fictional student with Down syndrome, apraxia of speech, and hearing loss. Lucas, just like his surname says, learns. That happens when lesson adaptations include collaborative practices and multiple modalities. The collaborative practices in this scenario include outside technology consultations for Lucas and related services from a

Specially Designed Instruction Documentation

 **Student:** Lucas Learns *Lucas is a concrete learner who enjoys interacting with peers. He has a peer mentor who sits with him at lunch and helps him to navigate the schedule and assignments. Lucas has Down syndrome, apraxia of speech, and hearing loss in his left ear. He has a combination of services on campus and online.*	**IEP states** • Provision of a wireless Bluetooth mic (from ReSound) to support hearing aids and amplify sounds • Access to headphones • CoWriter's word-prediction tools • Different pacing • More visuals to accompany text • Consultation with teacher of the deaf or hard of hearing • Multisensory approach for decoding and encoding • Personal word wall for customized spelling list • Oral and silent reading strategies for fluency and comprehension • Direct and explicit instruction • Hands-on opportunities • A handout of key concepts • Minilessons to support learning • Minimizing background noises • Peer mentor

Specially designed instruction provided:
- All accessibility tools for online instruction are activated (www.zoom.com/en/accessibility). Reduce noise with better classroom acoustics (www.asha.org/public/hearing/classroom-acoustics) to suppress some of the room noise and reverberation.
- Zoom settings are customized for Lucas to access the CoWriter word-prediction tools.
- Consultation with district or outside technology coordinator to determine if, how, and when to use the ReSound mic (www.resound.com/en-us/hearing-aids/accessories/micro-mic).
- Time-stamped cloud-recorded audio transcript shared via a link with Lucas's parents.
- Lucas and his parents are taught how to use Google Chrome's tools—for example, Read&Write extension to create a picture dictionary of vocabulary, how to use read-aloud tools, and how to create digital files of readings that are sent to his special education teacher.
- Sites like CommonLit (www.commonlit.org/en), Newsela (https://newsela.com), ReadWorks (www.readworks.org), Renaissance Learning (www.renaissance.com), *Smithsonian* magazine (www.smithsonianmag.com/category/teachers), and Magic School (www.magicschool.ai) are used to provide reading selections on his appropriate Lexile level.
- The speech-language pathologist offers guidance to Lucas's parents for at-home speech tips (for example, www.apraxia-kids.org/keep-calm-and-chatter-on). Teletherapy follows IEP guidelines for two twice-a-week thirty-minute sessions.
- Cues, prompts, and pictures are ongoing with private chats, emails, and visual reminders (documented in a digital file).

- Minilessons are offered on Lucas's independent reading level, with weekly progress monitoring and assessments given by his special education teacher (Flip recordings, https://info.flip.com/en-us.html).
- General education peer mentor schedules two weekly lunch meets with Lucas where they talk about school and interests; under teacher guidance, Lucas reviews his mathematics facts and solves one-step word problems with his peer mentor.
- Minilessons occur a minimum of three times each week, with a digital spelling list and a handout of weekly subject-specific key concepts provided.
- VAKT instruction is included with curriculum songs, images, photos, and guided physical, motor, and tactile connections (such as salt trays).
- Immersive Reader is used to separate and color code syllables.

Figure 5.11: Sample specially designed instruction documentation for a student with Down syndrome, apraxia of speech, and hearing loss.

speech-language pathologist, since that expertise is required for his hearing loss and apraxia of speech. Even if there is disagreement with providers, colleagues, or families, collaboration occurs because perspectives and expertise spin challenge and difference to solution.

Figure 5.12 provides an example of specially designed instruction documentation for a fictional student with behavioral challenges.

Specially Designed Instruction Documentation

 **Student:** Bill B. Hayve *Bill is often unaware of how his behavior negatively impacts himself and others.*	**IEP states** that a functional behavioral assessment (FBA) determined that his off-task behavior is anxiety driven. He'd rather act out then admit he didn't understand the assignment's requirements. This interferes with his learning and the learning of others. The paraprofessional assists with behavior management to help Bill to self-monitor his on-task behavior.

Specially designed instruction provided:
- Bill's checklist of expectations and norms is provided at the onset of each week and reviewed daily.
- He rates his behavior on a 1–5 scale, with 5 being the best behavior and 1 being the lowest performance; behaviors include, for example, listening without interrupting, dressing appropriately, and raising his hand to ask a question or contribute to discussions.
- Under the special education and general education teachers' guidance, the paraprofessional observes and records behavioral antecedents during an hourlong period each day. The para monitors Bill's goal setting chart (www.freeprintablebehaviorcharts.com/goal_setting_charts.htm).

Figure 5.12: Sample specially designed instruction documentation for a student with behavioral challenges.

continued →

- The special education teacher conferences with Bill at the end of each day to review daily emotional check-in and check-out sheets from Do2Learn (https://do2learn.com/activities/SocialSkills/EmotionCheckIn-Checkout/index.html) and to offer positive affirmations. These dated files are kept in his digital behavioral journal.
- Teachers incorporate the topic of football in the lessons, since Bill loves the game and plays Pop Warner; for example, they relate negative numbers to gaining and losing yards, and provide chapter books about football.
- As appropriate, Bill is given a choice of three out of five assignments that he completes with peers to offer him empowerment, encourage peer interactions, and avoid power struggles (the paraprofessional joins his group).
- Bill is required to document self-care in his daily routines—for example, eating habits, sleep, and exercise (push-ups, walking, and breathing and calming exercises). This is monitored, encouraged, and reinforced by his teachers, paraprofessional, and parents each day.

Inclusion professionals address Bill B. Hayve's anxiety by connecting to his preferred interest, football. They offer him voice-choice to avoid power struggles. (See the Offer Voice-Choice Assignments section, page 129 in chapter 6.) Teachers, families, and peers collaborate to instruct and monitor Bill with encouragement, feedback, and reinforcement. His emotional check-ins increase his metacognition as a self-regulated learner to deal with anxiety, since that is determined as the function of his behavior. Chapter 6 (page 125) deals with more specifics on managing anxiety.

Figure 5.13 provides an example of specially designed instruction documentation for a fictional student with autism.

Specially Designed Instruction Documentation	
 **Student:** Cara Can *Cara has autism and benefits from routine and structure. She is a visual learner and loves watching animated videos. Her word recognition and fact fluency are good, but Cara needs help to answer inferential reading comprehension questions and to solve multistep mathematics word problems. Cara has difficulties with fine motor tasks, written expression, following verbal directions, transitions, and social cues.*	**IEP states** - Redirection - Visuals provided - Praise and reinforcement - Occupational therapist and speech-language pathologist services twice a week, in small group - Communication supports - Family supports - Writing frames and rubrics - Transition supports - Social skill training - Instructional assistant - Reading supports; for example, main idea, sequencing, cause-effect, inferences - Mathematics problem-solving support with manipulatives; number lines, 100s chart, counters

Specially designed instruction provided:
- Visual task analysis and video modeling accompany multistep directions, abstract concepts, and new content that is not within Cara's prior knowledge.
- Cara has personalized pictures and visuals to record her emotions in a feelings book that is captioned (instructional assistant scribes her responses to *wh-* prompts).
- Daily visual schedule is kept near Cara's iPad.
- Subjects and breaks are listed in the same order each day.
- Social stories and scripts are provided for changes in schedule—for example, an interrupted online connection or a wrong key pressed.
- Praise and reminders accompany positive peer interactions—for example, turn taking, eye contact, or waiting to speak.
- Prize boxes and incentives are offered—for example, listening to animated videos.
- Personalized videos (made with Screencastify) given for small-group reading and mathematics instruction as praise for positive on-task behaviors, and as reminders—for example, no flapping arms, reduced repetitive movements.
- Related service providers (occupational therapists and speech-language pathologists) observe and offer her consultation and resources.
- Cara watches BrainPOP science videos, and she takes the interactive quizzes.
- The occupational therapist provides Cara's parents with an at-home learning packet from Learning Without Tears (www.lwtears.com) to practice with Mat Man (www.lwtears.com/blog/meet-mat-man) and to learn keyboarding skills (Spanish version sent). Writing and sensory tools sent home—for example, grip aids, weighted pencils.
- Headphones are paired to Cara's iPad.
- The instructional assistant observes and records Cara's verbal and nonverbal behavior for three consecutive dates each week and shares with teacher, who shares with the applied behavior analysis interventionist and family.
- Mathematics problem-solving chart and virtual manipulatives are provided (https://illuminations.nctm.org).
- Story maps and reading organizers compartmentalize details and elements from grade-level fiction and nonfiction articles (https://www.n2y.com/news-2-you).
- Weekly progress monitoring of reading and mathematics skills with oral and online quizzes.
- Cara's interest in animals is infused in reading and writing lessons (for example, wildlife stories, mathematics word problems with pets).
- Technology tools and sites accessed include word prediction tools, audio notes, text to speech (https://ttsreader.com), Text Compactor (www.textcompactor.com), Rewordify (https://rewordify.com), Vocaroo (https://vocaroo.com), Storyline Online (https://storylineonline.net), Colorín Colorado (www.colorincolorado.org).

Figure 5.13: Sample specially designed instruction documentation for a student with autism.

Cara Can's classification of autism does not lower expectations. Her goal remains to advance toward mastery. Her specially designed instruction and progress monitoring define the adaptations that include the weekly progress monitoring, collaboration with the OT on how to make social stories, and graphic organizers to visually sort information.

Conclusion

In conclusion, this chapter has highlighted the need to respond to inclusion challenges with the supports required. Proactive strategies include increased visuals, more collaboration, critical thinking skills, and the application of practices with trios of initials to ADMIRE, such as UbD and PBL. Whether strategies are high-tech such as those offered with AI, such as the rhyme.cool (2023) one about inclusion or a virtual field trip with Discovery Education to a museum or sports arena, or low-tech, such as running a highlighter across a blank page for a student to scribe answers within given parameters or providing a student access to an inflatable sprinkled seat cushion, the adaptations are CHILD specific—collaboratively planned, individualized, and data driven. Take a moment to reflect on the information and strategies you've read by completing the "Admiring How Inclusion Challenges Generate Solutions" reproducible at the end of this chapter (page 123). Lastly, how did you do on the toothpick exercise? See figure 5.14 to check your answers!

Toothpick Answers (from page 113)

1. Move 2 toothpicks to make 7 squares.

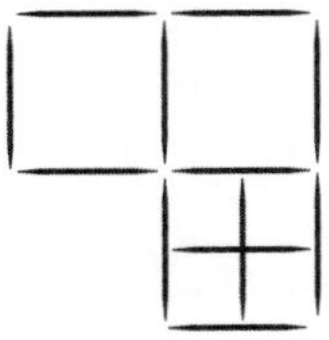

2. Move 4 toothpicks to make 10 squares.

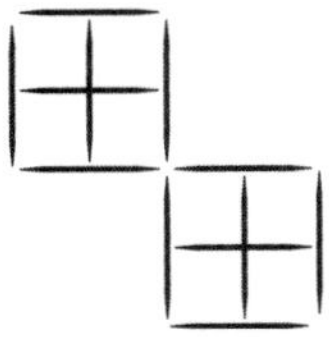

3. Remove 2 toothpicks to make 2 squares.

4. Move 3 toothpicks to make 3 squares.

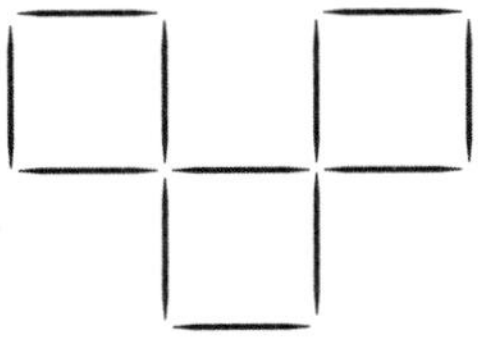

Source: © 2015 by Corwin Press. Adapted from Inclusion Strategies That Work! Research-Based Methods for the Classroom *(3rd ed.) by Toby J. Karten. Adapted with permission.*

Figure 5.14: Toothpick exercise answers.

Documenting Specially Designed Instruction

Use the following chart to document the specially designed instruction you use to address unique challenges students face in your classroom.

Specially Designed Instruction Documentation	
Student name: **Learning strengths and challenges:**	**Student's IEP states:**
Specially designed instruction provided:	

The ADMIRE Framework for Inclusion © 2024 Solution Tree Press • SolutionTree.com
Visit **go.SolutionTree.com/specialneeds** to download this free reproducible.

Admiring How Inclusion Challenges Generate Solutions

Use the following template to ADMIRE the actions to generate solutions. In the space provided, note which of the ADMIRE action items stood out to you from this chapter.

A **Assess and Activate**	
D **Decide and Delineate**	
M **Model and Monitor**	
I **Instruct and Involve**	
R **Reflect and Revise**	
E **Engage and Enrich**	

The ADMIRE Framework for Inclusion © 2024 Solution Tree Press • SolutionTree.com
Visit **go.SolutionTree.com/specialneeds** to download this free reproducible.

CHAPTER 6

Manage Inclusion Anxiety

Students, families, teachers, administrators, and other inclusion professionals encounter successes and challenges in inclusion classrooms. During this process, teachers experience stress as they manage classroom needs for students who learn and behave in diverse ways. Administrators encounter staffing and budget constraints to be in compliance with IDEA legislation. Family and student emotions include anxiety about what is known and not known, and what awaits. Students who fear being noticed as different, misunderstood, excluded, or unable to keep up with peers may exhibit anxiety that interferes with their learning.

In this chapter, we explore how inclusion teachers acknowledge and reduce inclusion anxiety. Knowing that inclusivity is a major factor in reducing anxiety in the classroom encourages teachers to include small-group activities to encourage peer cooperation and socialization. Offering voice-choice assignments is another way to inspire ownership and belonging. Teachers may consider MTSS as a pathway to empower students to be successful through targeted interventions. Finally, we consider how the four critical questions of a professional learning community (PLC) provide insight for teachers seeking to reduce anxiety in the inclusion classroom.

Acknowledge and Reduce Inclusion Anxiety

The National Institute of Mental Health (2023) outlines different levels of anxiety that include feelings and behavior that manifest themselves as worry, restlessness, panic, thoughts of being out of control, phobias, embarrassment, withdrawal, inattention, difficulties with concentration, irregular sleep patterns, irritability, avoidance, and impaired interactions with others in conversation, actions, and inactions. Inclusion anxiety in classrooms can lead to a feeling of discomfort, fear, or stress experienced for students who are part of a diverse classroom but feel different, excluded, or marginalized due to factors such as their race, culture, ethnicity, gender, sexual orientation, ability, or socioeconomic status. Many times, people with social anxiety magnify the little things (Carlson, 2013). Inclusion anxiety is a significant concern for individuals from marginalized groups.

Children and adolescents have a desire to belong and fit in with others. Inclusivity is a big part of suicide prevention and mental health awareness because, in all aspects of life, people deserve a seat at the table (Carlson, 2013). According to a study published in *Child Development*, social belongingness is a key factor in the development of self-esteem and well-being in young people (Wentzel & Asher, 1995). The study shared that children who felt socially accepted and connected to their peers are more likely to have positive self-perceptions and higher levels of life satisfaction. Neglected, rejected, excluded, or unpopular students experience feelings that influence what they hear, do, remember, and generally feel and think. Evidence suggests a positive association exists between self-efficacy and school performance. The effect of well-being on productivity for youth needs more study for correlation with academic engagement (Cárdenas, Lattimore, Steinberg, & Reynolds, 2022). The findings to date suggest that adolescent self-esteem, academic self-efficacy, and perceived social support are key factors that should be considered together to improve adolescent academic engagement (Zhao, Zheng, Pan, & Zhou, 2021).

A separate study published in *Frontiers in Psychology* outlines that social belongingness is positively associated with academic achievement and well-being among adolescents (Zhao et al., 2021). The study finds that adolescents who feel they are socially connected to their peers have higher levels of academic achievement and report greater life satisfaction. There is a need for parents and school educators to actively guide adolescents to improve their self-esteem and academic self-efficacy (Zhao et al., 2021).

An article from Child Mind Institute, "How Does Anxiety Affect Kids in School?" (Ehmke, 2023), speaks about the different characteristics that students manifest if they experience anxiety that range from avoidance to an upset stomach to disruptive or inattentive behavior. As an example, if a student is squirming in their seat and not paying attention, that is not always indicative of ADHD, but classroom anxiety could be the cause. If students are anxious in the classroom, then focusing on the lesson and ignoring the anxiety and a combination of worried thoughts overtaking their brain is challenging.

Adaptations provided in the inclusion classroom that a student may perceive as different and not on par with peers can lead to feelings that they don't really belong or are not on par with their peers, which leads to anxiety. Sometimes, reading adapted literature with more visuals or using a number line to solve subtraction problems draws unwanted attention, especially if the other students do not use those same aids. Inclusion anxiety can lead to negative outcomes such as decreased academic performance, increased absenteeism, and decreased motivation to participate in classroom activities.

Research shows that inclusion anxiety can have significant negative effects on individuals' mental health and well-being. For example, a study finds that exclusion experiences can lead to increased stress and negative emotions, as well as decreased self-esteem and feelings of belongingness (van Zomeren, Leach, & Spears, 2010). Social researchers (Williams, Forgas, & von Hippel, 2005) find that individuals who experienced exclusion report higher levels of anxiety and depression. Promoting inclusion and diversity can help to reduce the negative effects of exclusion and promote positive mental health outcomes.

Research shows that creating inclusive environments can help to reduce inclusion anxiety and promote positive mental health outcomes. For example, researchers John T. Jost, Aaron C. Kay, and Hulda Thorisdottir (2009) find that individuals exposed to diverse perspectives in their work environments report lower levels of anxiety and greater job satisfaction. Professional staff can be less overwhelmed by collaborating with others to share roles and responsibilities, whether they are co-teachers, general education or special education teachers, paraprofessionals, administration, or related service providers. Together, we grow, and together, we need to figure out how to decrease anxiety in students and in ourselves. Collaboration by students, families, and professionals to own the inclusive strategies is imperative to reduce anxiety. The *inclusion must-dos* should not create anxiety for adults (families and professionals) or students. Address anxiety in inclusion classrooms by implementing the following strategies.

- Create a welcoming and inclusive classroom environment where all students feel valued and respected on their level of performance, never compared to peers, but monitored within a growth paradigm with realistic feedback given to promote reflection and advancement.

- Encourage open and respectful communication among students and between students and the teachers, special education and general education staff, administration, related service providers, and families with a team-building approach that validates that **t**ogether, **e**veryone **a**chieves **m**ore (TEAM)!

- Incorporate diverse perspectives and experiences into classroom discussions, activities, and materials. This can be achieved through literature, nonfiction text, and multimedia, which range from exploring books with different versions of Cinderella to creating a learning plan that uses art as a tool for social justice as offered in Learning for Justice (www.learningforjustice.org).

- Include activities for peers to share their experiences and perspectives with multiple engagements, inquiry, and reflection, such as kinesthetic debates, cooperative groups, both project-based and problem-based units, podcasts, invited speakers, and more.

- Use inclusive language and avoid stereotypes and biases in classroom interactions and materials. Propagate people-first language with culturally responsive teaching.

- Provide support and resources for students, professionals, and families who may need additional assistance or accommodations to proactively reduce anxiety.

By implementing these strategies and monitoring the students, teachers can help foster a positive and inclusive classroom environment that supports the academic, social, linguistic, behavioral, and emotional well-being of students. Support, collaboration, reflection, compassion, and awareness pave the road to mastery.

> **Consider the following tips to ADMIRE belonging in the inclusion classroom.**
>
> **A** — **A**ssess and **a**ctivate the classroom and school environment to promote open and respectful communication among students and professionals.
>
> **D** — **D**ecide and **d**elineate empathy and adaptations as the class norm for those who know more and less, with any perceived pecking order banned, inside or outside school—whether that's in person or online.
>
> **M** — **M**odel mindfulness and **m**onitor students with emotional check-ins.
>
> **I** — **I**nstruct and **i**nvolve with culturally diverse perspectives and resources.
>
> **R** — **R**eflect and **r**evise interventions to honor the ability, backgrounds, identities, and social, emotional, and behavioral levels of the students and professionals.
>
> **E** — **E**ngage others to value acceptance, sans judgment, and **e**nrich the inclusion classroom with norms that respect difference.

Include Small-Group Activities

Students with IEPs, struggling learners, and the students who know more and less dig into the knowledge to learn, discuss, and co-construct understandings. With small-group activity, the larger class is broken up into cooperative peers who work at centers or stations. Peers work to complete academic assignments as they develop interpersonal skills. Educators and support staff rotate about to guide and offer feedback. This promotes socialization and collaboration with opportunities to converse with peers in small groups. Consider the following examples.

- A shy student who becomes overwhelmed in large groups may feel less anxious and more comfortable in a small-group discussion.
- A student who has difficulty paying attention in the context of the whole classroom can stay on task during a small-group activity.
- A student with oppositional defiance or one who has less self-efficacy as only one student in the whole class may experience more buy-in, interest, and motivation when given a voice with a small group of peers to select and complete learning tasks.

When structuring students into small groups, teachers guide and monitor but then step away so that the students take their own learning steps. The idea is to diminish anxiety and to promote thinking skills, not to just disseminate the knowledge.

PBIS World (www.pbisworld.com) has resources and ideas for behavior supports during academics. Often, students who have a lack of responsibility or are disorganized will complete tasks with more self-confident peers, alternate choices, modeling, and role playing as they learn to understand perspectives.

Offer Voice-Choice Assignments

Voice and choice can be used as part of instruction for practice, enrichment, assessment, and homework. Voice-choice assignments connect to student interest with multiple engagement, action, and expression. The idea is to offer students options, which lead to increased empowerment and ownership with a feeling of belonging and more control. Voice and choice are tools for inclusivity. Harvard Graduate School of Education's Project Zero (2018) talks about how perspective taking is difficult, and in order to scaffold the "my voice" part of voice and choice, students may need support considering their own perspectives and sensitivities. Voice considers points of view, identity, and student experiences.

Choice boards are one way to implement voice-choice during classroom activities and can be used across subjects and grades. Choice boards increase a student's own voice as they interact with others to complete assignments. This engagement option can spark curiosity and offer authenticity and relevancy by structuring students with alternative ways to demonstrate their mastery of a topic (Allen & Phillips, 2022). Teachers intentionally check for understanding by selecting tasks that best align with the standards being taught. Students collaboratively dig into the learning. As per individual needs, note that some students may choose to work independently. Most importantly, choice boards communicate the learning intentions for students, which is part of teacher clarity and student efficacy (Hattie, 2009; Hattie, Fisher, & Frey, 2017; Schultz & Phillips, 2021).

Figure 6.1 (page 130) contains a choice board students received to guide their response to reading *The Call of the Wild* (London, 1990). In this way, students choose from diverse options to demonstrate their understanding and solidify their knowledge. In this example, students use a choice board Think-Tac-Toe format for instruction and assessment. Choice boards offer differentiated instruction, with learner time and requirements contingent upon student skill set. As an option, choice boards may be completed cooperatively with peers, with three students in each group. Groups are formed by skill, interest, or random selection. Be aware of the chemistry between some students and monitor accordingly as they define and reinforce the small-group norms, roles, and assignment expectations. That includes infusing strategies such as team-building activities and rubrics, such as those created in Google Classroom. Ensure that the small- and cooperative-group configuration never stigmatizes students according to deficit or a pecking order of skill. Co-teachers should exercise caution to alternate who works with which groups and for which purpose. That includes small groups for practice, enrichment, assessment, instruction, and more. The beauty of the choice board is that it empowers students to

The Call of the Wild **Think-Tac-Toe**		
If you were one of the animals in this story, what would you say? Write this as cartoon dialogue like a graphic novel. You can free draw or use MakeBeliefsComix (https://makebeliefscomix.com).	If you were the author, instead of Jack London, how would you change any of the events? Write a brief paragraph with these transitional words to sequence the events; *First, Next, Later, After, Finally*. 	Draw a scene of something you read. Please add a caption. You can use a site like AutoDraw (www.autodraw.com) or pencil and paper, and then take a picture with your phone camera.
Would you rather live in California or in Canada? List three reasons why. 1. 2. 3.  	Create a song about the most exciting part of the book you have read so far.	Research more about gold in the Yukon. Share three facts from this site, accessed at the QR code. 
Predict what will happen in Buck's future in a short paragraph (at least three sentences).	Write a haiku that tells why you would or would not like Buck as your pet.	Reword this chapter 4 *Call of the Wild* quote in your own words: "Buck feels he deserves to be leader after winning the fight against Spitz. It was his by right. He had earned it, and he would not be content with less" (London, 1990, p. 20).

Figure 6.1: Sample choice board for The Call of the Wild *(London, 1990).*

select their learning, offering them guided control. Although the format remains the same, the complexity and content of a choice board vary and can include practice for past, current, and upcoming concepts across the curriculum.

Figure 6.2 contains a sample choice board students might receive from a mathematics teacher.

Mathematics Choice Board		
Directions: Choose three activities to complete a horizontal, vertical, or diagonal row. You can work individually or with peers. As an option, the full board can be completed for additional points. Check with your teacher if you have another idea for an activity. I (we) will complete the following boxes: #_____, #_____, #_____ by _____ (date) Student signatures: _____, _____, _____		
☐ Create one of the following about slopes: • Poem • Song • Picture	☐ Create a poster containing step-by-step directions to help another student understand how to round numbers to the: • Tens place • Hundreds place • Thousands place	☐ Create a foldable brochure with addition, subtraction, multiplication, and division pictures and facts. Include pictures and captions.
☐ Create a board game that tests your classmates' knowledge on linear equations.	☐ Free choice from textbook	☐ Create a word problem that uses at least two of these operations: • Addition • Subtraction • Multiplication • Division Solve each problem.
☐ Create a paragraph that uses these words: *add*, *subtract*, *multiply*, *divide*, *addend*, *sum*, *difference*, *factors*, and *product*.	☐ Create thirty multiplication flashcards on index cards. Check for accuracy with your text or online.	☐ Write a letter to your parents describing in detail five ways that people use mathematics.

Figure 6.2: Sample mathematics choice board.

To access choice board templates to use with your class, visit https://slidesmania.com/tag/choice-boards or see the "Create a Choice Board" reproducible at the end of this chapter (page 143).

Consider the following tips to ADMIRE voice-choice.

- **A**ssess how students will have a say in their learning and **a**ctivate a choice of inquiry-based activities.
- **D**ecide on what accountability looks like and **d**elineate ways to share the learning both in class and online with options connected to student perspectives.
- **M**odel how to lead and support peer discussion and **m**onitor small groups and individual students.
- **I**nstruct with academic and behavioral goals and **i**nvolve students in creating rules for engagement.
- **R**eflect on how students choose partners for group activity and discussion and **r**evise assessment choices.
- **E**ngage opportunities for students to take ownership and **e**nrich relationships and levels.

Empower Students to Be Successful

MTSS is an educational framework that offers three tiers of academic and behavioral support to students. It is a proactive way for educators to provide targeted interventions and support for students who have different academic levels, behaviors, and experiences to ensure they're successful. MTSS organization offers both teachers and students support and strategies that decrease and manage anxiety, trauma, emotional regulation, and depression (August, Piehler, & Miller, 2018).

MTSS aims to advance academic, social, and emotional needs, whether the starting point is at or above grade level. The MTSS framework is designed to offer interventions before challenges escalate (National Center on Intensive Intervention, n.d.).

Students and adults in classrooms, schools, homes, communities, countries, and the world display varying levels of cognition, behavior, physical stamina, attention, and proficiencies. Diversity exists, as does diverse reaction toward difference. This includes differences in level and attitude toward ability, culture, ethnicity, identity, and prior experiences. Teachers need to respond to the students who know more and the students who know less. Students who grow up in literacy-rich environments are often seated next to students who live displaced from their parents. Students who have different chromosomes than the typical forty-six require different supports. Some students escape war-torn countries, and some have passports they've used since birth as they've traveled the world first class with their families. Some students had childhoods that made them smile, and some saw things that they spend a lifetime wishing to erase. Educators simultaneously reach and teach each of those prototypes in the same classroom.

The MTSS framework includes three tiers or levels of support that can be used to manage and reduce stress and anxiety that students experience.

- **Tier 1 (universal, core supports for all students with differentiated instruction):** Teachers create a classroom environment that promotes emotional well-being and provides strategies to manage stress and anxiety. This benefits all students to acquire the knowledge and skills within a welcoming classroom environment, conducive to listening, learning, and smiling. Quieter areas and sensory calming breaks are included as part of Tier 1 core instruction.

- **Tier 2 (targeted support for students who need additional help in small-group instruction or extra practice for reinforcement):** Students who are identified as having heightened anxiety receive targeted interventions. This includes small-group sessions focused on building coping skills, emotional check-ins, stress management techniques, and self-regulation with a strategy such as Check-In/Check-Out, or CICO (www.panoramaed.com/blog/check-in-check-out-cico-intervention).

- **Tier 3 (intensive support for students with significant needs, including but not limited to individualized instruction, one-to-one tutoring, or specialized programs):** For students with severe anxiety that significantly impacts their functioning, more intensive interventions might be necessary. This could involve collaboration with school counselors, psychologists, and potentially even outside mental health professionals. Collaboration between educators, school counselors, mental health professionals, and families is crucial to implementing effective MTSS.

To implement MTSS in behavior, educators use data to identify students who may be at risk for behavior problems and provide targeted interventions to prevent those problems from escalating. For example, teachers use behavior checklists or observations to monitor student behavior and provide positive reinforcement for appropriate behavior. If a student continues to struggle with behavior and experiences anxiety, they may receive additional support through Tier 2 or Tier 3 interventions. The goal of MTSS in behavior is to create a positive and supportive school environment that promotes social and emotional well-being for all students with data-based individualization. By providing targeted interventions and support, educators can help students develop the social and emotional skills they need to succeed in school and in life.

In literacy, the MTSS framework is used for students who labor with reading comprehension, fluency, or phonics. In mathematics, educators use the data to identify students who are struggling with concepts to determine the appropriate support. Diagnostic instruction guides which areas need to be remediated, and that leads to specific targeted literacy and mathematics interventions within an MTSS framework. Then, formative assessments are given to monitor student progress and to adjust instruction accordingly.

The next sections offer literacy and mathematics connections within the MTSS framework. The SEL connections invite the evidence-based practices to connect to MTSS and PBIS in ways that students learn best to increase competencies and, conversely, manage and decrease the anxiety of being expected to perform at a level of academic competency without the appropriate supports. This includes concrete, representational, abstract, and virtual engagements (CRAVE), which allow the students to do it, speak it, link it, and own it (DSLO) while honoring their specially designed instruction.

Hence, let's put this multitude of initials into practice for literacy, mathematics, and more.

MTSS Literacy Connections

Let's look at what MTSS might look like in a literacy context. MTSS begins with screening and ongoing assessment to identify students who may be struggling with literacy skills. Figure 6.3 provides teachers a tool for observing and assessing a student's needs and planning appropriate supports.

The phrase "Do it, speak it, link it, and own it" (DSLO) emphasizes that student words and behavior impact gains. Many learners require engagement that helps them to internalize the skills. When they do something, they often remember it the next time. That applies to skills like vocabulary development and reading and listening comprehension to identify the main idea of a story or the gist of a conversation. The goal is to cultivate students who take the steps to gain acumen. Literacy skills occur with activities that invite effort and reflection. Literacy skills are integral ones that extend beyond inclusion classrooms to open many doors for successful postsecondary outcomes.

Noncognitive factors, such as behaviors, attitude, and strategies, affect reading achievement (Macdonald, Cirino, Miciak, & Grills, 2021). Research points to important implications for designing reading interventions that address anxiety-related cognitive interference and improve students' emotional well-being (Barnes, Grills, & Vaughn, 2023). Fun activities like games, creative projects, and physical exercise serve as outlets for stress and anxiety. They provide students with healthy ways to cope as they learn more difficult content and skills.

DSLO offers ways to engage with the literacy instruction to develop and increase self-confidence within the MTSS framework. DSLO in literacy helps students learn to decode, encode, and comprehend the reading to circumvent the inattention, anxiety, and other behaviors from interfering with reading and writing mastery.

1. **Do It!** Concrete demonstration with teacher direction and self-discovery (sans worksheets).

    As examples, students:

    - Toss or dribble a ball to create an oral story.
    - Play sight word hopscotch.
    - Write collaborative sentences and paragraphs.
    - Morph different parts of speech, such as *sun* to *sunny* or *teacher* to *teach* or *teachable*.

Literacy Standard or Concepts: _____ Grades: _____
Skills (Big Ideas): _____

Assessment and observation (formal or informal) to reveal difficulties with: (check all that apply)

☐ Phonemic awareness	☐ Fluency or automaticity	☐ Comprehension
☐ Abstract representations	☐ Time management	☐ Vocabulary
☐ Holding information in working memory	☐ Impulsivity	☐ Working independently
☐ Prerequisite skills	☐ Organization	☐ Cooperative work
☐ Anxiety, distractibility, _____ behaviors	☐ Confidence	☐ Other _____

MTSS Outcomes

Tier 1 core instruction: ALL students will _____.
Tier 2 small-group instruction—practice or remediation repetition: Students will _____.
Tier 3 more intensive instruction (small group or individualized): Students will _____.

Specially designed instruction notes (What? and How? Adapted content, methodology, or delivery of instruction, as per IEP)

Evidence-Based Practice

Practices include systematic and explicit instruction with visual representations, assessment-driven instruction, differentiation, distributive cumulative practice, personalization, peer-assisted and cooperative learning, error analysis, immediate specific feedback, think-alouds and verbalization, discussion, conferencing, journaling, cognitive-strategy instruction, step-by-step procedures, real-life and cross-disciplinary connections, models, and so on.

Literacy instruction includes:

- **CRAVE** (**c**oncrete, **r**epresentational, **a**bstract, **v**irtual, and **e**ngaging) UDL activities (http://udlguidelines.cast.org)
  AKA: DSLO: *Do It! Speak It! Link It! Own It!*
  C _____
  R _____
  A _____
  V _____
  E _____
- **SEL** (included in tiered instruction to heighten self-efficacy, self-determination, motivation, and so on)
  How? _____
  When? _____
  Where? _____
- **Enrichment** (critical thinking skills):
  Activities, centers, stations, forums, and ongoing projects will include _____.

Supports, resources, and roles for: general education and special education teachers and interventionists—paraprofessionals, related staff, administrators, family, students (time-frequency, type of supports)

Before (planning) _____
_____

During (instruction, monitoring, collecting data) _____
_____

Moving Forward (assessments, MTSS reflections, discussions, next steps) _____
_____

Source: Adapted from Karten, 2017c.

Figure 6.3: *MTSS literacy assessment tool.*

- Demonstrate vocabulary through pantomime and charades.
- Find words in classroom, text, or digital "scavenger hunts."
- Play *word family toss*, such as *big, dig, fig, pig, rig*.

2. **Speak It!** Specific language occurs with literacy talks, word walls, songs, stories, informal chats, cooperative forums, songs, and debriefing to link actions and concepts to precise academic vocabulary to create ongoing literacy discourse. Vocabulary is attached to text, such as setting, characters, sequencing, plot, resolution, and figurative language. Students can also engage tools such as read-aloud on Immersive Reader (access this book's webpage via **go.SolutionTree.com /specialneeds** for a link) and online sites, such as ReadWorks (www.readworks .org) and CommonLit (www.commonlit.org), to hear how to pronounce the words correctly before they speak them on their own. Immersive Reader has a tool to click that breaks up words into their syllables.

3. **Link It!** Concepts and representations are connected to paper or digital forums to increase fluency, vocabulary, written expression, and comprehension. Tools such as Vidtionary (www.vidtionary.com) can explain more difficult vocabulary with visuals and create a dictionary that students can reference for practice and reinforcement.

4. **Own It!** Students become the "reading or writing proprietors" who internalize knowledge. Teachers monitor progress with formal, informal assessment:
   - Fluency drills
   - Quizzes
   - Cooperative learns
   - Game-based assessment

MTSS Mathematics Connections

MTSS is not limited to literacy; it can also be applied to mathematics education to support students with varying levels of mathematics proficiency. Tier 1 represents core instruction in mathematics for all students, Tier 2 offers targeted interventions for students who need additional support, and Tier 3 provides intensive interventions for students with significant difficulties in mathematics. Screening and assessment identify students who may be struggling with these skills. Common assessments include mathematical fluency, number sense, problem-solving skills, and mathematical reasoning assessments. MTSS in mathematics includes evidence-based practices to make data-driven decisions for students to monitor progress and inform instructional decisions. Interventions are therefore responsive to individual learner levels.

Figure 6.4 provides teachers with a tool for observing and assessing a student's needs and planning appropriate supports. To plan for MTSS in your classroom, access the "Use an MTSS Planning Template" reproducible at the end of this chapter (page 144).

Literacy Standard or Concepts: _____ Grades: _____
Skills (Big Ideas): _____

Assessment and observation (formal or informal) to reveal difficulties with: (check all that apply)

☐ Number sense	☐ Recall, fluency, or automaticity	☐ Computational errors
☐ Abstract representations	☐ Attention to precision (carelessness)	☐ Conceptual deficits
☐ Holding information in working memory	☐ Impulsivity	☐ Working independently
☐ Prerequisite skills	☐ Organization or time management	☐ Cooperative work
☐ Anxiety, distractibility, _____ behaviors	☐ Confidence	☐ Other _____

MTSS Outcomes
Core instruction: ALL students will _____.
Small-group instruction—practice or remediation repetition: Students will _____.
More intensive instruction (small group or individualized): Students will _____.

Specially designed instruction notes (What? and How? Adapted content, methodology, or delivery of instruction, per IEP)

Evidence-Based Practice

Practices include systematic and explicit instruction with visual representations, assessment-driven instruction, differentiation, distributive cumulative practice, personalization, peer-assisted and cooperative learning, error analysis, immediate specific feedback, critical thinking skills, text read aloud, verbalization, mathematics discussion, conferencing, journals, cognitive-strategy instruction, step-by-step procedures, real-life and cross-disciplinary connections, models, pictures, reasoning abstractly and quantitatively, constructing arguments, perseverance, attention to detail, learner reflection, and so on.

Mathematics instruction includes:

- **CRAVE** (**c**oncrete, **r**epresentational, **a**bstract, **v**irtual, and **e**ngaging) UDL activities (http://udlguidelines.cast.org)
  AKA: DSLO: *Do It! Speak It! Link It! Own It!*
  C _____
  R _____
  A _____
  V _____
  E _____

- **SEL** (included in tiered instruction to heighten self-efficacy, self-determination, motivation, and so on)
  How? _____
  When? _____
  Where? _____

- **Enrichment** (critical thinking skills):
  Activities, centers, stations, forums, and ongoing projects will include _____.

Supports, resources, and roles for: general education and special education teachers and interventionists—paraprofessionals, related staff, administrators, family, students (time-frequency, type of supports)

Before (planning) _____
_____

During (instruction, monitoring, collecting data) _____
_____

Moving Forward (assessments, MTSS reflections, discussions, next steps) _____
_____

Source: Adapted from Karten, 2021.

Figure 6.4: *MTSS mathematics assessment tool.*

Mathematics exploration is a way to make sense of numbers with personal connection, real-world application, and multiple representation. Different engagements assist individual learners to manipulate the mathematical numbers and concepts, whether they require enrichment, practice, or remediation. Teachers of students of all levels are invited to use the DSLO strategies to encourage active engagement with mathematical concepts.

Anxiety causes a wide range of negative reactions to mathematics, from general worry to more severe anxiety for students with mathematics differences, such as dyscalculia and ADHD (Lockett, 2022). DSLO is a way to decrease that mathematics anxiety and swap worksheets with concrete, representational, abstract, and virtual engagement and discovery. Here are some concrete connections that replace *mathematics anxiety* with strategies such as movement, language, organization, and fun!

1. **Do It!** Concrete demonstration (sans worksheets) with teacher direction and self-discovery.

    As examples, students:

    - Collaboratively become part of a number line as they move forward and backward to solve equations.
    - Create a class human clock.
    - Juggle place value with number dot flashcards.
    - Stretch TheraBands to demonstrate different types of lines—for example, perpendicular, parallel, intersecting.
    - Stand in different parts of the room to represent ordered pairs.
    - Demonstrate fractions and ratios with reference to people—for example, kids to teachers and objects; fiction to nonfiction books.

2. **Speak It!** Specific language occurs with mathematics talks, word walls, songs, stories, informal chats, cooperative forums, and debriefing with actions given to academic vocabulary and mathematics discourse. Mathematics vocabulary is attached with terms like *fewer, more, less, equal, most, add, sum, subtract, greater than, less than, combine, estimate, measure, elapsed time, multiply, product, divide, divisor, dividend, vertical, horizontal, even, odd, prime, whole number, fraction, composite, perpendicular, parallel, ray, linear, nonlinear, sequential, random, coordinates, quadrants, equations, variable,* and *exponent*.

3. **Link It!** Students need to know that they are surrounded by mathematics in their lives whether or not they're taking a test. Concepts are connected to paper or digital forums with real-life connections and everyday application, whether that's temperature, weather, cooking a meal, shopping, or rolling dice. Practice includes mathematics fluency with multiple representation, and procedures. Some students also need mathematical headings to compartmentalize or link different responses under their headings.

4. **Own It!** Students become the "proprietors" who integrate the mathematical knowledge with demonstrations, reflections, examination, and internalization.

This includes, but is not limited to, formal and informal assessment, such as fluency drills, quizzes, ongoing applications, cooperative learns, and game-based assessment (ranging from Dominoes to mathematics baseball to online game-based options; see www.mathgames.com/math-games.html).

To plan for using DSLO in your classroom, access the "Create a DSLO Chart" reproducible at the end of this chapter (page 146).

Collaborative Framework

The four critical questions of a PLC (DuFour et al., 2024) apply to students educated in inclusion classrooms.

1. What do we want all students to know and be able to do?

    In an inclusion classroom, this question helps educators clarify their learning objectives for all students, including those with diverse learning needs who may be struggling learners and have IEPs. It encourages teachers to focus on essential learning outcomes that are meaningful and accessible to all students, regardless of their abilities or backgrounds. It also promotes differentiated instruction to meet individualized goals, minus the anxiety for the administrators, teachers, students, and families.

2. How will we know if they learn it?

    Inclusivity requires multiple means of assessment to gauge student progress accurately. Inclusion educators consider a variety of assessment methods, including formative and summative assessments, observations, and alternative assessments. Teachers adapt assessment strategies to accommodate diverse learning styles and abilities. Students need to view learning check-ups as paths to growth, not something that creates anxiety. This question encourages teachers to use both quantitative and qualitative data to assess student learning effectively.

3. How will we respond when some students do not learn?

    In an inclusive classroom, students have different skill sets and require different paces to understand and apply the knowledge. This question encourages teachers to plan for interventions and supports to address these differences. It involves collaborating with special education professionals, using response to intervention (RTI) strategies, and offering personalized assistance to students. Teachers can also explore assistive technologies and adapt instructional materials as needed as well as build in time for practice and repetition during units of study to increase mastery levels.

4. How will we extend the learning for students who are already proficient?

    Just as some students struggle with certain concepts, others excel and require enrichment opportunities. In an inclusive classroom, this question prompts educators to differentiate instruction to meet the needs of advanced learners to ensure they remain engaged and challenged. It encourages the creation of flexible learning environments where students can explore their interests and strengths.

As inclusion educators, let's connect these four questions to literacy, mathematics, and behavior and examine possible answers.

1. How will we match the essential literacy and mathematics standards to honor student skill sets?
    - Individual assessment of levels
    - Specially designed instruction
    - Tiered instruction, including whole class, small groups, and one-to-one
    - Consistency and fidelity
    - Reading decoding, encoding, comprehension, basic facts, +, −, ×, ÷, conceptual
    - Making sense of problems to reason and persevere
    - School-class-student-family norms
    - Instructional and behavioral goals
    - High expectations
    - Class organization
    - Quarterly and long-range expectations
    - Preteaching English language arts and mathematics academic language and vocabulary
    - Inferential-logical-word problem-solving skills
    - Verbal and written communications
    - Study-organizational skills
    - Technology supports
    - Teacher supports, such as resources and time
    - Personalization is culturally appropriate
    - Self-efficacy and self-determination
    - Collaboration among students, interventionists, and families
    - Ongoing advancements
    - Proactive UDL designs
    - Interactive responses
    - Literacy and mathematics discussions
    - Reflective practices

2. How will we determine students' literacy and mathematics levels at set time periods?
   - General education and special education teacher observation and personalization
   - Collaborative problem solving with team approach
   - Formative-summative-common assessments
   - Progress monitoring using weekly or unit quizzes and tests
   - Rubrics or metacognitive self-assessment checklists
   - Written records, digital portfolios, or mathematics notebooks
   - Student communications or reflections
   - Teacher-student literacy and mathematics conferences
   - Class participation
   - Pre-inter-post assessments
   - Student and class graphs
3. What evidence-based practices will we use to engage learners of different literacy, mathematics, and behavior skill sets?
   - Tier 1 intervention menu for core instruction
   - Webb's (1999) Depth of Knowledge and Bloom's (1956) taxonomy
   - Evidence-based practices (What Works Clearinghouse, https://ies.ed.gov/ncee/wwc/PracticeGuides)
   - Personalization, peer-to-peer, cooperative learning
   - Centers, forums, stations, multiple representations
   - Differentiated English language arts and mathematics instruction
   - VAKT-UDL mathematics and literacy interventions
   - Syllabication, structural analysis, decoding, encoding, syntactic structure, fact retrieval, and problem solving
   - English language arts and mathematics coaching and supports
   - Timely and specific feedback
   - *Do It! Speak It! Link It! Own It!*
   - Cumulative practice, compacting, reteaching
4. How will we continue to motivate and advance our learners?
   - Enrichment, empowerment, recognition, practice, personalization
   - Ongoing centers or forums using project-based learning (PBL)
   - UDL (www.cast.org)

- Cooperative learning
- PBIS (www.pbis.org)
- Technology, virtual manipulatives (https://toytheater.com/category/teacher-tools/virtual-manipulatives)
- Independent assignments and free choice
- Meaningful, appropriately leveled assignments strength paradigm
- Real-world literacy and mathematics applications
- Game-based learning
- "Show What You Know"
- High expectations

Incorporating the four critical questions of a PLC into the inclusion classroom setting fosters and promotes collaboration among teachers, increases student success rates, and ensures that all students have access to a high-quality education. Equity, diversity, and inclusion are essential in today's educational landscape.

Conclusion

Inclusion anxiety can lead to a feeling of discomfort, fear, or stress for students who are part of a diverse classroom but may feel different, excluded, or marginalized if they perceive themselves as being different and not on par with their peers. Educators play a critical role in addressing inclusion anxiety, since they are the ones who create a supportive environment for all students that values positive relationships, open communication, clear expectations, and peer supports. Inclusion classrooms are set up to empower everyone to collaborate, learn, and grow together. Differentiation is the norm, not the exception, to increase competency, not anxiety. Take a moment to reflect on the information and strategies you've read by completing the "Admiring Ways to Manage Inclusion Anxiety" reproducible at the end of this chapter (page 147).

Create a Choice Board

Fill in the following choice board template with activities relevant to an upcoming unit. Depending on student skill set and whether new or prior content is included, the academic expectations vary. While some learners complete one box of choice, other learners complete a diagonal, vertical, or horizontal row, or the full board.

Choice Board

Choose three activities to complete a horizontal, vertical, or diagonal row. You can work individually or with peers. As an option, the full board can be completed for additional points. Check with your teacher if you have another idea for an activity.

I (we) will complete the following boxes: #_____, #_____, #_____ by _____ (date)

Student signatures: _____, _____, _____

1.	2.	3.
4.	5.	6.
7.	8.	9.

The ADMIRE Framework for Inclusion © 2024 Solution Tree Press • SolutionTree.com
Visit **go.SolutionTree.com/specialneeds** to download this free reproducible.

Use an MTSS Planning Template

Whether MTSS supports academics, such as literacy or mathematics, or behavior, such as anxiety, the core knowledge is delivered in multiple ways to the whole class, small groups, and individual learners. Use this MTSS planner to plan for the tiered intervention.

Subject:	Marking period:
Weeks:	Dates:

Whole-class Tier 1 core interventions (academic or behavioral):

Tier 2 small groups with targeted interventions:

Tier 3 individualized with one-to-one, more intensive interventions:

Role of general educator:

Role of interventionist or special educator:

Role of instructional assistants or paraprofessionals:

Role of support teams:

page 1 of 2

The ADMIRE Framework for Inclusion © 2024 Solution Tree Press • SolutionTree.com
Visit **go.SolutionTree.com/specialneeds** to download this free reproducible.

Role of administrators:

Role of families:

Role of peers:

Role of guidance counselor:

Role of other personnel:

Related services:

Comments:

Source: Adapted from Karten, T. J. (2021). Inclusion strategies and interventions (2nd ed.). Bloomington, IN: Solution Tree Press.

Create a DSLO Chart

Use this DSLO chart to plan ways for students to do, speak, link, and own the knowledge. Remember that the first option is to provide alternate and multiple engagements, not to lower expectations by deleting difficult content.

DSLO Practices

1. *Do It!*

2. *Speak It!*

3. *Link It!*

4. *Own It!*

Admiring Ways to Manage Inclusion Anxiety

Use the following template to ADMIRE the actions to manage inclusion anxiety. In the space provided, note which of the ADMIRE action items stood out to you from this chapter.

A Assess and Activate	
D Decide and Delineate	
M Model and Monitor	
I Instruct and Involve	
R Reflect and Revise	
E Engage and Enrich	

CHAPTER 7

ADMIRE Wellness

Wellness belongs front and center for students, teachers, administrators, support staff, and families. That includes both personal and professional wellness. Inclusion competencies and supports differ; however, emotional well-being for students, families, and professionals is paramount.

Pfizer (n.d.) defines *wellness* as "the act of practicing healthy habits on a daily basis to attain better physical and mental health outcomes." By its nature, wellness looks different for each person. One person practices wellness when they take a walk or a jog; another when they are immersed in the lives of protagonists in books, movies, and video games. Things like coloring, listening to a favorite singer or band, visiting virtual calming rooms, and using fidget toys often promote wellness, as they decrease stress.

Wellness applies to the professional realm too, as educators may struggle to meet the many expectations placed on their time and resources. Given the communal nature of the classroom, wellness applies to both adults and students in the school setting. Administrators, teachers, students, and families manage diverse classroom, school, home, and individual inclusion needs. Academic demands, along with behavioral, physical, language, and sensory levels, present diverse challenges for teachers, students, and families. Wellness for all is within reach when teachers, students, and families work together. Together, we need to achieve individual and applicable definitions of wellness for preschool to secondary and postgraduate-level students.

In this chapter, we discuss competencies in the inclusion classroom that support wellness. Inclusion teachers are best equipped to encourage wellness in the classroom when they are practiced at supporting themselves. Using a ten-step intervention plan, educators can ensure well-being not only for themselves, but also for students and their families. Ultimately, wellness in the inclusion classroom hinges on a teacher's commitment to ADMIRE the personal and professional relationships that make up that classroom community.

Wellness Competencies

As with supports and adaptations in the inclusion classroom, a teacher's approach to wellness must focus on meeting students' diverse needs. Each student is ready to soar when they develop the competencies, which does not always coincide with when professionals begin the student-teacher and teacher-family relationships. Although starting levels differ, with collaboration and reflection, we need to consistently ADMIRE how to build the wellness and competencies of the students, families, and professionals. Support builds competencies. Competencies promote wellness for all.

Consider the following inclusion-based norms for developing wellness competencies (Karten, 2017b).

- Respond to student differences, levels, and potential with positive attitudes and actions.
- Set educational and functional goals for all learners, those with and without IEPs and labels of exceptionality.
- Focus on academics, along with practical applications in classrooms, homes, and communities, such as setting routines and schedules.
- Listen to one another's viewpoints and communications, even when there is disagreement on placement and services. Then, respectfully share knowledge to formulate moving forward plans.
- Value how coordination and collaboration promote advancements in the social-emotional, physical, and academic wellness of students, school staff, and families.
- Organize the inclusive environment with UDL approaches that honor diverse representation, engagement, and assessment to capitalize on each student's strengths.
- Motivate learners to try their best, and to accept errors as opportunities for growth, helping them to become eager to develop and apply knowledge and skills beyond the grade received.
- Apply competency-based inclusion strategies to promote positive yet realistic self-concepts for the learners so that they are prepared to achieve the rigor of the standards.
- Collaborate with students, family, and all staff with a mindful approach that advocates a same-team mentality.
- Figure out how to respond to stress with healthy emotions and behaviors.

Providing support for student wellness is most successful when we as teachers first ensure our wellness. Let's take a closer look at ensuring personal wellness for educators.

Support the Person in the Mirror

"Oh, mirror, mirror, on the wall! Who is the fairest of them all?" (Sharpsteen et al., 1937). The relationship you have with the person in the mirror is important. You matter. Self-regulation, self-care, and self-control influence self-esteem. How you feel about yourself and perceive your competencies affects your relationships and behaviors with students, families, professionals, and friends. Often, the school day's events spill over to personal relationships with friends and families, too. Let's digest this concept by *slicing your pie* (how you expend your energetic and emotional resources) and examining your approach to educator wellness. Read on for more explanation and application on how to support that person in the mirror with increased awareness, purpose, and organization.

Slicing My Pie

Achieving wellness means being kind to yourself, with increased awareness and control of how to slice your pie. All age groups and skill sets are invited to participate in this activity, which requires only a paper plate or hand-drawn circle and a writing implement.

I often tell teachers, administrators, students, and families that when they are feeling *stressed*, they need to spin that around to think *desserts* (*stressed* spelled backward!). Perceptions affect results. On a given day, inclusion teachers and school professionals face a plethora of events and situations generated by interactions with students, families, and colleagues. Professionals go home to their own children, families, and responsibilities, whether that is taking a continuing education course on campus or online, driving a carpool, or caring for an older parent. Students face pressure if they do or say the wrong thing in front of adults or peers. Some students and adults care and think more or less about their own wellness.

The reality we all share is that there are only twenty-four hours in a day, and you cannot be cloned. Specific prior knowledge includes knowing that a circle has 360 degrees and that 8 hours (one-third of the day) is recommended for eating. You are human, not a machine. Just some facts for thought! Let's concretize this SEL concept by *slicing our pies*.

I invite you to do this activity solo as a self-reflection and to share your product with others. In either case, simply follow these steps. (Note the fourth step is specific to sharing your pie.)

1. Think about your favorite pie, whether it is key lime, blueberry, pizza, cannoli, apple, pumpkin, mince, or other. If you don't like pie, select another food in the shape of a circle that makes you smile (for example, a donut, pancake, tortilla, or crepe).

2. Think about a typical twenty-four-hour school day and divide the circle into degrees to indicate personal and professional responsibilities and daily time divisions on a given professional day (Monday–Friday, if those are the school days). Share what's "on your plate" before, during, and after school hours.

3. Within each section of your pie, add a word that categorizes that part of your professional or personal day. Include the have-tos, whether that's being on bus duty in school or walking the dog. Also, include unrelated professional activities and the want-tos, such as cozying up to a book, going for a brisk walk, humming a tune, or watching a movie.

Figure 7.1 contains a sample "slicing my pie" activity.

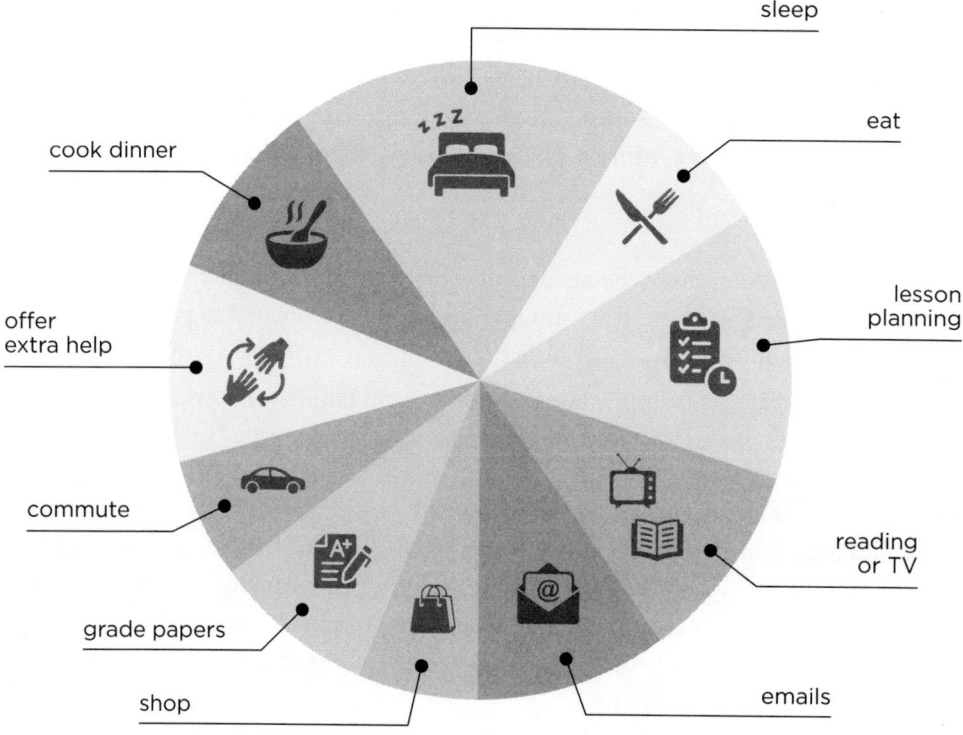

Figure 7.1: Sample "slicing my pie" activity.

After completing your pie, share it with a friend or colleague like a co-teacher or with a group of grade-level teachers or peers, or maybe share it with a spouse or friend.

After completing this activity, reflect on *your pie* to think about *which slices* need to be reduced or perhaps expanded. Also imagine, if you could share some of the roles and responsibilities or *have-tos* with others, how this would change your day. Healthy classroom environments promote a cooperative and personalized learning atmosphere that allows peers and colleagues to effectively work together to achieve goals and competencies with different levels of support. Teachers can complete this activity with students, customizing it for age and skill set, to create and share their pies with peers.

If you're feeling unwell, it's time to shift your daily responsibilities and add activities that support you to be more appropriately aligned with your capacity. Wellness means making time for activities that support us to manage stress, whether that is through mindfulness, meditation, talking to a friend, or another enjoyable activity.

Educator Wellness

Educator wellness includes the development of and reflection on positive routines, setting boundaries, developing confidence, relating well to others, and knowing oneself. That includes what, where, or when to eat, sleep, rest, move, and do things that make you and others smile.

Educators and authors Timothy D. Kanold and Tina H. Boogren (2022) describe the following four categories of wellness.

1. **Physical:** Physical wellness for inclusion educators involves maintaining good physical health. It includes practices such as regular exercise, proper nutrition, adequate sleep, and managing stress that is never planned, but often presented. Educators who prioritize physical wellness are more likely to have the energy and stamina needed to effectively teach and engage with students and each other. Physical health can impact one's ability to handle the demands and stresses of the teaching profession.

2. **Mental:** Mental wellness for inclusion educators focuses on their cognitive health. Maintaining mental wellness involves developing strategies for stress management, problem solving, and keeping a positive outlook, despite "inclusion hiccups." Optimistic outlooks, such as thinking that a glass is half full, is helpful. Mental health includes focusing on the advances, even though more progress is required. Interim celebrations inspire future strides. Access to mental health resources and support is essential for general and special educators, families, students, and administrators.

3. **Emotional:** Emotional wellness in education involves recognizing and managing emotions effectively. Teachers frequently encounter diverse student needs, and this can be emotionally taxing. Educators need to cultivate emotional intelligence, resilience, and self-care practices to prevent burnout and maintain their emotional well-being. Being in touch with their own emotions also enables educators to better support their students' emotional development.

4. **Social:** Social wellness for educators pertains to their relationships and interactions within the school, community, and beyond. Inclusion environments build relationships with colleagues, students, and families. Collaborating with other educators, sharing experiences, and seeking mentorship or peer support can enhance social well-being. Furthermore, educators who have a strong social support system are better equipped to handle the challenges of their profession to replace frustrations and perceived impasses with smiles and solutions.

Learning Forward, a prominent professional learning organization, has an article titled "8 Dimensions of Wellness for Educators" (Montoya & Summers, 2021). It reminds us of the importance of self-care, whether that's going to the gym or writing things in a gratitude journal. The school culture affects the wellness of students and teachers. Table 7.1 (page 154) provides an overview of the eight dimensions.

Table 7.1: Eight Dimensions of Wellness

1. Emotional	Awareness, acceptance, expression, adjusting, coping, relationships
2. Environmental	Classroom and school cleanliness, lighting, décor, comfort level
3. Intellectual	Creativity inspiration, opposite of stagnation, professional development, growth in knowledge and skills about how students learn with responsive pedagogy
4. Physical	Exercise, diet, mental well-being
5. Social	Healthy interactions with others with work-community balance
6. Spiritual	Not excluded to religion, but it also includes purpose and a sense of belonging with introspection and activities and resources such as mindfulness and reflections
7. Occupational	Meaningful work engagement, self-efficacy on the job *Who do you talk to at work?* *What patterns do you notice?*
8. Financial	Economic stability, equity, health benefits

Source: Adapted from Montoya & Summers, 2021.

Inclusion classrooms require educators to be particularly attentive to these dimensions of wellness, as they face unique challenges in meeting the diverse needs of their students. Educators in inclusion classrooms are both aware and adaptable, with the right degrees of structure and concern. They often work with students who have a wide range of emotional needs that require specific interventions to diffuse unwanted behaviors. That means understanding and managing both students and their own emotions to then be equipped to provide the effective support.

Professionals who stay updated on best practices for inclusive teaching can address the diverse learning needs of their students. Creating an inclusive and comfortable physical environment is essential in inclusion classrooms. This involves arranging the classroom layout to accommodate different learning styles and providing sensory-friendly spaces for students who need that release.

Inclusion professionals also need to find meaning and self-efficacy in their work. This means that inclusion teachers feel confident in their ability to meet the needs of all students. Inclusion professionals recognize the importance of their role in fostering an inclusion classroom. Collaboration catapults us and our shared students forward. Building positive relationships with all students, regardless of their abilities or backgrounds, is vital in inclusion classrooms. Inclusion professionals can foster an environment of inclusion and respect among students, promoting healthy social interactions.

By addressing these dimensions, educators can better support the academic, social, and emotional growth of all students in inclusive settings.

A Ten-Step Intervention Plan

The following ten steps highlight the critical inclusion intervention components that value academic achievement and emotional wellness for professionals, students, and families (Karten, 2017c). These steps define ability by students' strengths, not their deficits. They include needs-based instruction infused with evidence-based practices. Progress includes competencies and wellness in students, families, and professionals. This involves progress monitoring to reach the learning targets. Feedback and self-reflection play a crucial role in building competencies. The progress monitoring involves evaluating student learning, assessing the effectiveness of instruction, and making necessary adjustments to improve academic progress. In other words, where did they start, how are they doing now, and what other paths need to be paved?

Collaboration with inclusion facilitation, coaching, and feedback occurs to differentiate instruction to engage students effectively. Inclusion teachers are fluid and flexible to adapt to the ever-present evolving general and special education student needs presented within that inclusion classroom. Learning is a continuous entity for students, families, and professionals. It happens one step at a time to achieve academic acumen, personal wellness, and professional growth. Consider the following inclusion applications to ADMIRE.

1. **High expectations:** Opportunities for achievements within the core curriculum are universal for students of all ability levels. This includes students with and without IEPs. That means we focus on what students can do—their competencies and the supports needed to build those competencies. We redefine ability according to student strength. To promote increased awareness, consider an activity such as the *BioAbility Poem*. It invites students to explore how others with difference achieved accomplishments. The writing frame is an adaptation for students who lack syntactic and paragraph structure. Figure 7.2 (page 156) provides a poem you can use with students either with or without the graphics.

2. **Reflective learning:** Students and staff evaluate progress and reflect on the next steps to meet learning goals, looking at where they were, where they are, how they will proceed, what they achieved, and what lies ahead. Feedback and self-reflection respectively support and build competencies.

3. **Systematic, evidence-based practices:** Educators select systematic and explicit evidence-based practices to match social, emotional, and behavioral acumens and instructional levels at student skill sets. Consult reputable sites, such as What Works Clearinghouse from the Institute of Education Sciences (https://ies.ed.gov/ncee/WWC), the IRIS Center at Vanderbilt University (https://iris.peabody.vanderbilt.edu/pd-hours/school-district-platform/available-modules), and CAST (www.cast.org).

> **BioAbility Poem**
>
> _____ is a person who
> (First name of person chosen)
>
> is (was) _____, _____, _____.
> (Three adjectives that describe this person)
>
> **This person has (had) difficulties**
> Describe difference in one paragraph.
>
> _____
> _____
> _____
> _____
>
> **They loved**
> Describe strengths and abilities with real-life examples.
>
> _____
> _____
> _____
>
> **They learned to**
> Describe accomplishments and successes.
>
> _____
> _____
>
> **What they actually said or would say about themself** (share a quote).
>
> _____
> _____

Figure 7.2: BioAbility poem.

Visit **go.SolutionTree.com/specialneeds** for a free reproducible of this figure.

4. **Progress monitoring:** Progress monitoring is ongoing and shared with students, family, and all staff to guide literacy and mathematics instruction with ongoing assessments, discussion, and reflection. Progress monitoring includes the following.

   - Frequent and ongoing evaluation of student learning
   - Monitoring the effectiveness of instruction
   - Making instructional changes based on evaluations to improve students' academic progress (IRIS Center, n.d.c)

5. **Collaborative work:** Staff members work together by coaching one another and capitalizing on one another's competencies to deliver and differentiate tiered instruction to appropriately engage students.

6. **Challenges as opportunities:** Staff expect and welcome challenges as opportunities to strengthen individual, small-group, and whole-class instruction. For example, challenges can include scheduling issues, lack of resources, varying levels of student prior knowledge and interest, language and cultural differences, lower and higher degrees of staff and learner responsibility, and students who have more or less home support. Teachers who face challenges by planning for successful outcomes acknowledge the challenges, but they are also able to forge ahead with responsive and collaborative plans.

7. **Needs-based instruction and intervention:** Individual needs drive decisions and interventions.

8. **Fluidity and flexibility:** The system of intervention is fluid and flexible. Students are able to move within the tiers easily as they master academic and behavioral skills and learn new ones. Teachers monitor and change the course of the instruction or supports to honor student needs and levels.

9. **Focus on critical thinking:** Learners of all skill sets are critical thinkers. Inclusion learners reason effectively; use systems thinking, judgments, and decisions; and solve problems.

10. **Lifelong learning:** Educators, staff, and administrators develop effective lifelong learners. Learning is unavoidable and happens all the time. Lifelong learning is about creating and maintaining a positive attitude to achieve personal wellness and professional growth. If teachers learn, so do the students.

ADMIRE Relationships

Professional and personal relationships are complex. Relationships are not achieved with automaticity, but they require structure and time to develop. A new teacher requires more guidance on how to interact with colleagues and families. Co-teachers who have never worked together form healthy relationships as they get to know each other, their diverse students, and the curriculum.

If they've never taught that subject or grade before, then it becomes more complicated, but it can be seen as an opportunity for growth, especially with the support of colleagues. I navigated this experience with a special education teacher who was assigned to a German class, although she didn't speak the language. At first glance, this seems like a terrible idea—how was she going to provide instruction about a subject she's unfamiliar with? Initially, she didn't take the news well, and I worried she wouldn't have the capacity to fill the role. Serving as the inclusion facilitator, I coached her to shift her thinking about the situation: Given that it was a German 1 class, the students didn't know the language either. Then, I invited her to think about how she would approach learning the language and to translate that to the student instruction. That included all of the inclusion principles and how to ADMIRE German, even though prior experience differed.

No matter the situation, as educators, we communicate as professionals, whether there is agreement or disagreement with a methodology for instruction for the whole class, small groups, or individual students. Administrators who pair educators as co-teachers also need to think about roles, experiences, and compatibility (Karten, 2015).

Figure 7.3 illustrates how inclusion professionals, students, and families are the core. The spokes are the evidence-based practices that surround the people who collaboratively evolve and revolve with their application.

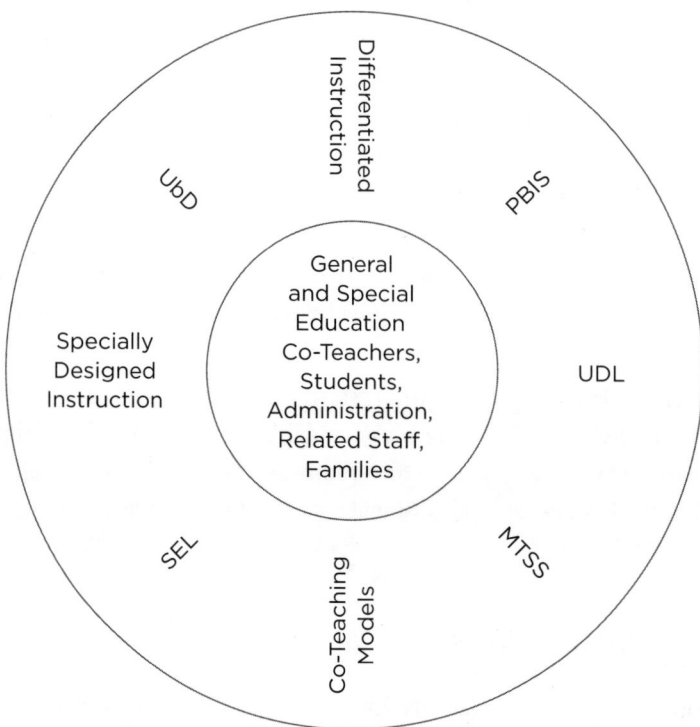

Source: *Adapted from Karten, 2019.*
Figure 7.3: Core relationships and evidence-based practices.

Inclusion competencies and supports cannot happen without the people they serve and their relationships with one another.

Figure 7.4 contains a graphic organizer that reminds us that inclusion wellness hinges on people, places, and things. Consider using the online template to brainstorm the people, places, and things in your context that support your well-being. Consider using this resource with students around the topic of well-being in addition to content-specific topics.

Wellness cannot be achieved if the inclusion stakeholders in the first column, *the people*, are overwhelmed. Figure 7.5 (page 160) features a chart that visually reinforces several concepts discussed in the ADMIRE inclusion framework. As noted by the bus, plane, train, boat, and car, depending on the *inclusion topography*, the learning paths require different vehicles to explore, expand, embrace, engage, and empower wellness.

People, Places, and Things Chart		
Name: Elements of an Inclusion Classroom **Directions:** Identify the people, places, and things to consider in a successful inclusion classroom.		
People	**Places**	**Things**
Students with and without IEPs	General education classroom	IEPs
Families	Self-contained	Technology
Administration	Resource room	Inclusion principles
General education teachers	Community	Attitudes
Special education teachers	Out-of-district placement	Beliefs
Caregivers	Specials, like art, music, physical education, and world language	Biases
Parents	Hallway	Collaboration
Related service providers (speech-language pathologists, occupational therapists, and physical therapists)	Bathroom	Discrimination
Outside agencies	Cafeteria	Acceptance
Guidance counselors	LRE (least restricted environment)	A way of life
School psychologists	World	Friendship
Medical staff (nurse, audiologist, and so on)	Side-by-side	Respect
Mobility trainers	Life	Independence
Write a paragraph describing the important people, places, and things you read about. Use three words from each column.	Use this space to write your paragraph. Inclusion, a way of life, is contingent on its people, places, and things for students with and without IEPs to experience successful outcomes. This means that general education and special education teachers, along with families and related service providers, collaborate with each other to diminish barriers. Inclusion principles remind us that we are a community of learners.	
Nine words used: community, life, general education, special education, students, families, teachers, providers, principles		

Source: Adapted from Karten, 2017c.

Figure 7.4: *Sample people, places, and things chart.*

	LEARNING PATHS 🚌 ✈ 🚆 ⛵ 🚗				
	EXPLORE	**EXPAND**	**EMBRACE**	**ENGAGE**	**EMPOWER**
E to the fifth 👣	Choice boards	Progress monitoring	Evidence-based practices	Norms	Yourself
	PBIS	Self-efficacy	Data	VAKT	Students
	Strengths and interests	Peer collaboration	Inclusion principles	Inquiry	Families
	Adaptations	Professional development	Differences	Small-group discussion	Colleagues

Figure 7.5: *"E to the fifth" learning paths.*

Consider the following examples of learning paths a teacher might choose given this chart.

- *Explore* choice boards to disengage power struggles.
- *Expand* professional development by slotting time to plan ideas during scheduled faculty meets.
- *Embrace* the inclusion principles with ongoing applications.
- *Engage* inquiry to promote higher-level thinking skills.
- *Empower* yourself, students, families, and colleagues with the knowledge and skills to advance.

Pause for a moment and consider ways you might navigate these learning paths in your classroom.

It's important to recognize that imperfections are often more valuable than perfections, what blogger John Spacey (2020) calls *perfect imperfection*. People possess complex and diverse strengths and abilities. No matter how altruistic a character in a story is, they often draw increased reader interest by their imperfection or deviation from the norm. Spacey shares seven examples of perfect imperfection: likability, craft, asymmetry, wabi-sabi (a Japanese art that makes the basic interesting), uniqueness, complexity, and perfection of the whole. Think about how an item you create by hand, that may have imperfections, has unique value when compared to a manufactured version. A superhero may have extraordinary abilities, but part of their charm lies in their vulnerability. Sometimes, what is perceived as a flaw turns into an admirable trait. In art, asymmetrical design is often more appealing than uniformity. In addition, while individual parts may not be perfect, the whole itself has value and individual character when the parts complement one another.

The same is true with inclusion. As educators, we must do our best to create inclusion environments that contribute to student well-being while acknowledging the imperfections along the way. Let's ADMIRE inclusion as a *perfectly imperfect* way to educate our learners as they learn and advance side by side in schools and in life.

The letter in this book's introduction (page 1) emphasizes how inclusion professionals are the architects who, together with students and their families, build one *inclusion floor* at a time. Each of the chapters in this book offers ways that we live and breathe the inclusion principles with evidence-based practices and the knowledge and scaffolding required. As inclusion professionals, we include planning, prep, resources, support, reflection, dedication, respect, compassion, and collaboration.

As the author, I am a passionate believer that inclusion is more than doable, but it's something to continually ADMIRE. Here's the last wrap-up to summarize a few salient points to ADMIRE inclusion through the lenses of academic, emotional, social, and physical wellness.

- **A**ssess who needs more, who needs less, and who needs different engagement and **a**ctivate mega-, macro-, and micro-inclusion plans with UDL.
- **D**ecide on how to differentiate instruction for content and process, and **d**elineate how high expectations apply to all students across the subjects, whether or not a student has an IEP.
- **M**odel "can do and will do" attitudes, and **m**onitor complexities and competencies on the inclusion journey toward mastery.
- **I**nstruct with discrete task analysis, and **i**nvolve the other stuff (for example, MTSS, game-based learning, humor, neuroscience, DI, PBL, PBIS, SEL, UbD, voice-choice, music, art, movement, VAKT).
- **R**eflect on adaptations and pacing for the whole class, cooperative centers, and individual learners, and **r**evise inclusion lessons based on data and progress monitoring.
- **E**ngage critical thinking skills with ongoing small-group peer interactions within inclusion classrooms, and **e**nrich outcomes with eyes focused on how current levels of academic achievement and functional performance guide the next steps to achieve advancements.

Conclusion

Inclusion wellness fosters belonging and promotes advancement. Wellness includes cultivating relationships in class and school environments that allow students to feel safe and valued. It requires collective effort from administrators, educators, students, support staff, families, and the community to create an inclusive environment that nurtures the well-being of all its members. Wellness is front and center in the inclusion classroom to help the professionals support students and families to meaningfully belong, participate, and contribute benefit to themselves and others. Take a moment to reflect on the information and strategies you've read by completing the "Admiring Wellness" reproducible at the end of this chapter.

Admiring Wellness

Use the following template to ADMIRE the actions to promote wellness. In the space provided, note which of the ADMIRE action items stood out to you from this chapter.

A — Assess and Activate	
D — Decide and Delineate	
M — Model and Monitor	
I — Instruct and Involve	
R — Reflect and Revise	
E — Engage and Enrich	

The ADMIRE Framework for Inclusion © 2024 Solution Tree Press • SolutionTree.com
Visit **go.SolutionTree.com/specialneeds** to download this free reproducible.

Epilogue

To wrap up *The ADMIRE Framework for Inclusion*, let's engage with this book's academic content in the following ways.

- A word cloud
- True or false questions
- An edutaining pictograph
- An online collaborative platform

Yes, this epilogue contains text, but the multiple presentations and engagements with visuals such as word clouds, icons, guided questions, and an online platform remind professionals to differentiate. I invite you to view these models and to then think about the multiple ways you'll assess and activate, decide and delineate, model and monitor, instruct and involve, reflect and revise, and engage and enrich your inclusion environments.

Inclusion Word Cloud

Inclusion professionals assess and activate, decide and delineate, model and monitor, instruct and involve, reflect and revise, and engage and enrich positive actions in inclusion environments with multiple practices and modalities.

Figure E.1 (page 166) features a word cloud generated with Word It Out (https://worditout.com/word-cloud/create) using this book's key vocabulary. Notice that the word *students* is the largest, as they are the largest focus. The words *professionals*, *model*, *environment*, *learning*, *practices*, and *classroom* appear bolder and larger because of their significance in inclusion classrooms. This representation of information is offered as a model to reinforce the value of visuals.

How might word clouds benefit your students to connect to and reinforce the *big* ideas for their academic content?

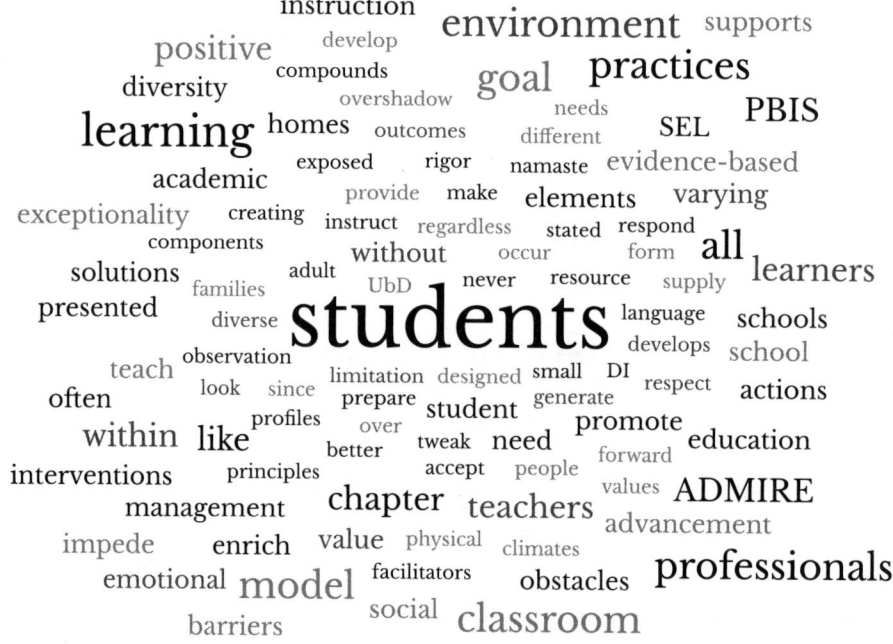

Figure E.1: ADMIRE inclusion word cloud.

True or False Questions

Respond to the following statements in figure E.2 as *true* or *false* and return to the specific chapters to review the content in more detail and discuss application with your colleagues.

Chapter 1: What Students and Staff Need to Know
_____ When we ADMIRE inclusion, we honor the implications of neuroscience to deliver the content to students whose brains may need something different to solidify what is taught into their working memories.
Chapter 2: Think Individuals, Not Categories
_____ Each student enters an inclusion classroom with various ability levels, prior successes, interests, needs, likes, and dislikes.
Chapter 3: Connect to the Realities That Teachers, Students, and Families Face
_____ We look at how students respond to interventions and then visually, physically, academically, and collaboratively organize the classroom, school, and home environment and practices.

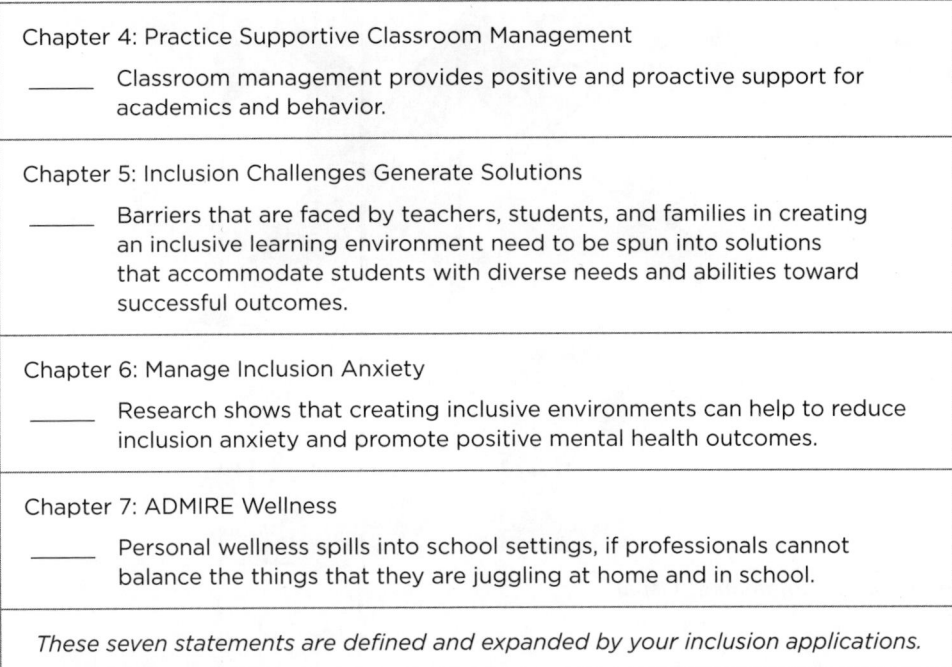

Chapter 4: Practice Supportive Classroom Management
_____ Classroom management provides positive and proactive support for academics and behavior.
Chapter 5: Inclusion Challenges Generate Solutions
_____ Barriers that are faced by teachers, students, and families in creating an inclusive learning environment need to be spun into solutions that accommodate students with diverse needs and abilities toward successful outcomes.
Chapter 6: Manage Inclusion Anxiety
_____ Research shows that creating inclusive environments can help to reduce inclusion anxiety and promote positive mental health outcomes.
Chapter 7: ADMIRE Wellness
_____ Personal wellness spills into school settings, if professionals cannot balance the things that they are juggling at home and in school.
These seven statements are defined and expanded by your inclusion applications.

Figure E.2: ADMIRE inclusion true or false.

An Edutaining Pictograph

As noted throughout the book, fun activities, edutainment (ADMIRE model 65, from table I.1, page 4), and academic rigor are compatible elements that form strong compounds that bond the learning to students' lives. Edutainment offers multiple pathways for students to learn, such as playing online games and watching videos (Giraldo, Jenkins, & Tungatarova, 2022). Studies have shown that play can enter classrooms way beyond the preschool years (Parker, Thomsen, & Berry, 2022). Play fosters cognitive, social, emotional, creative, and physical skills through active and iterative learning engagement (Giraldo et al., 2022). Some students need *razzle* and *dazzle* to better attend, engage, and understand concepts they've never encountered before and may not care much about. Figure E.3 (page 168) offers a visual representation of edutainment.

When fun enters inclusion classrooms, there's a window of learning opportunities to evolve, grow, and soar. With its grouped icons and shapes, this image is analogous to inclusion classrooms, where we complement one another to evolve, grow, and soar. When education bonds with entertainment, that promotes growth and advancements.

Figure E.3: Edutainment visual.

A Digital Platform

Last but not least, this online resource is offered to assess and activate, decide and delineate, model and monitor, instruct and involve, reflect and revise, and engage and enrich your inclusion practices.

The ADMIRE Padlet is an online resource that provides digital interaction, representation, and engagement with the sixty-five ADMIRE actions. It includes classroom examples, research applications, activities, and revisitation with our text. You are invited to peruse these resources for further application in your inclusion environments. You're welcome to comment on the Padlet as well. As our title states, we as professionals collaboratively *ADMIRE the inclusion framework with positive strategies that pave the way for students of all abilities.* Scan the QR code to access the Padlet.

What happens next depends on your environmental supports and the fidelity to ADMIRE inclusion. I look forward to your positive response to the invitation in our introduction.

References and Resources

Ainscow, M., Dyson, A., & Weiner, S. (2013). *From exclusion to inclusion: Ways of responding in schools to students with special educational needs.* Berkshire, England: CfBT Education Trust. Accessed at https://files.eric.ed.gov/fulltext/ED546818.pdf on November 6, 2023.

Ainsworth, L. (2022, March 29). *Common formative assessments 2.0* [Blog post]. Accessed at www.larryainsworth.com/blog/common-formative-assessments-20 on November 6, 2023.

Allen, M., & Phillips, M. (2022, January 24). *Using choice boards to boost student engagement.* Accessed at www.edutopia.org/article/using-choice-boards-boost-student-engagement on November 6, 2023.

Alter, P., & Haydon, T. (2017). Characteristics of effective classroom rules: A review of the literature. *Teacher Education and Special Education, 40*(2), 114–127.

American Chemical Society. (2023, August 16). *What is a chemical reaction?* Accessed at www.acs.org/middleschoolchemistry/lessonplans/chapter6/lesson1.html on November 6, 2023.

American Psychiatric Association. (2013). *Diagnostic and statistical manual of mental disorders* (5th ed.). Washington, DC: Author.

Angelou, M. (1978). *And still I rise.* New York: Random House.

Angelou, M. (2008). *Letter to my daughter.* New York: Random House.

Armstrong, P. (2010). *Bloom's taxonomy.* Accessed at https://cft.vanderbilt.edu/guides-sub-pages/blooms-taxonomy on June 8, 2023.

Armstrong, T. (2016). *The power of the adolescent brain: Strategies for teaching middle and high school students.* Alexandria, VA: ASCD.

Arway, T. L. (2023, April 6). *MTSS: More than alphabet soup.* Accessed at www.nea.org/professional-excellence/student-engagement/tools-tips/mtss-more-alphabet-soup on November 6, 2023.

ASCD. (2009, April 1). *What research says about . . . / Small-group intervention for ELLs.* Accessed at www.ascd.org/el/articles/small-group-intervention-for-ells on March 4, 2024.

August, G. J., Piehler, T. F., & Miller, F. G. (2018). Getting "SMART" about implementing multi-tiered systems of support to promote school mental health. *Journal of School Psychology, 66,* 85–96. https://doi.org/10.1016/j.jsp.2017.10.001

Autism Speaks. (n.d.). *Social skills and autism.* Accessed at www.autismspeaks.org/social-skills-and-autism on April 10, 2024.

Babik, I., & Gardner, E. S. (2021). Factors affecting the perception of disability: A developmental perspective. *Frontiers in Psychology, 12.* https://doi.org/10.3389/fpsyg.2021.702166

Barnes, E. D., Grills, A. E., & Vaughn, S. R. (2023, July 3). *Relationships between anxiety, attention, and reading comprehension in children.* Accessed at https://assets.researchsquare.com/files/rs-3088436/v1/1a677ba1-e372-4ae0-9953-b2f712ce9e90.pdf?c=1688391269 on November 6, 2023.

Barrera, I., & Corso, R. M. (2003). *Skilled dialogue: Strategies for responding to cultural diversity in early childhood.* Baltimore: Brookes.

Baru, J. S., Bloom, D. A., Muraszko, K., & Koop, C. E. (2001). John Holter's shunt. *Journal of the American College of Surgeons, 192*(1), 79–85.

Baumgardner, D. J. (2019). Social isolation among families caring for children with disabilities. *Journal of Patient-Centered Research and Reviews, 6*(4), 229–232.

Belland, B. R., Glazewski, K. D., & Ertmer, P. A. (2009). Inclusion and problem-based learning: Roles of students in a mixed-ability group. *Research in Middle Level Education, 32*(9), 1–19.

Belsky, G. (n.d.). *What is executive function?* Accessed at www.understood.org/en/articles/what-is-executive-function on April 10, 2024.

Bill & Melinda Gates Foundation. (2024). *Diversity, equity, and inclusion.* Accessed at www.gatesfoundation.org/about/diversity-equity-inclusion on April 10, 2024.

Birnbaum, D., & Ryan, M. (2016, March 1). *"People v. O.J. Simpson" star Sterling K. Brown on playing Chris Darden and how his view of the verdict changed.* Accessed at https://variety.com/2016/tv/features/people-v-o-j-simpson-sterling-k-brown-chris-darden-1201692561/ on March 1, 2024.

Bloom, B. S. (Ed.). (1956). *Taxonomy of educational objectives: The classification of educational goals; Handbook I: Cognitive domain.* New York: McKay.

Bloom, B. S. (1976). *Human characteristics and school learning.* New York: McGraw-Hill.

Bradshaw, C. P., Mitchell, M. M., & Leaf, P. J. (2010). Examining the effects of schoolwide positive behavioral interventions and supports on student outcomes: Results from a randomized controlled effectiveness trial in elementary schools. *Journal of Positive Behavior Interventions, 12*(3), 133–148.

Bradshaw, C. P., Reinke, W. M., Brown, L. D., Bevans, K. B., & Leaf, P. J. (2008). Implementation of school-wide positive behavioral interventions and supports (PBIS) in elementary schools: Observations from a randomized trial. *Education and Treatment of Children, 31*(1), 1–26.

Brooks, G. (n.d.). *In the arts: My grandmother is waiting for me to come home.* Accessed at https://realblackgrandmothers.com/arts-grandmother-waiting-come-home/in-the-arts/ on March 6, 2024.

Bruner, J. S. (1961). The act of discovery. *Harvard Educational Review, 31*, 21–32.

Capp, M. J. (2017). The effectiveness of universal design for learning: A meta-analysis of literature between 2013 and 2016. *International Journal of Inclusive Education, 21*(8), 791–807.

Cárdenas, D., Lattimore, F., Steinberg, D., & Reynolds, K. J. (2022). Youth well-being predicts later academic success. *Scientific Reports, 12*, Article 2134.

Carlson, E. N. (2013). Overcoming the barriers to self-knowledge: Mindfulness as a path to seeing yourself as you really are. *Perspectives on Psychological Science, 8*(2), 173–186.

Carrington, S., Tangen, D., & Beutel, D. (2019). Inclusive education in the Asia Indo-Pacific region. *International Journal of Inclusive Education, 23*(1), 1–6.

CAST. (n.d.). *About Universal Design for Learning.* Accessed at www.udlcenter.org/aboutudl on March 5, 2024.

Centers for Disease Control and Prevention (CDC). (2023, March 24). *Prevalence and characteristics of autism spectrum disorder among children aged 8 years—Autism and developmental disabilities monitoring network, 11 sites, United States, 2020.* Accessed at www.cdc.gov/mmwr/volumes/72 /ss/ss7202a1.htm?s_cid=ss7202a1_w on April 10, 2024.

Center for Parent Information and Resources. (2022). *Inclusion in the classroom.* Accessed at www .parentcenterhub.org/inclusion on April 10, 2024.

Center for Parent Information and Resources. (2024, May). *Other health impairment.* Accessed at www.parentcenterhub.org/ohi/#idea on November 6, 2023.

Center for Teaching Excellence. (2024, March 18). *Intercultural competence.* Accessed at https:// cteresources.bc.edu/documentation/intercultural-competence/#466998682-bpw2aa on April 10, 2024.

Chick, N. (2013). *Metacognition.* Accessed at https://cft.vanderbilt.edu/guides-sub-pages/metacognition on September 19, 2023.

Coerr, E. (1999). *Sadako and the thousand paper cranes* (R. Himler, Illus.). New York: Puffin.

Cologon, K. (2022). Is inclusive education really for everyone? Family stories of children and young people labelled with "severe and multiple" or "profound" "disabilities." *Research Papers in Education, 37*(3), 395–417. https://doi.org/10.1080/02671522.2020.1849372

Colorín Colorado. (n.d.). *How to create a welcoming classroom environment for ELLs.* Accessed at www .colorincolorado.org/article/how-create-welcoming-classroom-environment on March 7, 2024.

Cosier, M., Causton-Theoharis, J., & Theoharis, G. (2013). Does access matter? Time in general education and achievement for students with disabilities. *Remedial and Special Education, 34*(6), 323–332.

Curwin, R. L., Mendler, A. N., & Mendler, B. D. (2018). *Discipline with dignity: How to build responsibility, relationships, and respect in your classroom* (4th ed.). Alexandria, VA: ASCD.

Dalton, E. M. (2017). Beyond universal design for learning: Guiding principles to reduce barriers to digital & media literacy competence. *Journal of Media Literacy Education, 9*(2), 17–29.

Davis, A. (2016, March 8). *Voice recording with Google Docs* [Blog post]. Accessed at https:// readwriterespond.com/2016/03/voice-recording-with-google-docs on October 13, 2023.

Davis, K., & Gavidia-Payne, S. (2009). The impact of child, family, and professional support characteristics on the quality of life in families of young children with disabilities. *Journal of Intellectual & Developmental Disability, 34*(2), 153–162.

Dawson, P., & Guare, R. (2010). *Executive skills in children and adolescents: A practical guide to assessment and intervention* (2nd ed.). New York: Guilford Press.

Dawson, P., & Guare, R. (2018). *Executive skills in children and adolescents: A practical guide to assessment and intervention* (3rd ed.). New York: Guilford Press.

Demir, I., Sener, E., Karaboga, H. A., & Basal, A. (2023). Expectations of students from classroom rules: A scenario-based Bayesian network analysis. *Participatory Educational Research*, 10(1), 424–442. http://dx.doi.org/10.17275/per.23.23.10.1

Deutscher, R. R., Holthuis, N. C., Maldonado, S. I., Pecheone, R. L., Schultz, S. E., & Wei, R. C. (2021). *Project-based learning leads to gains in science and other subjects in middle school and benefits all learners.* San Rafael, CA: Lucas Education Research. Accessed at www.lucasedresearch.org/wp-content/uploads/2021/01/LTP-Research-Brief.pdf on November 6, 2023.

Dewey, J. (1916). *Democracy and education: An introduction to the philosophy of education.* New York: Macmillan.

Dewey, J. (1938). *Experience and education.* New York: Macmillan.

Dickens, C. (2012). *A tale of two cities.* New York: Penguin Classics.

Dray, B. J., & Wisneski, D. B. (2011). Mindful reflection as a process for developing culturally responsive practices. *Teaching Exceptional Children*, 44(1), 28–36.

DuFour, R., DuFour, R., Eaker, R., Many, T. W., Mattos, M., & Muhammad, A. (2024). *Learning by doing: A handbook for Professional Learning Communities at Work* (4th ed.). Bloomington, IN: Solution Tree Press.

Dunlosky, J., Rawson, K. A., Marsh, E. J., Nathan, M. J., & Willingham, D. T. (2013). Improving students' learning with effective learning techniques: Promising directions from cognitive and educational psychology. *Psychological Science in the Public Interest*, 14(1), 4–58.

DuPaul, G. J., & Stoner, G. (2014). *ADHD in the schools: Assessment and intervention strategies* (3rd ed.). New York: Guilford Press.

DuPaul, G. J., Weyandt, L. L., O'Dell, S. M., & Varejao, M. (2009). College students with ADHD: Current status and future directions. *Journal of Attention Disorders*, 13(3), 234–250.

Durlak, J. A., Weissberg, R. P., Dymnicki, A. B., Taylor, R. D., & Schellinger, K. B. (2011). The impact of enhancing students' social and emotional learning: A meta-analysis of school-based universal interventions. *Child Development*, 82(1), 405–432.

Egilson, S. T., & Traustadottir, R. (2009). Participation of students with physical disabilities in the school environment. *American Journal of Occupational Therapy*, 63(3), 264–272.

Ehmke, R. (2023, October 30). *How does anxiety affect kids in school?* Accessed at https://childmind.org/article/classroom-anxiety-in-children on November 6, 2023.

English Standard Version Bible (ESV). (2016). Wheaton, IL: Crossway.

Espada, M. (2006). *The republic of poetry: Poems.* New York: Norton.

Felver, J. C., Celis-de Hoyos, C. E., Tezanos, K., & Singh, N. N. (2016). A systematic review of mindfulness-based interventions for youth in school settings. *Mindfulness*, 7(1), 34–45.

Ferlazzo, L. (2023, May 2). *How teachers are using artificial intelligence in classes today* [Blog post]. Accessed at www.edweek.org/technology/opinion-how-teachers-are-using-artificial-intelligence-in-classes-today/2023/05 on September 19, 2023.

Fischer, H. (1964). The psychology of Piaget and its educational applications. *International Review of Education*, 10(4), 431–440.

Flatow, I. (Host). (2006, January 20). A conversation with Temple Grandin [Audio podcast episode]. In *Short Wave*. Accessed at www.npr.org/2006/01/20/5165123/a-conversation-with-temple-grandin on January 10, 2024.

Flint, L. J. (2010). Using life-story research for gifted education: Part three: Implications for practice. *Gifted Children*, *4*(2), 1–5.

Fox, D. (2000). Classroom assessment data: Asking the right questions. *Leadership*, *30*(2), 22–23.

Frank, A. (1952). *Anne Frank: The diary of a young girl* (B. M. Mooyaart-Doubleday, Trans.). New York: Bantam Books.

Freeman, J., Simonsen, B., McCoach, D. B., Sugai, G., Lombardi, A., & Horner, R. (2016). Relationship between school-wide positive behavior interventions and supports and academic, attendance, and behavior outcomes in high schools. *Journal of Positive Behavior Interventions*, *18*(1), 41–51. https://doi.org/10.1177/1098300715580992

Friend, M. (2020). *Interactions: Collaboration skills for school professionals* (9th ed.). Hoboken, NJ: Pearson.

Friend, M., & Bursuck, W. D. (2019). *Including students with special needs: A practical guide for classroom teachers* (8th ed.). New York: Pearson.

Frost, R. (1977). *North of Boston* (E. C. Lathem, Ed.). New York: Dodd.

Galla, B. M., Wood, J. J., Tsukayama, E., Har, K., Chiu, A. W., & Langer, D. A. (2014). A longitudinal multilevel model analysis of the within-person and between-person effect of effortful engagement and academic self-efficacy on academic performance. *Journal of School Psychology*, *52*(3), 295–308.

Gathercole, S. E., Alloway, T. P., Kirkwood, H. J., Elliott, J. G., Holmes, J., & Hilton, K. A. (2008). Attentional and executive function behaviours in children with poor working memory. *Learning and Individual Differences*, *18*(2), 214–223.

George, P. S. (2005). A rationale for differentiating instruction in the regular classroom. *Theory Into Practice*, *44*(3), 185–193.

Ghosh, N. (2021). CBR practice and inclusion: Persons with disabilities in northeast India. *Disability, CBR and Inclusive Development*, *32*(4), 114–133.

Giangreco, M. F., Shogren, K. A., & Dymond, S. K. (2020). Educating students with severe disabilities: Foundational concepts and practices. In F. Brown, J. McDonnell, & M. E. Snell (Eds.), *Instruction of students with severe disabilities: Meeting the needs of children and youth with intellectual disabilities, multiple disabilities, and autism spectrum disorders* (9th ed., pp. 1–27). New York: Pearson.

Giraldo, J.-P., Jenkins, R., & Tungatarova, A. (2022, June 9). *The case for edutainment: Rethinking how we can enable multiple pathways to learning for all children* [Blog post]. Accessed at www.unicef.org/blog/edutainment-multiple-pathways-learning on November 6, 2023.

Grandin, T., & Moore, D. (2021). *Navigating autism: 9 mindsets for helping kids on the spectrum*. New York: Norton.

Haegele, J. A., Wilson, W. J., Zhu, X., Bueche, J. J., Brady, E., & Li, C. (2021). Barriers and facilitators to inclusion in integrated physical education: Adapted physical educators' perspectives. *European Physical Education Review*, *27*(2), 297–311.

Hanková, M., & Vávrová, S. (2016). Emotional and social needs of integrated disabled students in secondary school environment. *Proceida, 217*, 229–238.

Hannigan, J., Hannigan, J. D., Mattos, M., & Buffum, A. (2021). *Behavior solutions: Teaching academic and social skills through RTI at Work.* Bloomington, IN: Solution Tree Press.

Hart, B., & Risley, T. R. (2003, Spring). The early catastrophe: The 30 million word gap by age 3. *American Educator, 27*(1), 4–9.

Harvey, N. (2018). *Mindful little yogis: Self-regulation tools to empower kids with special needs to breathe and relax.* London: Singing Dragon.

Hattie, J. (2009). *Visible learning: A synthesis of over 800 meta-analyses relating to achievement.* New York: Routledge.

Hattie, J., Fisher, D., & Frey, N. (2017). *Visible learning for mathematics, grades K–12: What works best to optimize student learning.* Thousand Oaks, CA: Corwin.

Haynes, J. (n.d.). *Seven teaching strategies for classroom teachers of ELLs.* Accessed at http://ftp.everythingesl.net/inservices/seven_teaching_strategies_clas_06140.php on April 10, 2024.

Heward, W. L., Alber-Morgan, S. R., & Konrad, M. (2022). *Exceptional children: An introduction to special education* (12th ed.). Hoboken, NJ: Pearson.

Hinton, S. E. (1967). *The outsiders.* New York: Viking.

Holahan, C. J., Ragan, J. D., & Moos, R. H. (2017). Stress [Reference module]. *Neuroscience and Biobehavioral Psychology.* https://doi.org/10.1016/B978-0-12-809324-5.05724-2

Holmqvist, M., & Lelinge, B. (2021). Teachers' collaborative professional development for inclusive education. *European Journal of Special Needs Education, 36*(5), 819–833.

Howard-Jones, P. A. (2014). Neuroscience and education: Myths and messages. *Nature Reviews Neuroscience, 15*(12), 817–824.

Hughes, L. (n.d.). *Dream boogie.* Accessed at www.poetryfoundation.org/poems/151091/dream-boogie on March 6, 2024.

Iberlin, J. M. (2017). *Cultivating mindfulness in the classroom.* Bloomington, IN: Marzano Resources.

Individuals With Disabilities Education Improvement Act of 2004, Pub. L. No. 108-446 § 300.115 (2004).

IRIS Center. (n.d.a). *Available modules.* Accessed at https://iris.peabody.vanderbilt.edu/pd-hours/school-district-platform/available-modules on November 6, 2023.

IRIS Center. (n.d.b). *Page 5: Exceptionalities.* Accessed at https://iris.peabody.vanderbilt.edu/module/div/cresource/q2/p05 on November 6, 2023.

IRIS Center. (n.d.c). *Progress monitoring: Mastery measurement vs. general outcome measurement.* Accessed at https://iris.peabody.vanderbilt.edu/wp-content/uploads/modules/pmm/pdf/IRIS_PM_InfoBrief_011420.pdf on November 6, 2023.

Jensen, E. (2005). *Teaching with the brain in mind* (2nd ed.). Arlington, VA: ASCD.

Jonassen, D. (2003). Using cognitive tools to represent problems. *Journal of Research on Technology in Education, 35*(3), 362–381.

Jost, J. T., Kay, A. C., & Thorisdottir, H. (2009). *Social and psychological bases of ideology and system justification.* New York: Oxford University Press.

Jury, M., Perrin, A.-L., Rohmer, O., & Desombre, C. (2021). Attitudes toward inclusive education: An exploration of the interaction between teachers' status and students' type of disability within the French context. *Frontiers in Education, 6.* https://doi.org/10.3389/feduc.2021.655356

Kanold, T. D., & Boogren, T. H. (2022). *Educator wellness: A guide for sustaining physical, mental, emotional, and social well-being.* Bloomington, IN: Solution Tree Press.

Kart, A., & Kart, M. (2021). Academic and social effects of inclusion on students without disabilities: A review of the literature. *Education Sciences, 11*(1), Article 16. https://doi.org/10.3390/educsci11010016

Karten, T. J. (2007). *More inclusion strategies that work! Aligning student strengths with standards.* Thousand Oaks, CA: Corwin.

Karten, T. J. (2008a). *Embracing disabilities in the classroom: Strategies to maximize students' assets.* Thousand Oaks, CA: Corwin.

Karten, T. J. (2008b). *Inclusion activities that work! Grades 3–5.* Thousand Oaks, CA: Corwin.

Karten, T. J. (2008c). *Inclusion activities that work! Grades 6–8.* Thousand Oaks, CA: Corwin.

Karten, T. J. (2008d). *Inclusion activities that work! Grades K–2.* Thousand Oaks, CA: Corwin.

Karten, T. J. (2010a). *Inclusion lesson plan book for the 21st century.* Lake Worth, FL: National Professional Resources.

Karten, T. J. (2010b). *Inclusion strategies that work! Research-based methods for the classroom* (2nd ed.). Thousand Oaks, CA: Corwin.

Karten, T. J. (2015). *Inclusion strategies that work! Research-based methods for the classroom* (3rd ed.). Thousand Oaks, CA: Corwin.

Karten, T. J. (2017a). *Building on the strengths of students with special needs: How to move beyond disability labels in the classroom.* Alexandria, VA: ASCD.

Karten, T. J. (2017b). *Inclusion mastery: Competency-based strategies for students and staff.* West Palm Beach, FL: Learning Sciences International.

Karten, T. J. (2017c). *Navigating the core curriculum: RTI strategies to support every learner.* Bloomington, IN: Solution Tree Press.

Karten, T. J. (2019). *Mindfulness in the inclusive classroom.* Lake Worth, FL: National Professional Resources.

Karten, T. J. (2021). *Inclusion strategies and interventions* (2nd ed.). Bloomington, IN: Solution Tree Press.

Karten, T. J., & Murawski, W. W. (2020). *Co-teaching do's, don'ts, and do betters.* Alexandria, VA: ASCD.

Kauffman, J. M., Hallahan, D. P., Pullen, P. C., & Badar, J. (2018). *Special education: What it is and why we need it* (2nd ed.). New York: Routledge.

Kazmi, A. B., Kamran, M., & Siddiqui, S. (2023). The effect of teacher's attitudes in supporting inclusive education by catering to diverse learners. *Frontiers in Education, 8.* https://doi.org/10.3389/feduc.2023.1083963

Kerry, T. (2015). *Cross curricular teaching in the primary school: Planning and facilitating imaginative lessons* (2nd ed.). New York: Routledge.

Kim, J., & Kwon, M. (2018). Effects of mindfulness-based intervention to improve task performance for children with intellectual disabilities. *Journal of Applied Research in Intellectual Disabilities, 31*(1), 87–97.

Kingsley, E. P. (1987). *Welcome to Holland.* Accessed at www.emilyperlkingsley.com/welcome-to-holland on November 6, 2023.

Kolb, D. A. (1984). *Experiential learning: Experience as the source of learning and development.* Englewood Cliffs, NJ: Prentice-Hall.

Komunyakaa, Y. (2001). *Pleasure dome: New and collected poems.* Middletown, CT: Wesleyan University Press.

Kotter, J. P., & Cohen, D. S. (2002). *The heart of change: Real-life stories of how people change their organizations.* Boston: Harvard Business Review Press.

Larmer, J. (2015, July 13). *Project-based learning vs. problem-based learning vs. X-BL* [Blog post]. Accessed at www.edutopia.org/blog/pbl-vs-pbl-vs-xbl-john-larmer on August 11, 2015.

Learning Disabilities Association of America. (n.d.). *Graphic organizers.* Accessed at https://ldaamerica.org/info/graphic-organizers on November 6, 2023.

Lewis, C. S. (1994). *The lion, the witch, and the wardrobe* (P. Baynes, Illus.). New York: HarperCollins.

Lickteig, A. (2023). Interdisciplinary instruction. In A. Lickteig & C. R. Short (Eds.), *Effective teaching in the secondary classroom* (pp. 55–57). EdTech Books. Accessed at https://edtechbooks.org/effective_teaching_in_the_secondary_classroom/interdisciplinary_instruction on April 10, 2024.

Lindsay, G. (2007). Educational psychology and the effectiveness of inclusive education/mainstreaming. *British Journal of Educational Psychology, 77*(1), 1–24.

Lockett, E. (2022, November 16). *Tackling math anxiety: From diagnosis to treatment and more.* Accessed at www.healthline.com/health/anxiety/math-anxiety on September 19, 2023.

London, J. (1990). *The call of the wild.* New York: Dover.

Longfellow, H. W. (2001). *The midnight ride of Paul Revere* (C. Bing, Illus.). Brooklyn, NY: Handprint Books.

Low, K. (2023, November 16). *Parents with ADHD raising children with ADHD.* Accessed at www.verywellmind.com/help-for-parents-who-have-adhd-20875 on March 5, 2024.

Lucas Education Research. (n.d.). *Rigorous project-based learning is a powerful lever for improving equity.* San Rafael, CA: Author. Accessed at www.lucasedresearch.org/wp-content/uploads/2021/08/Equity-Research-Brief.pdf on November 6, 2023.

Macdonald, K. T., Cirino, P. T., Miciak, J., & Grills, A. E. (2021). The role of reading anxiety among struggling readers in fourth and fifth grade. *Reading and Writing Quarterly, 37*(4), 382–394.

MasterClass. (2022, September 26). *Palindromes defined: 9 types of palindromes.* Accessed at www.masterclass.com/articles/palindromes-explained on November 6, 2023.

McCandliss, B. D. (2010). Educational neuroscience: The early years. *Proceedings of the National Academy of Sciences, 107*(18), 8049–8050.

McGill Smith, P. (n.d.). *You are not alone: For parents when they learn that their child has a disability.* Accessed at www.parentcenterhub.org/notalone on November 6, 2023.

McGregor, G., & Vogelsberg, R. T. (1998). *Inclusive schooling practices: Pedagogical and research foundations.* Pittsburgh, PA: Allegheny University of the Health Sciences.

McTighe, J., & Wiggins, G. (2012). *Understanding by Design® framework.* Alexandria, VA: ASCD. Accessed at https://files.ascd.org/staticfiles/ascd/pdf/siteASCD/publications/UbD_WhitePaper0312.pdf on April 10, 2024.

Meyer, A., Rose, D. H., & Gordon, D. (2014). *Universal design for learning: Theory and practice.* Wakefield, MA: CAST Professional Publishing.

Montoya, A., & Summers, L. L. (2021, February). *8 dimensions of wellness for educators.* Accessed at https://learningforward.org/journal/looking-ahead/8-dimensions-of-wellness-for-educators on November 6, 2023.

Murata, A. (2013). Diversity and high academic expectations without tracking: Inclusively responsive instruction. *Journal of the Learning Sciences, 22*(2), 312–335.

National Association for Gifted Children. (n.d.). *Myths about gifted students.* Accessed at nagc.org/page/myths-about-gifted-students on November 6, 2023.

National Center for Education Statistics. (2023, May). *Students with disabilities.* Accessed at https://nces.ed.gov/programs/coe/indicator/cgg on March 5, 2024.

National Center for Education Statistics. (n.d.). *Table 204.30: Children 3 to 21 years old served under Individuals With Disabilities Education Act (IDEA), Part B, by type of disability: Selected years, 1976–77 through 2017–18.* Accessed at https://nces.ed.gov/programs/digest/d18/tables/dt18_204.30.asp?current=yes on March 5, 2024.

National Center on Accessible Educational Materials. (2023). *Defining the term "accessible."* Accessed at https://aem.cast.org/get-started/resources/aem-takeaways/defining-term-accessible on April 10, 2024.

National Center on Intensive Intervention. (n.d.). *Intensive intervention and MTSS.* Accessed at https://intensiveintervention.org/special-topics/mtss on November 6, 2023.

National Institute of Mental Health. (2023, April). *Anxiety disorders.* Accessed at www.nimh.nih.gov/health/topics/anxiety-disorders on November 6, 2023.

Neuschwander, C. (1997). *Sir Cumference and the first round table: A math adventure* (W. Geehan, Illus.). Watertown, MA: Charlesbridge.

Office of Educational Technology. (2023, May). *Artificial intelligence and the future of teaching and learning: Insights and recommendations.* Washington, DC: U.S. Department of Education. Accessed at https://tech.ed.gov/files/2023/05/ai-future-of-teaching-and-learning-report.pdf on March 6, 2024.

Open Society Foundations. (2019). *The value of inclusive education.* Accessed at www.opensocietyfoundations.org/explainers/value-inclusive-education on April 10, 2024.

Palacio, R. J. (2012). *Wonder.* New York: Knopf.

Parker, R., Thomsen, B. S., & Berry, A. (2022). Learning through play at school: A framework for policy and practice. *Frontiers in Education, 7.* https://doi.org/10.3389/feduc.2022.751801

Pas, E. T., Ryoo, J. H., Musci, R. J., & Bradshaw, C. P. (2019). A state-wide quasi-experimental effectiveness study of the scale-up of school-wide positive behavioral interventions and supports. *Journal of School Psychology, 73*, 41–55.

Pfizer. (n.d.). *What is wellness?* Accessed at www.pfizer.com/health-wellness/wellness/what-is-wellness on September 19, 2023.

Phillips, K. W. (2014, October 1). *How diversity makes us smarter: Being around people who are different from us makes us more creative, more diligent and harder-working.* Accessed at www.scientificamerican.com/article/how-diversity-makes-us-smarter/?redirect=1 on November 6, 2023.

Plucker, J. A., & Callahan, C. M. (2014). Research on giftedness and gifted education: Status of the field and considerations for the future. *Exceptional Children, 80*(4), 390–406.

Polirstok, S. (2015). Classroom management strategies for inclusive classrooms. *Creative Education, 6*(10), 927–933.

Project Zero. (2018). *Voice and choice.* Accessed at https://pz.harvard.edu/resources/voice-and-choice on November 6, 2023.

Qi, J., & Ha, A. S. (2012). Inclusion in physical education: A review of literature. *International Journal of Disability, Development and Education, 59*(3), 257–281.

Quenemoen, R. F., & Thurlow, M. L. (2017). Standards-based reform and students with disabilities. In J. M. Kauffman, D. P. Hallahan, & P. C. Pullen (Eds.), *Handbook of special education* (2nd ed., pp. 203–217). New York: Routledge.

Raath, S., & Hay, A. (2016). Self-efficacy: A South African case study on teachers' commitment to integrate climate change resilience into their teaching practices. *Cogent Education, 3*(1). https://doi.org/10.1080/2331186X.2016.1264698

Rao, K., & Meo, G. (2016). Using universal design for learning to design standards-based lessons. *SAGE Open, 6*(4). https://doi.org/10.1177/2158244016680688

Rawe, J. (n.d.). *How to teach kids with dyslexia to read.* Accessed at www.understood.org/articles/how-do-you-teach-a-child-with-dyslexia-to-read on October 13, 2023.

Rea, P. J., McLaughlin, V. L., & Walther-Thomas, C. (2002). Outcomes for students with learning disabilities in inclusive and pullout programs. *Exceptional Children, 68*(2), 203–222.

Renzulli, J. S., & Reis, S. M. (1997). *The schoolwide enrichment model: A how-to guide for educational excellence* (2nd ed.). New York: Prufrock Press.

rhyme.cool. (2023). *rhyme.cool* [Large language model]. Accessed at https://rhyme.cool/ on March 5, 2024.

Ridderinkhof, A., de Bruin, E. I., Blom, R., & Bögels, S. M. (2018). Mindfulness-based program for children with autism spectrum disorder and their parents: Direct and long-term improvements. *Mindfulness, 9*(3), 773–791.

Riddle, A. (2022, October 18). *4 ways to use CommonLit to support differentiation* [Blog post]. Accessed at www.commonlit.org/blog/4-ways-to-use-commonlit-to-support-differentiation-52499caab441 on October 17, 2023.

Roberge, M.-É., & Alokha, Y. O. (2022). Establishing an effective dialogue to support diversity, inclusion, and the learning outcomes. *Journal of Business Diversity, 22*(2). https://doi.org/10.33423/jbd.v22i2.5494

Rodgers, R., & Hammerstein, O. (1951). *Getting to know you* [Song]. New York: Angel Records.

Rose, D. H., & Meyer, A. (2002). *Teaching every student in the digital age: Universal design for learning.* Alexandria, VA: ASCD.

Rosen, P. (n.d.). *The challenges of twice-exceptional kids.* Accessed at www.understood.org/en/friends-feelings/empowering-your-child/building-on-strengths/gifted-childrens-challenges-with-learning-and-attention-issues on March 4, 2024.

Rosenthal, E. J. (2001). *His song: The musical journey of Elton John.* New York: Billboard Books.

Salend, S. J., & Garrick Duhaney, L. M. (1999). The impact of inclusion on students with and without disabilities and their educators. *Remedial and Special Education, 20*(2), 114–126.

Sawyer, R. K. (Ed.). (2006). *The Cambridge handbook of the learning sciences.* New York: Cambridge University Press.

Schaaf, R. (n.d.). *Overcoming a "that's the way we have always done it" mindset in schools.* Accessed at www.ednewsdaily.com/overcoming-a-thats-the-way-we-have-always-done-it-mindset-in-schools on June 12, 2024.

Schonert-Reichl, K. A., Oberle, E., Lawlor, M. S., Abbott, D., Thomson, K., Oberlander, T. F., et al. (2015). Enhancing cognitive and social-emotional development through a simple-to-administer mindfulness-based school program for elementary school children: A randomized controlled trial. *Developmental Psychology, 51*(1), 52–66.

Schultz, K., & Phillips, M. (2021, November 30). *Aligning curricular decisions with student voice.* Accessed at https://achievethecore.org/peersandpedagogy/aligning-curricular-decisions-with-student-voice on November 6, 2023.

Semple, R. J., Reid, E. F. G., & Miller, L. (2005). Treating anxiety with mindfulness: An open trial of mindfulness training for anxious children. *Journal of Cognitive Psychotherapy, 19*(4), 379–392.

Sewell, A. (2011). *Black Beauty.* New York: Signet Classics.

Sharma, U., & Sokal, L. (2016). Can teachers' self-reported efficacy, concerns, and attitudes toward inclusion scores predict their actual inclusive classroom practices? *Australasian Journal of Special Education, 40*(1), 21–38.

Sharpsteen, B., Morey, L., Jackson, W., Hand, D., Cottrell, W., & Pearce, P. (Directors). (1937). *Snow White and the seven dwarfs* [Film]. New York: RKO Radio Pictures.

Shoda, V. P., & Yamanaka, T. (2021). A study on instructional humor: How much humor is used in presentations? *Behavioral Sciences, 12*(1), 7.

Smith, C. (2020). *How culturally responsive lessons teach critical thinking.* Accessed at www.learningforjustice.org/magazine/spring-2020/how-culturally-responsive-lessons-teach-critical-thinking on November 6, 2023.

Spacey, J. (2020, July 2). *7 examples of perfect imperfection* [Blog post]. Accessed at https://simplicable.com/talent/perfect-imperfection on October 27, 2023.

Speare, E. G. (2011). *The sign of the beaver.* Boston: Sandpiper.

Stefanski, A., Valli, L., & Jacobson, R. (2016). Beyond involvement and engagement: The role of the family in school-community partnerships. *School Community Journal, 26*(2), 135–160.

Stenning, A., & Bertilsdotter-Rosqvist, H. (2021). Neurodiversity studies: Mapping out possibilities of a new critical paradigm. *Disability and Society, 36*(9), 1532–1537.

Szidon, K., & Franzone, E. (2009). *Task analysis: Steps for implementation.* Madison, WI: National Professional Development Center on Autism Spectrum Disorders, Waisman Center, University of Wisconsin. Accessed at https://autismpdc.fpg.unc.edu/sites/autismpdc.fpg.unc.edu/files/TaskAnalyis_Steps_0.pdf on May 7, 2024.

Telethon Kids Institute. (n.d.). *Intellectual disability.* Accessed at www.telethonkids.org.au/our-research/research-topics/intellectual-disability on June 18, 2024.

Thomas, J. W. (2000, March). *A review of research on project-based learning.* Accessed at www.bobpearlman.org/BestPractices/PBL_Research.pdf on March 6, 2024.

Thoreau, H. D. (2004). *Walden: A fully annotated edition* (J. S. Cramer, Ed.). New Haven, CT: Yale University Press.

Turnbull, A., Turnbull, R., & Wehmeyer, M. L. (2013). *Exceptional lives: Special education in today's schools* (7th ed.). Upper Saddle River, NJ: Merrill.

Understood Team. (n.d.). *Four benefits of inclusive classrooms.* Accessed at www.understood.org/en/articles/4-benefits-of-inclusive-classrooms on April 10, 2024.

UNICEF. (2017, September). *Inclusive education: Understanding Article 24 of the Convention on the Rights of Persons With Disabilities.* Geneva, Switzerland: Author. Accessed at www.unicef.org/eca/sites/unicef.org.eca/files/IE_summary_accessible_220917_0.pdf on November 6, 2023.

United Federation of Teachers. (n.d.). *Specially designed instruction.* Accessed at www.uft.org/teaching/students-disabilities/specially-designed-instruction on November 6, 2023.

United Nations. (n.d.). *Convention on the Rights of Persons with Disabilities (CRPD).* Accessed at www.un.org/development/desa/disabilities/convention-on-the-rights-of-persons-with-disabilities.html on November 6, 2023.

University of Nebraska Medical Center. (n.d.) *Understanding depth of knowledge and cognitive complexity.* UNMC College of Medicine. Accessed at https://www.unmc.edu/mmi/training/sepa/teachers/teacher-resource-webb-bloom-taxonomy.pdf on April 10, 2024.

U.S. Department of Education. (2024). *Individuals with Disabilities Education Act (IDEA) - 1401 CFR §1401.30.* Accessed at https://sites.ed.gov/idea/statute-chapter-33/subchapter-i/1401/30 on June 18, 2024.

U.S. Department of Education. (n.d.a). *About IDEA.* Accessed at https://sites.ed.gov/idea/about-idea on November 6, 2023.

U.S. Department of Education. (n.d.b). *Individuals with Disabilities Education Act (IDEA): Part A: Section 1401.* Accessed at https://sites.ed.gov/idea/statute-chapter-33/subchapter-i/1401/30 on April 10, 2024.

van Gog, T., & Sweller, J. (2015). Not new, but nearly forgotten: The testing effect decreases or even disappears as the complexity of learning materials increases. *Educational Psychology Review, 27*(2), 247–264.

VanTassel-Baska, J., Feng, A. X., Swanson, J. D., Quek, C., & Chandler, K. (2009). Academic and affective profiles of low-income, minority, and twice-exceptional gifted learners: The role of gifted program membership in enhancing self. *Journal of Advanced Academics, 20*(4), 702–739.

van Zomeren, M., Leach, C. W., & Spears, R. (2010). Does group efficacy increase group identification? Resolving their paradoxical relationship. *Journal of Experimental Social Psychology, 46*(6), 1055–1060.

Volavková, H. (Ed.). (1993). *I never saw another butterfly: Children's drawings and poems from Terezín Concentration Camp, 1942–1944* (Expanded 2nd ed.). New York: Schocken Books.

Vygotsky, L. S. (1978). *Mind in society: The development of higher psychological processes.* Cambridge, MA: Harvard University Press.

Wang, L., & He, C. (2020). Review of research on portfolios in ESL/EFL context. *English Language Teaching, 13*(12), 76–82.

Wanzer, M. B., Frymier, A. B., & Irwin, J. (2010). An explanation of the relationship between instructor humor and student learning: Instructional humor processing theory. *Communication Education, 59*(1), 1–18.

Wearmouth, J. (2023). *Special educational needs and disability: The basics* (4th ed.). New York: Routledge.

Webb, N. (1999). *Alignment of science and mathematics standards and assessments in four states* (Research Monograph No. 18). Madison, WI: National Institute for Science Education. Accessed at https://files.eric.ed.gov/fulltext/ED440852.pdf on March 6, 2024.

Wentzel, K. R., & Asher, S. R. (1995). The academic lives of neglected, rejected, popular, and controversial children. *Child Development, 66*(3), 754–763.

Wiggins, G., & McTighe, J. (2005). *Understanding by design* (Expanded 2nd ed.). Alexandria, VA: ASCD.

Will, M., & Najarro, I. (2022, April 18). *What is culturally responsive teaching?* Accessed at www.edweek.org/teaching-learning/culturally-responsive-teaching-culturally-responsive-pedagogy/2022/04 on November 6, 2023.

Williams, K. D., Forgas, J. P., & von Hippel, W. (Eds.). (2005). *The social outcast: Ostracism, social exclusion, rejection, and bullying* (1st ed.). New York: Psychology Press.

Willis, J. (2021, November 5). *How cooperative learning can benefit students this year.* Accessed at www.edutopia.org/article/how-cooperative-learning-can-benefit-students-year on November 6, 2023.

Wisconsin Department of Public Instruction. (2017, January). *Formative assessment: 10 key questions.* Accessed at www.studocu.com/ph/document/university-of-manila/cost-accounting/formative-assessment-10-key-questions/35591563 on March 6, 2024.

Wu, E. H. (2013). The path leading to differentiation: An interview with Carol Tomlinson. *Journal of Advanced Academics, 24*(2), 125–133.

Zhao, Y., Zheng, Z., Pan, C., & Zhou, L. (2021). Self-esteem and academic engagement among adolescents: A moderated mediation model. *Frontiers in Psychology, 12.* https://doi.org/10.3389/fpsyg.2021.690828

Index

A

abilities, 85
abstract conceptualization, 84
    offering examples, 85
academic vocabulary. *See* vocabulary
accessible restrooms, 97
accommodations, 24, 51–52, 85
    date-driven, 93
    individualized support, 82–83
    modeling and monitoring, 86
achievements, 5
acknowledging and reducing inclusion anxiety, 125–128
    tips to ADMIRE belonging in the inclusion classroom, 128
active experimentation, 84
    offering examples, 85
adaptability, 36
adaptations, 107, 160–161
    critical thinking skills, 112–113
    perceived as different, 126
    project-based learning, 110–111
    UbD framework, 111–112
    visual supports, 107–110
adapting instruction to meet students' needs, 6, 24
    students with autism, 40–42
adaptive tools, 104
ADDitude magazine, 55
ADHD. *See* attention deficit/hyperactivity disorder
adjusting complexity and delivery, 6, 98–101
    challenge generates solution, 99
    sample cross-cultural student connection, 100
administrators, 4, 24
    part of the co-teaching process, 17
    vital partners, 7

ADMIRE inclusion framework, 2
    both forms of PBL, 111
    classroom management, 76
    competencies, 20–26
    core relationships and evidence–based practices, 158
    "E to the fifth" learning paths, 160
    exceptionality as a difference, 32–43
    inclusion principles, 85–86, 92–93
    relationships, 157–161
    sample people, places, things chart, 159
    student realities, 43–46
    UbD tips, 112
    voice-choice, 132
ADMIRE Padlet, 168
admiring how inclusion challenges generate solutions, 123
admiring individuals, not categories, 47
admiring supportive classroom management practices, 94
admiring the realities of teachers, students, and families, 74
admiring ways to manage inclusion anxiety, 147
admiring wellness, 163
admiring what students and staff need to know, 28
affirmations, 84
    instructing and involving, 92
"After Apple-Picking" (Frost), 43
age-appropriate emojis, 81
AI-generated song, 97
algebra tiles, 38
all students, 4
    can experience belonging and growth, 75
    high expectations for, 12
"all very determined students deserve infinitely more opportunities than schools have ever offered" paradigm, 30
American Chemical Society lesson plans, 89–90
anchor and sponge activities, 5, 25

"And Still I Rise" (Angelou), 43
Angelou, M., 43
Anne Frank (Frank), 91
anticipating barriers to inclusion, 6
anxiety, 78
    about mathematics, 138–139
    hidden disorders, 37
    inclusion, 125–147
    levels of, 125–126
applying the ADMIRE model, 6
appropriate education and intervention, 30
    embracing the strength paradigm, 35–37
    key in inclusion classrooms, 9
apraxia of speech
    specially designed instruction documentation, 116–117
art, 161
artificial intelligence (AI), 96
    generated song, 97
assess and activate, 3–4
    awareness, 49–53
    defining inclusion, 21–22, 28
    inclusion principles, 92
    individuals, not categories, 32–33
    managing inclusion anxiety, 128
    mindfulness, 55
    supportive classroom strategies, 86–87, 89, 91
    voice-choice, 132
    wellness, 161
assessments, 4
    common, 141
    embedded, 22, 24
    formative, 4, 32, 141
    metacognition self-assessment checklists, 141
    MTSS literacy assessment tool, 135
    pre-inter-post, 141
    summative, 141
assistive technologies, 88, 139
attention deficit hyperactivity disorder (ADHD), 12, 75
    enrichment, 25
    hidden, 37
    mathematics anxiety, 138
    supporting students with, 39–40
attention needs
    specially designed instruction documentation, 115
attention to detail, 37
attitudes toward inclusion, 2–3, 104–105
audio materials, 91
augmented and alternative communication devices, 41–42
autism, 2, 24, 30, 40–42, 75
    hidden, 37
    specially designed instruction documentation, 118–119
Autism Read and Write Pro, 41

Autism Speaks, 42
avoiding stereotypes, 127
awareness of student realities, 49–53

B

barriers to inclusion, 98
baseline levels, 4
behavioral challenges
    specially designed instruction documentation, 117–118
belonging
    need for, 125–126
    voice and choice, 129–132
benefits and challenges for peers and adults, 20
bias, 97–98
    avoiding, 127
big text picture, 36
BioAbility Poem, 155–156
Blooket website, 90
Bloom, B. S., 10–11, 24, 141
Bloom's taxonomy, 24, 141
Boardmaker, 41
Body Scan website, 54
Boogren, T. H., 153
Bookshare website, 91
Brooks, G., 43
Brown, S. K., 102
Bruner, J., 83
building relationships, 49–74, 85
By the End of the Week Inclusion Strategies Education (BE WISE) planner, 62
    template, 64–65
    TIP value inquiry, 66

C

calculating the formula weight of compounds, 6
The Call of the Wild (London)
    choice board, 129–130
    Think-Tac-Toe, 130
Calm website, 41, 54
Calm–Down Bottles, 54
The Cambridge Handbook of the Learning Sciences (Sawyer), 84
can do and will do attitude, 12
    modeling, 161
Canvas, 44
Center for Applied Special Technology (CAST), 19
Center for Parent Information and Resources, 40
centers, forums, stations, multiple representations, 141
challenges as opportunities, 157
challenges to inclusion (*see also* challenges generate solutions), 107
characteristics of exceptionality, 29
    functional skills, 29–31
    student diversity as an asset, 6

Index

ChatGPT, 96
check-in and check-out (CICO), 133
Chem4Kids website, 90
Child Development, 126
Child Mind Institute, 54, 126
Children and Adults with Attention-Deficit/Hyperactivity Disorder (CHADD), 40
children of migrant workers, 35
choice boards, 129–132, 160
    The Call of the Wild (London), 130
    create a choice board, 143
    mathematics, 131
    templates, 132
Choiceworks, 41
chronic health conditions, 37
"Circle of Life" (John), 101
circles of relationships, 101
"City of Glass" (Espada), 43
CL. *See* cooperative learning
class organization, 140
class participation, 141
ClassDojo, 81, 91
classroom norms
    creating, 27
    sample, 23
classroom rules, 80–82
climate for inclusion acceptance, 104–105
    perception versus reality, 107
    we all have value, 106
    what is "normal," 105
cloze notes, 91
coaches, 4, 24
Coerr, E., 91
cognitive apprenticeship, 83
collaboration, 84, 114, 154
    engaging and enriching, 93
    with colleagues, students, and families, 12, 16–17, 133, 140
    with families, 69–70
collaborative framework, 5, 139–142
    four critical questions of a PLC, 139–140
collaborative instruction, 14
collaborative partners, 13
collaborative practices with students, families, and colleagues, 86
collaborative problem solving with team approach, 141
collaborative staff, 4
collaborative work, 156
collaborative writing, 33
collaborative, high-tech, individualized, low-tech, data-driven approaches (CHILD), 113–120
    samples of specially designed instruction documentation, 115–119

college and career prep goals, 5, 25
Colorín Colorado, 79
common assessments, 141
common challenges, 6
common myths about inclusion, 9–11
    is not appropriate for all students with disabilities, 10
    is too expensive, 10
    means that students with disabilities will receive less individualized attention, 10
    places too much burden on teachers, 10
CommonLit website, 37, 56, 136
communicating with students, families, and colleagues, 85
    engaging and enriching, 93
communication apps, 41
comparing political systems, 6
competencies, 150, 20–22
    assess and activate, 21–22
    decide and delineate, 22–23
    engage and enrich, 25–26
    instruct and involve, 24
    model and monitor, 23–24
    reflect and revise, 24–25
concrete experience, 84
    offering examples, 85
concrete, abstract, and virtual connections
    engaging and enriching, 93
connecting to the realities that teachers, students, and families face, 49
    admiring the realities of teachers, students, and families, 74
    assess and activate awareness, 49–53
    collaborating with families, 69–70
    decide and delineate inclusion structures, 54–55
    interest survey, 71–72
    learner profile, 73
    planning with and for learners, 56–69
consistency and fidelity, 140
Convention on the Rights of Persons with Disabilities (UNICEF), 11
cooperative centers, 161
cooperative learning (CL), 5, 20, 24, 91, 141–142
cooperative peer writes, 33
core relationships and evidence-based practices, 158
co-regulation, 77–78, 113
co-teaching models, 14, 16–17
    activating strengths, 89
    delineating responsibility, 89
    parallel lessons, 91–92
create a choice board, 132, 143
create a DSLO chart, 14, 146
creating classroom norms, 22, 27
creating inclusive environments, 127–128

creativity, 5, 37
credible sources, 33
critical thinking skills, 2, 24, 112–113
    activities, 104
    engaging, 161
    focus on, 157
    modeling, 32
    toothpick exercise, 113
cross-curricular connections, 5, 25, 33, 99
    sample, 100
cross-curricular instruction, 99
cultivating a positive classroom environment, 6
cultural diversity, 35
    enrichment, 25
    respecting, 33
culturally diverse learners, 12, 21
culturally diverse perspectives, 127–128
culturally responsive teaching, 79–80
    defined, 79
culture, 4, 85

D

Daily Agenda and Special Highlights (DASH) planner, 62
    sample, 63
daily planning. *See* micro planning
data-driven accommodations and modifications, 114
    reflecting and revising, 93
Davis, A., 43
Davis, K., 13
deafness, 30
decide and delineate, 3–4
    defining inclusion, 22–23, 28
    differentiated instruction, 43
    inclusion principles, 92
    inclusion structures, 54–55
    individuals, not categories, 32–34
    managing inclusion anxiety, 128
    mindfulness, 55
    supportive classroom strategies, 86–87, 89, 91
    voice-choice, 132
    wellness, 161
decoding, 140–141
defining inclusion, 6, 9
    ADMIRE the competencies, 20–26
    admiring what students and staff need to know, 28
    common myths about inclusion, 9–11
    creating classroom norms, 27
    inclusion in research, 15–20
    seven questions to guide a definition, 11–15
desired outcomes, 92
determining students' literacy and mathematics levels, 141
developmental delays, 31

Dewey, J., 83
DI. *See* differentiated instruction
Dickens, C., 101
differentiated instruction (DI), 5, 18, 20, 24, 44–46, 91, 142, 161
    English and mathematics, 141
    individualized support, 82–84
    instructing and involving, 92
    supportive classroom management, 77
    use in planning, 57
digital pens, 24
discrete task analysis, 25, 78, 82–85, 103
    assessing and activating, 92
    defined, 83
distributed practice, 113
diversity, 75
DIY Stress Balls, 54
"do it, speak it, link it, own it" (DSLO), 134–135, 138, 141
    create a DSLO chart, 146
Do2Learn, 41, 50
documentation, 25
    of specially designed instruction, 122
Down syndrome
    specially designed instruction documentation, 116–117
"Dream Boogie" (Hughes), 43
DSLO. *See* "do it, speak it, link it, own it"
Dunlosky, J., 113
dyscalcula
    hidden, 37
    mathematics anxiety, 138
Dyscalculia.org, 45
dysgraphia, 24, 37, 96
dyslexia, 24, 38
    hidden, 37

E

"E to the fifth" learning paths, 160
each student's starting point varies, 11
edifice of inclusion, 1
educational apps, 41
educator wellness, 153–154
    emotional, 153–165
    environmental, 154
    financial, 154
    intellectual, 154
    mental, 153
    occupational, 154
    physical, 153–154
    social, 153–154
    spiritual, 154
edutainment, 5, 25
    pictographs, 165, 167–168

efforts and progress through portfolios, 4
Ehmke, R., 126
"8 Dimension of Wellness for Educators" (Montoya & Summers), 153–154
elaborative interrogation, 113
embedded assessments, 22, 24
embedded feedback, 38
embracing the strength paradigm with appropriate instruction, 35–37
emotional difference, 2
    hidden, 37
emotional disturbance, 30
emotional wellness, 153–154
emotionally safe environments, 12, 89, 105
empathy, 37, 49, 102, 128
    inclusion fosters, 10
empowering students to be successful, 132–134, 141
    MTSS literacy connections, 134–136
    MTSS mathematics connections, 136–139
encoding, 140–141
encouraging acceptance, 128
Endless Alphabet, 41
engage and enrich, 3, 5
    defining inclusion, 25–26, 28
    differentiated instruction, 45
    inclusion principles, 92
    individuals, not categories, 33–34
    managing inclusion anxiety, 128
    mindfulness, 55
    supportive classroom strategies, 86, 88, 90–92
    voice-choice, 132
    wellness, 161
engagements and processes, 5
English and mathematics coaching and supports, 141
English learners (ELs), 35, 79
    gap between them and non-EL classmates, 35
    visuals help, 108–109
enrichment, 141
ensuring teaching well-being, 7
environmental wellness, 154
Espada, M., 43
establishing prior knowledge, 85
ethnicity, 85
evidence of learning
    defining inclusion, 23–24
    examples and nonexamples, 4
evidence of performance, 87
evidence-based practices, 4, 14, 16–18, 57, 155, 160
    core relationships and, 157
    overview, 18–19
    to engage learners of different literacy, mathematics, and behavioral skills sets, 141

examples and nonexamples, 4, 15, 33
exceptionality as a difference, not a deficit, 32–34
exclusion experiences, 126–127
executive function
    creating assists, 42–43
    defined, 42
exit cards, 104
expect the unexpected, 57
expectations (*see also* high expectations), 81–82
experiential learning theory (Kolb), 84
experiential learning, 84
externalizing, 37

F

face-to-face conversations, 50
Fact Monster, 91
fact retrieval, 141
Factor Football, 103
fading assistance, 5, 40
families, 4, 81, 160
    collaborating with, 12, 16, 24, 39, 69–70
    communicating with, 76
    honoring their culture, 34
    roles in student achievement, 13
feedback, 102, 155
    timely and specific, 141
figurative language, 33
financial wellness, 154
First Then Visual Schedule, 41
502 plans, 20–21, 31
flight plans, 57
fluidity and flexibility, 157
focus on critical thinking, 157
focusing on functional skills, 29–31
    admiring individuals, not categories, 47
    exceptionality as a difference, 32–34
    recognizing diversity as a strength, 34–43
    student realities, 43–46
formative assessments, 4, 32, 141
fostering a growth mindset, 85
"4 Ways to Use CommonLit to Support Differentiation" (CommonLit), 56
four Cs of behavior, 82
Frank, A., 91
Frayer model, 14–15
free choice, 142
Free Printable Behavior Charts website, 81
Frost, R., 43
fun atmosphere, 85
functional communication training, 88
functional skills, 29
    focusing on, 29–31

G

game-based educational apps, 81
game-based learning, 142, 161
gamified learning, 103
Garrick Duhaney, L. M., 20
Gavidia–Payne, S., 13
gender, 85
general education and special education teacher observation and personalization, 141
"Getting to Know You" (Rodgers & Hammerstein), 49
giftedness, 42–43
    defined, 43
Glasson, E. M., 13
goals, 87
GoNoodle website, 41, 55
Google Classroom, 39, 44, 129
Google Docs, 43
Google Forms, 50, 78
Google Scholar, 91
Google Slides, 45
Grandin, T., 42
graphic organizers, 45, 108
graphing quadratic equations, 6
greater than and less than in sets, 6
growth mindset, 85
    modeling and monitoring, 92

H

Ha, S. S., 32
Hammerstein, O., 49
Harvard Graduate School of Education, 129
Haynes, J., 79
Headspace app, 41
health impairments, 30
Healthy Brain Network, 55
hearing impairments, 12, 30
    adaptations, 24
    hidden, 37
    specially designed instruction documentation, 116–117
heartfelt affirmations, 77–78
hidden disabilities, 37–38
hierarchy of inclusion classroom sample participation data collection form, 68
high expectation, 85, 140, 142, 155
    deciding and delineating, 92
    for *all* students, 12, 21
higher- and lower-level learners, 5, 25
    engaging, 33
higher-order thinking, 24
highlighters, 45
high-low technology options, 5, 14, 45
high-tech inclusion classes, 114
history class, 90
    staff communications, 90
    strategies to ADMIRE, 91–92
Holter, J., 96, 98
homeless students, 35
how can students with different ability levels and skills simultaneously benefit from being taught in an inclusion classroom, 13–14
"How Does Anxiety Affect Kids in School?" (Ehmke), 126
Hughes, L., 43
humor, 161

I

I can and will statements, 89
I Never Saw Another Butterfly (Volavková), 91
I spy, 112
icons, 108
IDEA. *See* Individuals with Disabilities Education Improvement Act
IEPs. *See* individualized education programs
illustrations and learning visualizations, 5, 25
Immersive Reader, 91, 104, 136
including small-group activities, 128–129
inclusion
    ADMIRE framework, 2–3
    ADMIRE principles, 85–87, 92–93
    ADMIRE the competencies, 20–26
    admiring what students and staff need to know, 28
    attitudes toward, 2–3
    characteristics, 15
    common myths about, 9–11
    creating classroom norms, 27
    defining, 6, 9–28
    definition, 9, 15
    examples, 15
    in research, 15–20
    is a way of life, 11
    legal right under IDEA, 10
    nonexamples, 15
    principles, 160
    seven questions to guide a definition, 11–15
    structures, 54–55
    supportive classroom management, 75–94
    think individuals, not categories, 29–47
    topography, 157
inclusion anxiety. *See* managing inclusion anxiety
inclusion challenges generate solutions, 95
    adaptations, 107–113
    adjusting complexity and delivery, 98–101
    admiring how inclusion challenges generate solutions, 123
    climate for inclusion acceptance, 104–107

collaborative, high-tech, individualized, low-tech, data-driven approaches, 113–120
    documenting specially designed instruction, 122
    innovations, inventions, and solutions, 96–98
    proactive inclusion, 101–104
    toothpick exercise answers, 121
inclusion classrooms
    benefit all students, 13–14
    most importance ingredients, 12
inclusion in research, 15–16
    benefits and challenges for peers and adults, 20
    collaboration, 16–17
    evidence-based practices, 16
    professional development, 17–19
the "inclusion is not appropriate for all students with disabilities" myth, 10
the "inclusion is too expensive" myth, 10
the "inclusion means that students with disabilities will receive less individualized attention" myth, 10
inclusion observations, notes, and future plans, 67
the "inclusion places too much burden on teachers" myth, 10
Inclusion Strategies That Work! (Karten), 85
inclusion word cloud, 165–166
incorporating diverse perspectives, 127
independent assignments, 142
individual assessment of levels, 140
individualized education programs (IEPs), 1, 29–31, 51–52
    AI and, 96
    classifications, 20–21
    collaborative input, 30
    goals, 22
individualized support, 82, 114
    accommodations and modifications, 82–83
    discrete task analysis, 83–84
    supportive classroom management, 76
Individuals With Disabilities Education Improvement Act (IDEA), 9–11, 14, 31
    importance of, 29–30
individuals, not categories, 29
    admiring individuals, not categories, 47
    exceptionality as a difference, 32–34
    focusing on functional skills, 29–31
    recognizing diversity as a strength, 34–43
    student realities, 43–46
inferential-logical-word problem-solving skills, 140
infographics, 108
infusing VAKT sensory elements, 85
innovations, inventions, and solutions, 96–98
    AI-generated song, 97
inquiry, 160
Institute of Education Sciences, 155
instruct and involve, 3–5
    defining inclusion, 24, 28
    differentiated instruction, 45
    inclusion principles, 92
    individuals, not categories, 33–34
    managing inclusion anxiety, 128
    mindfulness, 55
    supportive classroom strategies, 86, 88, 90–91
    voice-choice, 132
    wellness, 161
instructional and behavioral goals, 140
instructional assistants, 88
instructional models, 5
intellectual differences, 2, 30
    enrichment, 25
intellectual wellness, 154
interactive responses, 140
interactive whiteboards, 81
interest survey, 50, 71–72
interleaved practice, 113
internalizing, 37
International Dyslexia Association, 45
interventions honoring students' reality, 128
iPads, 24, 41, 96
IRIS Center (Vanderbilt University), 155

J
John, E., 101
Jost, J. T., 127
Journal of Youth and Adolescence, 126

K
Kahoot! website, 90
Kanold, T. D., 153
Karten, T. J., 1, 85
Kay, A. C., 127
kinesthetic debates, 91
The King and I (Rodgers & Hammerstein), 49
Kingsley, E. P., 69–70
knowledge about individual students, 12
knowledge about the curriculum, 12
Kolb, D. A., 84
Komunyakaa, Y., 43
KWL charts, 91

L
language and vocabulary
    assess and activate, 33
    decide and delineate, 33
    engage and enrich, 33
    instruct and involve, 33
    model and monitor, 33
    proficiency, 21
    reflect and revise, 33

language needs, 4
learner downtime, 78
learner profiles, 50–53, 73
    samples, 51–53
learning activities, 4
Learning Ally, 45, 91
learning celebrations, 5, 76–77
learning differences, 12
Learning Disabilities Association of America, 45
learning disabilities, 30
Learning for Justice website, 79, 127
Learning Forward, 153
learning in action, 83
learning needs, 115
learning norms, 4, 22
    delineating, 32
learning paths, 160
learning targets, 4
    mapping out, 25
least restrictive environment (LRE), 6, 14, 29
lesson objectives, 5
lessons with discrete task analysis, 5
letting data guide your next steps, 85
Lewis, C. S., 101
lifelong learning, 157
line readers, 45
The Lion, the Witch, and the Wardrobe (Lewis), 101
literacy and mathematics discussions, 140
literacy
    "do it, speak it, link it, own it" (DSLO), 134–135
    MTSS connections, 134–136
    MTSS literacy assessment tool, 135
London, J., 129–130
low-tech approaches, 114

M

macro planning, 57–58, 161
    sample, 61
making sense of problems to reason and persevere, 140
managing inclusion anxiety, 6, 125
    acknowledging and reducing anxiety, 125–128
    admiring ways to manage inclusion anxiety, 147
    collaborative framework, 139–142
    create a choice board, 143
    create a DSLO chart, 14
    empowering students to be successful, 132–139
    including small-group activities, 128–129
    offering voice-choice assignments, 129–132
    use an MTSS planning template, 144–145
manipulatives, 38
    mathematical, 112
Marsh, E. J., 113

matching literacy and mathematics standards to honor student skill sets, 140
mathematical manipulatives, 112
mathematics
    anxiety, 138–139
    assess and activate, 34
    decide and delineate, 34
    engage and enrich, 34
    instruct and involve, 34
    model and monitor, 34
    MTSS assessment tool, 137
    MTSS connections, 136–139
    reflect and revise, 34
    sample choice board, 131
    values, 106
    visuals for, 110
mathematics walks, 6–7
mathisfun.com, 104
McTighe, J., 19, 112
meaningful, appropriately leveled assignments strength paradigm, 142
meditation apps, 55
mega planning, 57–58, 161
    sample, 59–60
mental rehearsal, 89
mental wellness, 153
Merriam-Webster, 45
metacognition, 5, 83
    self-assessment checklists, 141
micro planning, 57, 62–69, 161
    BE WISE planning template, 64–65
    hierarchy of inclusion classroom sample participation data collection form, 68
    inclusion observations, notes, and future plans, 67
    sample DASH micro planner, 63
    WISE TIP Value inquiry, 66
Mindful Breathing Using Shapes, 55
Mindful Practices for Kids with Autism, 55
Mindful Walking, 55
mindfulness
    modeling, 128
    practices, 54–55
Mindfulness in Education Network, 55
MindUp Curriculum, Grades PreK–12, 55
mixed-ability grouping, 88
mnemonics, 91, 113
model and monitor, 3–4
    defining inclusion, 23–24, 28
    differentiated instruction, 44
    inclusion principles, 92
    individuals, not categories, 32–34
    managing inclusion anxiety, 128

mindfulness, 55
supportive classroom strategies, 86–89, 91
voice-choice, 132
wellness, 161
Model Me Going Places, 41
modeling
appropriate inclusion etiquette, 105
can do and will do attitudes, 161
chemical reactions, 89
desired outcomes, 85
with guided practice, 40
modifications
data-driven, 93
individualized support, 82–83
modifications, 24, 51–52, 85
month-by-month planning. *See* macro planning
Montoya, A., 153–154
more and least restrictive environments, 6, 14
more knowledgeable other (MKO), 58
motivating and advancing learners, 141–142
movements, 161
MTSS. *See* multitiered system of supports (MTSS)
multiple disabilities, 30
multiple modalities, 56
multitiered system of supports (MTSS), 5, 161
empowering students, 125, 132–134
evidence-based practice, 18, 20, 24
literacy connections, 134–136
mathematics connections, 136–139
planning template, 136, 144–145
supportive classroom management, 77
tiers, 133
use in planning, 57
music, 161
"My Grandmother Is Waiting for Me to Come Home" (Brooks), 43

N

Nathan, M. J., 113
National Center for Education Statistics, 9
National Center for Learning Disabilities, 45
National Center on Accessible Educational Materials, 56
National Institute of Mental Health, 125
needs-based instruction and intervention, 157
negativity thwarts growth, 2
Network for Grateful Living, 55
neurodiversity, 32
neuroscience, 161
on diversity, 16
Neuschwander, C., 99
norms, 160

O

occupational wellness, 154
offering adaptations for students with autism, 40–42
creating executive function assists, 42–43
offering more challenges, 87
offering self- and co-regulation, 38
offering voice-choice assignments, 129–132
sample choice board for *The Call of the Wild*, 130
sample mathematics choice board, 131
one-to-one instruction, 88
ongoing advancements, 140
ongoing centers or forums using PBL, 141
online collaborative platform, 165, 168
online computational drills, 103
open-ended responses, 4, 32
require higher-order thinking, 24
opportunities for advancement, practice, reinforcement, and repetition, 5
organization, 92
orthopedic impairments, 30
Orton-Gillingham instruction, 38
The Outsiders (Hinton), 6

P

pacing, 5, 79, 161
Palacio, R. J., 111–112
ParentSquare, 69
PBIS. *See* positive behavioral interventions and supports
PBIS World website, 129
PBL. *See* project-based learning
peer collaboration, 160
peer monitors, 87–88
peer supports, 88
through small-group activities, 128–129
peer-to-peer learning, 141
perception versus reality, 107
what do you see, 107
perfect imperfection, 160–161
personalization is culturally appropriate, 140
personalization, 141
Pfizer, 149
PhET website, 56, 90
phone apps, 39
Photos for Class website, 110
physical education class, 86–87
staff communications, 87
strategies to ADMIRE, 87–88
physical impairments, 12
physical wellness, 153–154
Piaget, J., 82
Pics4Learning, 110

picture boards, 88
planned ignoring, 102
planning for diverse skills and behaviors, 38–39
planning for outcomes, 85
planning with and for learners, 56–58
    macro planning, 58, 61
    mega planning, 58–60
    micro planning, 62–69
Plato, 96
Plexers website, 104
portfolios, 24, 91, 101
    digital, 141
positive attitudes, 2
positive behavioral interventions and supports (PBIS), 14, 85, 134, 142, 160–161
    evidence-based practice, 18, 20
    individualized support, 82
    instructing and involving, 92
    lowers rates of problem behavior, 77
    supportive classroom management, 77
    tiers of support, 81–82
    use in planning, 57
    website, 81
positive classroom environment, 76–79, 93
    classroom rules, 80–82
    culturally responsive teaching, 79–80
    reach before you teach, 77
positive reinforcement, 39, 89, 102
positives before negatives, 93
poverty, 35
PowerPoint, 45
practice, 141
    for social skills, 85
PRC-Saltillo website, 42
pre-inter-post assessments, 141
prerecorded poems, 45
preteaching English and mathematics language and vocabulary, 140
prior knowledge, 21
    assessing and activating, 86, 89, 91–92
prior successes, 4
prioritizing ADMIRE inclusion principles, 6
proactive inclusion, 101–104
    defined, 101
    student documentation tool, 103
proactive UDL designs, 140
problem solving, 141
problem-based learning. *See* project-based learning
procedures, 4
processing differences, 37
professional development, 17–19, 102, 160
    to achieve successful outcomes, 12

professional learning community (PLC)
    four critical questions, 125, 139–140
professional learning experiences. *See* professional development
progress monitoring, 156, 160
    using weekly or unit quizzes and tests, 141
Project Zero (Harvard Graduate School of Education), 129
project-based learning (PBL), 5, 14, 19–20, 24, 33, 110–111, 161
    ongoing centers or forums using, 141
    use in planning, 57
Proloquo2Go, 41
Proverbs 22:6, 45
providing individualized support, 6
providing opportunities for movement, 39

Q

Qi, J., 32
quarterly and long-range expectations, 140
quizlet flashcards, 90

R

The Raisin Meditation, 55
ramps, 97, 107
Rawe, J., 43
Rawson, K. A., 113
reach before you teach, 77–78
read-alouds, 32
reading
    assess and activate, 32
    decide and delineate, 32
    decoding, 140
    encoding, comprehension, 140
    engage and enrich, 33
    instruct and involve, 33
    model and monitor, 32
    reflect and revise, 33
ReadWorks website, 38, 136
real-life photos, 108
real-world literacy and mathematics applications, 142
recognition, 141
recognizing hidden and visible characteristics, 37–38
recognizing student diversity as a strength, 34–35
    creating executive function assists, 42–43
    embracing the strength paradigm with appropriate instruction, 35–37
    offering adaptations for students with autism, 40–42
    planning for diverse skills and behaviors, 38–39
    recognizing hidden and visible characteristics, 37–38
    supporting students with ADD and ADHD, 39–40
reflect and revise, 3, 5
    defining inclusion, 24–25, 28
    differentiated instruction, 45

inclusion principles, 92
individuals, not categories, 33–34
managing inclusion anxiety, 128
mindfulness, 55
supportive classroom strategies, 86, 88, 90–91
voice-choice, 132
wellness, 161
reflective learning, 155
reflective observation, 84
offering examples, 85
reflective practices, 140
reinforcing abstract and representational concepts, 6
Reis, S. M., 43
related service providers, 4, 88
relationships, 157–161
core relationships and evidence-based practices, 158
"E to the fifth" learning paths, 160
sample people, places, things chart, 159
Remind Hub, 39
reminders for nurturing relationships, 7
Renzulli, J. S., 43
repeated practice, 88
resilience, 36
resources to practice supportive classroom management, 6
respect, 105
encouraging, 127–128
for differences, 4, 23
modeling, 33, 87
respect, empathy, accountability, consistency, healing (REACH), 77
response to intervention (RTI) strategies, 139
Rewordify website, 91
rhyming games, 112
Rodgers, R., 49
routines and expectations, 81–82
setting, 6
tiered universal interventions, 82
rubrics or metacognitive self-assessment checklists, 141
rubrics, 4, 85, 91

S
Sadako and the Thousand Paper Cranes (Coerr), 91
Salend, S. J., 20
sample cross-cultural student connection, 100
sample mathematics choice board, 131
sample people, places, things chart, 159
sample social story, 108
sample visual tool, 109
samples of specially designed instruction documentation, 115–119
Sawyer, R. K., 84
scaffolding, 12–14, 83, 102, 112
"my voice," 128

school rules, 4, 22
school-class-student-family norms, 140
science class, 88
staff communications, 88
strategies to ADMIRE, 89–90
SEL. *See* social and emotional learning
self-determination, 140
self-efficacy, 85, 140, 160
instructing and involving, 92
self-explanation, 113
self-reflection, 155
self-regulation, 4, 22, 85, 91, 102
sensory corners, 78
sensory sensitivities, 42
hidden, 37
sensory regulation apps, 41
setting routines and expectations, 6
seven questions to guide a definition of inclusion, 11
how can students with different ability levels and skills simultaneously benefit from being taught in an inclusion classroom, 13–14
what are the most important ingredients of an inclusion classroom, 12
what does inclusion look like, 11–12
what professional learning experiences do teachers in inclusion environments require to achieve successful outcomes, 12
what roles to family members play, 13
when would inclusion be an inappropriate placement, 14–15
who are collaborative partners, 13
"show what you know," 142
The Sign of the Beaver (Speare), 80
Sir Cumference and the First Round Table (Neuschwander), 99
"Slam, Dunk, & Hook" (Komunyakaa), 43
slant boards, 38
slicing my pie, 151–152
sample activity, 152
Slidesmania.com, 132
small-group activities. *See* including small–group activities
small-group discussions, 160
small-group peer interactions, 161
Smithsonian magazine, 38
social and behavioral differences, 12
social and emotional learning (SEL), 85, 161
apps, 41
connection to academic achievement, 22
connections, 134
social narratives, 85
social stories, 41
social wellness, 153–154
socioeconomic levels
influence vocabulary, 35

Socratic discussions, 91
sound amplification systems, 24
Spacey, J., 160
speaking and listening
    assess and activate, 33
    decide and delineate, 34
    engage and enrich, 34
    instruct and involve, 34
    model and monitor, 34
    reflect and revise, 34
Speare, E. G., 80
special dyslexia font, 45
special education staff, 4
specially designed instruction, 31, 140
specific learning disability, 75
    defined, 38
speech and language impairment, 30
Speech Blubs, 41
speech-language difference
    hidden, 37
speech-language providers, 33
spiritual wellness, 154
staff communications, 43–44
    general education teacher, 88, 90
    physical education teacher, 87
Starfall app, 41
step-by-step organization, 4, 33, 78
Storyline Online, 56
strategies to ADMIRE
    history class, 91–92
    physical education class, 78–88
    science class, 89–90
strength paradigm, 35–37
    planning for diverse skills and behaviors, 38–39
strengths and interests, 160
stress, 151–152
structural analysis, 141
student and class graphs, 141
student anxiety. *See* anxiety; inclusion anxiety
student behavior, 4
    monitoring, 33
student communications or reflections, 141
student documentation tool, 103
student motivation, 33
student realities, 29, 43, 86
    differentiated instruction, 44–46
    physical education, 86–88
    reflecting and revising, 86
    science, 88–90
    staff communications, 43–44
    U.S. history, 90–92
student strengths, 87
    modeling and monitoring, 92
students
    achieve mastery at different times, 10–11
    are not identical, 11
    levels, 4
    part of the co-teaching process, 17
    roles, 4
    who are gifted, 35
    with and without exceptionality have strengths, 10
students with autism
    monitoring their behavior, 88
    offering adaptations for, 40–42
study guides, 91
study-organizational skills, 140
successful outcome criteria, 5
Sudoku, 104, 112
summarizing current research, 6
summative assessments, 141
Summers, L. L., 153–154
supplemental instruction, 24
support the person in the mirror, 151
    educator wellness, 153–154
    slicing my pie, 151–152
supporting students with ADD and ADHD, 39–40
supportive classroom management, 75
    ADMIRE, 76
    ADMIRE inclusion principles, 85–87, 92–93
    admiring supportive classroom management practices, 94
    individualized support, 82–85
    positive environment, 76–81
    routines and expectations, 81–82
    student realities, 87–92
supports, 5, 25, 31
Sweller, J., 56
syllabication, 141
syntactic structure, 141
systematic, evidence-based practices, 155

T

A Tale of Two Cities (Dickens), 101
tapping diverse strengths, 6
tapping out symbols, 38
teacher supports, 140
Teachers of English to Speakers of Other Languages (TESOL), 79
    online blog, 79
teachers' sense of self-efficacy, 2
teacher-student conferences, 141
teaching students to explain their reasoning, 38
technology supports, 41, 140, 142

Tell About Yourself (TAY) survey, 50
ten-step wellness intervention plan, 7, 155–157
    challenges as opportunities, 157
    collaborative work, 156
    fluidity and flexibility, 157
    focus on critical thinking, 157
    high expectations, 155
    lifelong learning, 157
    needs-based instruction and intervention, 157
    progress monitoring, 156
    reflective learning, 155
    systematic, evidence-based practices, 155
Text Compactor website, 91
text read aloud, 96
text-to-speech tools, 45
That's the Way We Always Did It (TTWWADI) syndrome, 20
theory of cognitive development (Piaget), 82
Think-Tac-Toe, 130
Thoreau, H. D., 80
Thorisdottir, H., 127
Tier 1 intervention menu for core instruction, 141
tiered instruction, 141
Tiered Universal Interventions, 81–82
time frames, 4
    deciding and delineating, 33, 92
time to plan and prepare, 12
timelines, 5
    revising as needed, 33
tips to ADMIRE belonging in the inclusion classroom, 128
Tobii Dynavox, 42
Toca Boca app, 41
toothpick exercise, 113
    answers, 121
TouchChat, 41
TouchMath, 38
Toytheater.com, 142
Transformative Life Skills and Dynamic Mindfulness, 54
transitions, 4
traumatic brain injury, 30
treating errors as learning opportunities, 38
true or false questions, 165–167
trust, 77–78
trust, empowerment, academics, co-regulation, heartfelt (TEACH), 77
TTWWADI. See *That's the Way We Always Did It* syndrome
Turnbull, A., 13
Turnbull, R., 13
twice-exceptional learners, 12, 35

U

UbD. *See* Understanding by Design
UDL. *See* Universal Design for Learning
Understanding by Design (UbD), 5, 85, 111–112, 161
    evidence-based practice, 19–20, 24
    instructing and involving, 92
    supportive classroom management, 77
    use in planning, 57
Understanding Dysgraphia website, 45
understanding inclusion fosters, 10
UNICEF, 11
unifix cubes, 38, 107
Universal Design for Learning (UDL), 4, 45, 141, 150, 160
    evidence-based practice, 19–20, 24
    mathematics and literacy interventions, 141
    modeling and monitoring, 92
    planning with and for learners, 56–58
    practices, 85
    proactive designs, 140
    supportive classroom management, 77
    use in planning, 57, 62
use an MTSS planning template, 144–145

V

VAKT. *See* visual, auditory, kinesthetic, and tactile elements
validation, 85
    instructing and involving, 92
van Gog, T., 56
Vanderbilt University, 1555
verbal and written communications, 140
verbalization, 89
Vidtionary website, 56, 110, 136
virtual manipulatives, 142
vision impairments, 12, 24, 30
    adaptations, 25
    audio materials, 91
    hidden, 37
    specially designed instruction documentation, 115
visual aids, 89
visual cues, 85
Visual Dictionary Online, 110
visual examples, 33
visual representation of a concept, 22–23
visual scheduling apps, 41
visual supports, 107–110
    sample social story, 108
    sample visual tool, 109
    visuals for mathematics problem-solving strategies, 110
visual, auditory, kinesthetic, and tactile (VAKT) elements, 5, 14, 24, 45, 51–52, 56, 79, 85, 91, 160–161
    instruct and involve, 86
    instructing and involving, 92
    involving to make reading 3-D, 33
    mathematics and literacy interventions, 141
visualization of success, 89

visuals for mathematics problem-solving strategies, 110
vocabulary, 33, 91, 136
    appropriate instruction, 35–37
    evidence-based practices, 18
    socioeconomic levels influence, 35
    tiers, 36
voice typing tools, 24
voice-choice, 129–132, 161
Volavková, H., 91
Vygotsky, L. S., 58

W

we all have value, 106
Webb, N., 24, 141
Webb's Depth of Knowledge, 24, 141
WebQuests, 104
weekly planning. *See* micro planning
Wehmeyer, M. L., 13
"Welcome to Holland" (Kingsley), 69–70
wellness, 149
    ADMIRE relationships, 157–161
    admiring wellness, 163
    competencies, 7, 150
    support the person in the mirror, 151–154
    ten-step intervention plan, 155–157
what are the most important ingredients of an inclusion classroom, 12
what does inclusion look like, 11–12
what is "normal," 105
what professional learning experiences do teachers in inclusion environments require to achieve successful outcomes, 12
what roles do family members play, 13
what students and staff need to know. *See* defining inclusion
What Works Clearinghouse, 141, 155
when would inclusion be an inappropriate placement, 14
    inclusion Frayer model, 15

who are collaborative partners, 13
whole-class support, 88
whole-part-whole lessons, 5, 33
Wiggins, G., 19, 112
Willingham, D. T., 113
willingness to grow and learn, 12
Wonder (Palacio), 111–112
word prediction
    programs, 38, 96
    strategies, 110
working memories, 92
World-Class Instructional Design and Assessment (WIDA), 36
Would You Rather? website, 104
writer's notebooks, 45
writing
    assess and activate, 33
    decide and delineate, 33
    engage and enrich, 33
    instruct and involve, 33
    model and monitor, 33
    reflect and revise, 33
    routines, 33
written records, digital portfolios, or mathematics notebooks, 141

Y

Yale Center for Dyslexia and Creativity, 45
yearly planning. *See* mega planning
yin-yang of cognitive and affect skills, 22
yoga, 89
    stagnation, 95

Z

zone of proximal development (Vygotsky), 58, 85
    assessing and activating, 92

Inclusion Strategies and Interventions, Second Edition
Toby J. Karten
In a world filled with diverse students, inclusive education is more important than ever. Rely on the second edition of this user-friendly guide to help you provide a strong learning path for all students, with a focus on special needs.
BKF963

Watch, Listen, Ask, Learn
Belinda Dunnick Karge
Written for current and aspiring administrators and teacher leaders, this book offers action items, case studies, and reproducible tools to help you stay in front of special education law, know and support your learning services team, and ensure students with disabilities receive equitable, inclusive education.
BKG080

Yes We Can!
Heather Friziellie, Julie A. Schmidt, and Jeanne Spiller
Utilizing PLC practices, general and special educators must develop collaborative partnerships in order to close the achievement gap and maximize learning for all. The authors encourage *all* educators to take collective responsibility in improving outcomes for students with special needs.
BKF653

The General Education Teacher's Guide to Autism
Barbara Boroson
In this engaging title, you will find answers to all your questions about students on the autism spectrum in inclusive classrooms. Collect the information and strategies you need to create an effective, welcoming, and supportive environment for these neurodiverse students.
BKG055

Solution Tree | Press a division of Solution Tree

Visit SolutionTree.com or call 800.733.6786 to order.

Wait! Your professional development journey doesn't have to end with the last pages of this book.

We realize improving student learning doesn't happen overnight. And your school or district shouldn't be left to puzzle out all the details of this process alone.

No matter where you are on the journey, we're committed to helping you get to the next stage.

Take advantage of everything from **custom workshops** to **keynote presentations** and **interactive web and video conferencing**. We can even help you develop an action plan tailored to fit your specific needs.

Let's get the conversation started.

Call 888.763.9045 today.

SolutionTree.com